MODERN
CULTURAL
ANTHROPOLOGY

THIRD EDITION

MODERN CULTURAL ANTHROPOLOGY

AN INTRODUCTION

PHILIP K. BOCK
THE UNIVERSITY OF NEW MEXICO

ALFRED A. KNOPF   NEW YORK

Third Edition
987654321
Copyright © 1969, 1974, 1979 by Philip K. Bock

Library of Congress Cataloging in Publication Data

Bock, Philip K
  Modern cultural anthropology.

  Bibliography: p.
  Includes index.
  1. Ethnology. I. Title.
GN315.B57   1978   301.2   78-13107
ISBN 0-394-32218-5

Cover Credit: Werner Bischof/Magnum

Acknowledgments are gratefully extended to the following authors and publishers for their kind permission to quote from copyrighted works:
Oxford University Press for excerpts from *The Nuer* by E. E. Evans-Pritchard.
Northwestern University Press for excerpts from *Dahomean Narrative* by M. J. Herskovits and F. Herskovits.

Manufactured in the United States of America

To my parents,
Eugene and Clara Bock,
and to the memory of
my teachers
Robert Redfield
and Clyde Kluckhohn

PREFACE

This book has been substantially revised and abridged since the last edition. It should now be suitable for use as the sole text in a quarter course or as one of several texts in a semester course.

I have modified the contents in several ways. Linguistic theory has a less prominent place, although the analogy between language structure and culture is retained. I have deleted many unessential examples and a few larger sections including the chapter on social space and time. Some materials that were formerly treated separately are now combined. The chapter on enculturation now precedes that on language acquisition, and the chapters on field methods and comparative methods have been merged. New material, both conceptual and illustrative, has been added, especially in Chapter Five where ethnic groups and social classes receive greater attention and in Chapter Ten where moral values and sociobiology are discussed. Sexist thought and vocabulary has been eliminated. Recommended readings are up-to-date, and citations are now in standard anthropological form.

Despite these changes, the book still focuses on cultural diversity and the ways that cultural systems—language, social structure, technology, and ideology—function to satisfy human biological and social needs. In our anxiety to communicate the latest ideas to our beginning students, I believe we frequently overlook the fundamental lessons of anthropology which we, as professionals, take for granted. Therefore, I have continued to emphasize the integrity of cultural systems and the importance of a relativistic approach to the understanding of other cultures. The instructor may supplement this emphasis with his or her own perspective on cultural process and evolution.

I wish to acknowledge here the able assistance of my daughter, Marian Bock, who looked with fresh eyes at a manuscript that has become overly familiar to me and who made dozens of valuable suggestions for revision. I have also profited from the criticisms of Louis A. Hieb, and of my editors at Knopf: Barry Fetterolf, Harriet Prentiss, and Anna Marie Muskelly. I would also like to thank copyeditor Barbara Salazar.

PHILIP K. BOCK

Albuquerque, New Mexico

April 1978

CONTENTS

MODERN
CULTURAL
ANTHROPOLOGY

PART ONE
THE PATHWAY
TO HUMANITY

Anthropology is the study of human beings: what they are and how they got that way. To understand the ABCs of human anatomy, behavior, and culture, it is necessary to study the process of becoming human, both in the history of our species as a whole and in the development of individuals. In this part of the book we shall survey the pathway to humanity, considering first the evolution of *Homo sapiens* from earlier and simpler forms of life, and then the process by which human children acquire the language and customs of their community.

The remainder of the book is concerned with the diversity of human customs—social, technological, and ideological—which have developed as adaptations of particular human groups to their respective environments. The more we learn about the ways people in other societies have ordered their lives, the greater perspective we gain on our own society. One of the most important lessons that anthropology teaches is that simply being brought up in a given society, speaking a given language, makes it extremely difficult for the individual to understand or appreciate other ways of life. The tendency for people to consider their own way of life the best and to use their own customs as a standard in evaluating others is called *ethnocentrism.* A certain amount of this attitude is probably healthy, for when people lose all faith in their own society they tend to sicken and die. But excessive ethnocentrism can prevent us from recognizing the good, beautiful, and useful things in other societies. To gain the greatest benefit from your journey on the pathway to humanity it will be essential to keep an open mind. *Bon voyage*!

CHAPTER ONE
THE BIOLOGICAL BACKGROUND

THE PRIMATE PATTERN

The way that we look and behave and the way the world looks to us are the result of hundreds of millions of years of biological evolution. The origin of the fact that there are two human sexes lies over a billion years in the past, in the development of sexual reproduction in simple one-celled organisms. We owe the fact that we are warm-blooded and hairy, rather than cold, clammy, and covered with scales, to the emergence of the mammals less than 200 million years ago. On the other hand, the fact that we have five digits at the end of each limb is a characteristic that we share not only with our fellow mammals but with the reptiles as well, indicating a common source much further back.

Human beings are members of the mammalian order *Primates.* Primates are animals whose evolution as a distinct group has been going on for only about 70 million years. There is some important evidence for this affiliation right on the tips of your fingers: only primates (among the mammals) have flat nails, rather than sharp claws, on their fingers. All primates are "grasping" animals; most (apes, monkeys, and prosimians) live in or around trees, and their long, mobile fingers tipped with flat nails are useful for getting a good grip on a tree limb and for handling nearby objects.

Unlike the other four-limbed mammals, primates don't trot around on the ground, sniffing and poking at things with snouts. Rather, they tend to sit up or perch on hind limbs, make noises, look around, and explore with "hands." Life in trees calls for good vision rather than keen scent, and nearly all the primates do have acute color vision. Also, most primates have eyes that face forward (rather than out to the sides), and can see objects in three dimensions—a handy trick if you are going to go leaping from tree to tree.

Monkeys and apes are noted for their natural curiosity. Recent laboratory experiments have shown that monkeys will do quite a bit of work for no reward other than the chance to manipulate or even gaze at some unfamiliar object. Human infants also demonstrate exploratory behavior and curiosity. It is not clear whether any of our direct ancestors ever got around by swinging from branch to branch, but humans do share the apes' highly mobile shoulders, arms, and fingers. Only humans and the higher primates can throw accurately.

Most of the primates who live in groups tend to form *dominance hierarchies.* Within a troop of baboons (a type of monkey in which this characteristic has been carefully studied), each male has an established position in relation to every other male—above, equal, or below, depending on the outcome of a sequence of confrontations. This hierarchy is similar to the "pecking order" established among the chickens of every barnyard, and to the prestige systems of human communities, primitive and civilized.

Our primate ancestors shared the following: long, highly mobile arms and hands; a relatively large brain adapted to control those hands; stereoscopic color vision; various vocal abilities; curiosity; and a tendency to establish dominance within a social group.

The higher primates also tend to have rather extended childhoods—long periods during which they depend on adults for satisfaction of their basic needs. Many young animals, on their own within the first year of life, attain full physical and social maturity soon afterward. The young of many nonmammalian species never even see their "parents." Mammals are born alive, develop slowly, and require the presence of an adult female if they are to survive. This need for care is particularly lengthy in apes and humans—a chimpanzee depends on maternal care for about two years, and does not reach its adult size until it is eight to twelve years old; comparable figures for human young in most societies are six to eight years of dependence and full growth at the age of about twenty.

This prolonged period of dependence was accentuated by our ancestors' development of a taste for meat. In a tropical environment, getting enough roots or wild fruit is best accomplished individually, and tools are only occasionally useful. But a hunting way of life makes the whole group dependent upon the strength, cunning, and tool-making skill of the adult males, and their willingness to share the kill. Human children must depend upon their parents for both sustenance and knowledge; their need for food reinforces the learning of group tradition.

Much of what is learned during primate childhood involves getting along with other members of the group. All group-living animals must make some such adjustments. In the case of social insects and birds, most of the required behavioral patterns are built into the animal at birth. But primates have few such instincts. Brainy animals that they are, they also learn to communicate with one another by means of rather subtle gestures and vocal sounds. Such arbitrary, group-specific, and socially learned signals are not yet language, but they do represent a step in the direction of true speech.

THE ORIGIN OF HUMANITY

Our precultural ancestors were curious, communicative, and capable of complex interactions with one another and with their environment. There is no reason to think that they did not make at least sporadic use of tools. Recent studies of chimpanzees in the wild have revealed that these apes frequently use sticks and other natural objects in ways learned from other members of the group. There is no absolute break between the tool-using and tool-making of the apes and that of early humans; however, our ancestors' ability to shape natural objects into useful forms was carried further and applied to increasingly durable materials. Tool-making is one of the most characteristic activities of humans, and has had important consequences for the evolution of our species.

If we define ourselves as "tool-making animals," it follows that wherever there is found a consistent pattern of tool-making, human beings have been present. One of the major advantages of defining ourselves in this way lies in the fact that stone tools are much more likely to persist unchanged for thousands of years than the organic remains of the people who made them. Most of our evidence for the age and whereabouts of ancient humans comes from the tools they left behind. Fortunately, these tools also give clues to the kinds of activities in which our ancestors engaged.

The Earliest Hominids

In geological deposits that date back roughly five million years, anthropologists have discovered the beginnings of a continuous tradition of tool-making. The very earliest tools have been discovered in eastern Africa, but later deposits have been found in many other parts of the world. In some cases, the fossilized remains of the tool-makers have also been found. We call these creatures *hominids* to indicate their membership in the biological family to which modern humans belong, the Hominidae. Classifying them in this way also sets them apart from the ape family, technically known as the Pongidae. (See Figure 1.1.)

The best known of the early hominids are classified as members of the subfamily Australopithecinae. This subfamily includes *Australopithecus africanus,* a small hominid first discovered in 1924; *Australopithecus robustus,* a larger species; and several other fossils that have been given a confusing variety of names. The Australopithecinae are popularly referred to as "man-apes" or "ape-men." They may not be direct ancestors of our own species, but they certainly illustrate the kind of transitional creature that links humans with their simpler primate ancestors.

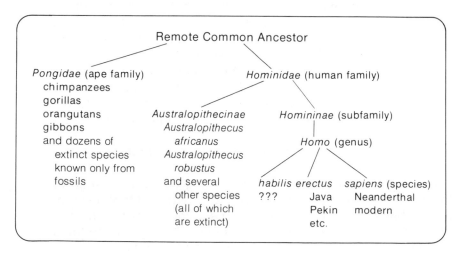

FIGURE 1.1 Classification of *Homo sapiens* and Our Closest Biological Relatives

As Charles Darwin noted long ago, the living apes and modern humans share so many anatomical and biochemical characteristics that they must all be descended from a common (primate) ancestor. In their millions of years of separate evolution, however, the pongids and the hominids developed systematic differences. Three of these differences are of special importance:

1. All the Hominidae are *bipedal,* that is, they walk upright on two feet rather than going on all fours or swinging by their arms.
2. The *brains* of the Hominidae are much larger than those of any ape of comparable size, and certain qualitative changes doubtless accompany this quantitative change.
3. Unlike the apes, who are primarily vegetarians and who have evolved long, pointed canine teeth for defense, the *teeth* of the Hominidae are relatively unspecialized and are adapted to a mixed diet of meat and vegetable foods.

These three general characteristics of the hominids are related to one another and to the unique tool-making capacities of our ancestors. The ability to walk upright leaves the forelimbs free for exploring and manipulating parts of the environment. The intellectual improvement that presumably accompanied increased brain size made possible the manufacture of more effective tools. And as tools became more effective, the anatomical characteristics that they replaced—such as large cutting and grinding teeth—became gradually less prominent. (This is an oversimplified statement of an extremely complex process, but it does illustrate how the human body and human culture evolved together.)

During the Australopithecine stage, from roughly five million years ago to less than a million years ago, the hominid brain was still comparatively small, but upright posture and bipedal locomotion were gradually perfected. These changes, together with increasing reliance on cultural means of adaptation, led to the next stage of human evolution.

Homo Erectus and *Homo Sapiens*

The next stage of human evolution is represented by the fossil remains of *Homo erectus*. These members of our own genus (*Homo*) lived throughout much of the Old World for perhaps as long as half a million years. They were effective tool-makers,

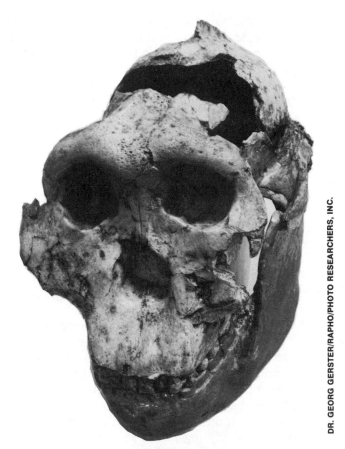

DR. GEORG GERSTER/RAPHO/PHOTO RESEARCHERS, INC.

The reconstructed skull of an Australopithecine discovered in 1959 by Dr. Louis Leakey in Bed I of Olduvai Gorge, Tanzania, East Africa. Leakey called this fossil "Zinjanthropus," and established its age at over 1,750,000 years. Most anthropologists today regard it as a member of the species Australopithecus robustus. *Whatever its classification, this early hominid walked erect, had a large brain, and most likely manufactured pebble tools of the Oldawan type.*

manufacturing a variety of stone and bone implements. Below the neck, their skeletons cannot be distinguished from our own. Their brains, however, were intermediate in size between those of apes and modern humans, and their skulls were quite rugged: the bones were thick, with heavy brow ridges above the eye sockets; the top of the skull was relatively flat and low, leaving no space for forehead; the jaw was large, chinless, and projecting; and the teeth were huge, though clearly human in form.

Examples of *Homo erectus* are the well-known Java and Pekin "ape-men" (formerly classified as the genus *Pithecanthropus*), as well as several more recent discoveries from North and East Africa. *Homo erectus* was an efficient hunter, and, judging by the presence of hearths, charcoal, and charred animal bones in the cave of Pekin man, had mastered the use of fire.

Consider for a moment the importance of the control of fire to the survival and development of humanity. Though fire is a chemical process rather than a physical object, it becomes a special type of tool when it is brought under control and used purposively. This tool gave people a way of releasing energy from organic substances to provide warmth, light, and protection from predators, and to cook food. In the hostile environment of the Ice Age, the control of fire was a great aid to survival.

Anthony F. C. Wallace has pointed out some striking implications of the control of fire. Groups of humans who had mastered the complex techniques of building, maintaining, and transporting fire had an advantage not only over wild animals but over other groups that had not mastered these techniques, or that perhaps could not master them because they were less intelligent than the fire-users. Wallace points out that considerable intelligence, foresight, and skill are required to control fire, as are constant subliminal attention and probably some division of labor within a group. Groups that lacked these intellectual abilities would gradually be eliminated, as would individuals within the more successful groups who were incapable of learning the essential skills (Wallace 1970: 65–72).

The invention of tools and techniques whose use required skill and intelligence favored the skillful and intelligent in the struggle for survival. Before the development of complex tools, nature tended to favor individuals with strength, speed, agility, or natural defenses. Intelligence was a helpful but secondary factor. Now, for the first time in the history of life, brains—not automatic reflexes—became the key to survival. The brain of *Homo erectus* expanded until it reached a size equal to that of the smaller-brained men and women of today (see Figure 1.2).

Neanderthals, the first well-known representatives of our own species, *Homo sapiens,* date back more than a hundred thousand years. Despite comic-strip stereotypes, their brains were on the average larger than ours. Neanderthals developed an elaborate tool-kit (known as the Mousterian culture), including stone scrapers for making clothing from animal skins. They buried their dead and apparently conducted rituals in connection with the skulls of slain bears.

The skulls of most European Neanderthals were thick and

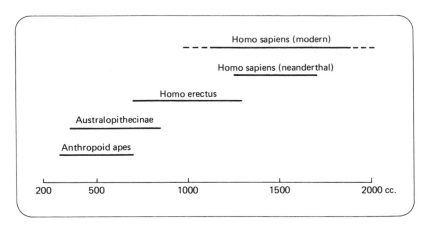

FIGURE 1.2 Range of Brain Sizes in Some Living and Fossil Primates (in cubic centimeters)

quite flat with heavy brow ridges, and the teeth were large and set into heavy, usually chinless jaws. Heavy brow ridges linger on in some modern races, but teeth and jaws have changed. As tools gradually took over the cutting, tearing, and crushing functions formerly performed by teeth, human teeth became smaller and the supporting bones of the face and jaw were reduced and rearranged. The chin, which had been absent in *Homo erectus* and only feebly developed in the Neanderthals, became more prominent, adding strength at a critical point to the jaw, which had become lighter and more fragile.

The earliest known fully modern humans date back only thirty to forty thousand years. Skulls from Combe Capelle and Cro-Magnon in France are not radically different from ours, though the Combe Capelle specimen has a rather weak chin and fairly prominent brow ridges. The skull is globular, encasing the highly developed brain in a thin sheet of bone. The face is almost vertical, with the jaws pulled back under the face.

These modern-looking hunters lived near the end of the great Ice Age. They pursued their game on both sides of the Mediterranean and in other parts of the Old World. They had several new techniques for making tools from various natural materials besides stone. On pieces of ivory and antler, and on the walls of their caves, they left the earliest known sculpture and pictorial art. These representations have been interpreted in a number of ways; they are probably attempts to portray those aspects of nature that were most important to these people, and perhaps to control them through portrayal.

Since the time of the Neanderthals, human bodies have

changed very little. Most of the changes have been directly related to a limited number of basic inventions, among them the development of weapons and cutting tools, the control of fire, the use of natural and artificial shelters (including that portable type of shelter called clothing), and the invention of improved ways of getting food by hunting, fishing, and, much later, cultivation. All these inventions have affected the human body. For example, our relative hairlessness is most likely related to the use of clothing, which makes a hairy body both unnecessary and unsanitary. There are close relationships between what we *do* and what we are (Bock 1977).

CULTURE AND RACE

The anthropologist uses *culture* to refer to a much broader range of phenomena than this term covers in ordinary speech. A classical anthropological definition of culture was presented

TOM MCHUGH/PHOTO RESEARCHERS, INC.

An example of Upper Paleolithic cave art from a site near Ariège, France, depicts animals wounded by spears.

by Sir Edward B. Tylor in 1871: "Culture . . . is that complex whole which includes knowledge, belief, art, morals, law, custom, and any other capabilities and habits acquired by man as a member of society." More recently, Robert Redfield has suggested that culture may be briefly defined as "the conventional understandings, manifest in act and artifact, that characterize societies" (1941:132). In both of these definitions the emphasis is on the ideas and ideals learned and shared by the members of a social group. For Redfield, as for Tylor, the tools and hearths of *Homo erectus* are *not* the culture of these ancient people, though they are *evidence* from which students of prehistory infer the presence of a cultured, tool-making animal. Such objects are the material results of "capabilities and habits" shared within human groups. We cannot "see" the culture. But from regularities in the form and distribution of things that we can observe, we are able to infer the existence of "conventional understandings."

The notion of culture is introduced here to distinguish between *culturally* regulated behavior, which is transmitted by learning, and *genetically* regulated behavior, which is transmitted by mating. Some differences among human groups have nothing to do with learning. These are called *racial* characteristics; they are the result of biological adaptation to different environments and are transmitted genetically through sexual reproduction. Some groups of people have only straight hair, others have naturally wavy hair; some have dark skin, others have little skin pigmentation; some are highly resistant to certain diseases, others are more susceptible; and so on. We cannot always understand the advantage conferred by racial characteristics, but the vast majority have come about by the evolutionary process of adaptation. The difference between genetically and culturally determined characteristics is fundamental. In one case, people look or behave as they do because they are "born that way." In the other case, they look or behave as they do because they are "brought up that way." One of the most important jobs of the anthropologist is to find out which is which.

Most of the really striking differences among human groups are culturally determined. The language that you speak, the tools that you use, the foods that you prefer, the career that you choose, your ideas about the beautiful and the supernatural— all depend primarily on the culture of the group in which you are brought up. Every normal human being has the biological capacity to learn *a* language, *a* technology, and *a* social code;

but *which* an individual will learn depends on place and time of birth, not on racial heredity.

Racial differences stem from the continuing biological evolution of human groups. Over many generations, each human population becomes adapted to a particular environment. Anthropology studies the biological and cultural adaptations of peoples to changing environments. Racial differences are interesting examples of human adaptability; however, the doctrine of *racism,* which asserts the superiority of one human group over others, receives *no scientific support* from any of the fields of anthropology.

THE FIELDS OF ANTHROPOLOGY

Anthropology is characterized by its breadth of interest in people and their creations. Ideally, an anthropologist is prepared to study every facet of human life, in all times and places. Anthropologists, to a greater extent than other social scientists, like to travel to strange places and work with exotic peoples at firsthand; they like to experience their materials directly. Like other natural scientists, they tend to bring back specimens for further study and display. Clyde Kluckhohn used to say that the main difference between anthropology and sociology is that sociologists have no museums.

Such a broad range of interests involves the danger of shallowness, and in an age of specialization it was perhaps inevitable that a division of labor would be established within the field of anthropology. The main subdivisions of the field are *physical anthropology* and *cultural anthropology.* Physical anthropologists are biologists with an interest in the evolutionary history of our species (including the process of race formation) and with an appreciation of the relevance of culture to human behavior. Cultural anthropologists, on the other hand, are primarily concerned with the material and social forms that humans have created throughout history, to cope with their environment and with each other.

Within cultural anthropology are a number of subdivisions. Prehistoric *archaeology* is the subfield that studies the material remains of cultures lacking written records, both for their intrinsic interest and with the goal of reconstructing the total pattern of life of people long dead.

Anthropological *linguistics* is concerned with the languages of all peoples, past and present. It looks at language from two general points of view: the *structural* approach is used to find out how languages work by analyzing their parts and describing how these parts go together; the *historical* approach is employed to reconstruct the form and relationships of languages that are no longer spoken. Language is treated in this book as a part of culture; its study can throw light upon many aspects of culture history and culture change.

The rest of cultural anthropology falls under the heading of *general ethnology*—the study of "peoples." It may be divided into three subfields, though these divisions reflect different emphases rather than clear-cut breaks, and there is a great deal of overlap among them. They are *ethnography,* which deals with the description of ways of life of particular social groups; *ethnology,* which emphasizes the comparison of cultures, the reconstruction of culture history, and the study of culture change; and *social anthropology,* which also emphasizes comparisons of cultures, but with the aim of generalizing about the nature of human societies and the relationships among social groups. (See Figure 1.3.)

Despite differences of approach and emphasis, most anthropologists hold as an ideal the notion of an integrated approach to humanity. Our bodies, our languages, and our ways of life must be understood in relation to one another. As Sol Tax once wrote, "Whether we are archaeologists or linguists, students of the arts or of geography, whether we study the behavior of ba-

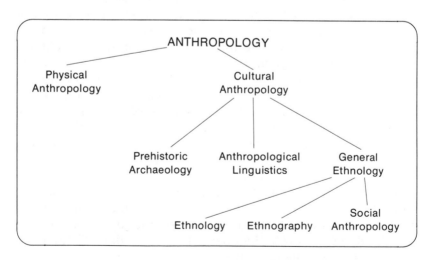

FIGURE 1.3 The Subfields of Cultural Anthropology

boons or the refinements of the human mind, we all call ourselves anthropologists" (1964:23). And all anthropologists are
trying to answer the question: What does it mean to be human?

RECOMMENDED READING

John E. Pfeiffer, *The Emergence of Man*, 3d ed. New York: Harper &
    Row, 1978. A highly readable, anecdotal account of human origins,
    with good material on primate behavior and recent archaeological
    discoveries as well as accounts of contemporary hunters and gath-
    erers.

Clifford J. Jolly and Fred Plog, *Physical Anthropology and Archaeol-
    ogy*. New York: Knopf, 1976. A well-written and profusely illustrated
    textbook on these subfields of anthropology, including up-to-date
    materials on the evolution of cultural diversity, the origins of food
    production, and the rise of civilization.

J. Z. Young, *An Introduction to the Study of Man*. New York: Oxford
    University Press, 1974. Probably the most comprehensive and au-
    thoritative single volume devoted to human development and vari-
    ation. Written with style and wit, it includes sections on psychology,
    culture, and behavior.

Robbins Burling, *Man's Many Voices*. New York: Holt, Rinehart & Win-
    ston, 1970. A useful if somewhat technical survey of methods and
    findings in anthropological linguistics.

David E. Hunter and Phillip Whitten, eds., *Encyclopedia of Anthropol-
    ogy*. New York: Harper & Row, 1976. A useful reference work cov-
    ering all the fields of anthropology, with clear definitions and in-
    formative articles.

CHAPTER TWO
THE PROCESS OF ENCULTURATION

EARLY STAGES OF ENCULTURATION

The traditions of a society begin to affect children before they are born. Recent research indicates that unborn children are not the passive parasites that they have long been thought to be. They are aware of light and darkness, hear and respond to loud noises, feel and react to pain, suck their thumbs, and actually drink the amniotic fluid. All societies have beliefs about unborn children and traditional interpretations of the various signs of pregnancy. Pregnant women are expected to behave in special ways: to exercise, rest, sleep in certain positions, eat (or refrain from eating) certain foods, avoid unpleasant sights or upsetting experiences, or (commonly) abstain from sexual relations for a period of time. Relatively little is known about the long-term consequences of such stimuli upon the developing child, but it seems highly likely that the behavior (particularly the diet) of a pregnant woman has some effects on the fetus. Some kinds of maternal behavior clearly affect the unborn child. Inadequate nutrition for the mother greatly increases the likelihood of spontaneous abortion or of stillbirth. Venereal disease is transmitted to the unborn child; children have been born addicted to various narcotics, while the effects of synthetic drugs such as thalidomide upon the developing fetus can be most serious.

Contemporary American culture includes a wide variety of beliefs about the way an expectant mother should behave. Some of these beliefs have sound scientific bases, and when followed can be shown to benefit both the mother and her unborn child. For example, it is generally believed that a woman should drink cow's milk during the latter part of her pregnancy; medical experiments have shown the importance of milk (or some other good source of protein and calcium) to the baby's development.

Other common American beliefs seem reasonable, but their scientific validity is still unproved. Contrasting beliefs in other cultural systems should make us suspend judgment about their effects. For example, in the United States and most European countries, a woman close to her time of delivery is expected to avoid strenuous tasks: she will usually quit her job a few weeks before the baby is due, rest a good deal, avoid traveling or lifting heavy objects, and so forth. In many other societies, a woman is expected to keep working at her usual tasks up to the last minute. Some anthropological reports tell of women who "turn aside from the path" to bear their children, catching up with their companions soon after. In some of these societies, the child's *father* then takes to bed to recover from the childbirth experience—a custom known as the *couvade*. (Recent interpretations of this custom may be found in Munroe and Munroe 1975: 124–133 and Rivière 1974.)

A number of current American beliefs have no rational basis. For example, most Americans are at least familiar with the notion that one can tell the sex of a baby from its position in the womb or from its degree of activity (boys are thought to kick more), and many people feel that it is bad luck to buy or send gifts of baby clothes before the child is born. Such beliefs are of dubious scientific validity, but they are nevertheless of great interest to the anthropologist, for they indirectly reveal facets of the culture that may not be consciously expressed—expectations about sex differences in behavior or anxieties about childbirth.

What is meant by the statement that such beliefs or customs are "part of American culture"? It means that American culture recognizes a *category of persons,* "women in late pregnancy," and associates with this category certain *plans for action,* such as drinking milk and avoiding strenuous tasks. Most Americans are aware of this category. They are also familiar with these plans for action, and with the conventional association between the category and the plans. If an American woman says, "That's too heavy for me to lift in my condition," most people will assume that she is pregnant.

It is the thesis of this book that the categories and plans that compose a culture *influence* but do not determine the behavior of the members of a society. That is, the presence of a rule or custom does not automatically produce compliance in persons who are familiar with it. Real behavior is always variable. Even in the simplest societies, variation is found among individuals, between subgroups, and over time. Ethnographers attempt to discover patterns and regularities in group behavior, but as part of this they must also analyze the causes of intra-cultural variation (see Pelto and Pelto 1975).

Customs Surrounding Childbirth

The circumstances surrounding the birth of a child differ greatly from place to place. The birth may be private and almost mysterious, with only the mother and a few female relatives in attendance, or it may be quite public with children and male relatives wandering in and out. There may be skilled midwives in attendance, or only a woman who has had many children. The mother may have to do everything for herself or she may be massaged and given herbal concoctions to ease the birth and the passage of the placenta.

Among the Dinka of Sudan (North Africa), children and men are excluded from the special hut in which delivery takes place. This is in part because the mother, if she is having a difficult delivery, will be encouraged to confess the names of all her lovers! Dinka believe that a difficult birth is usually a divine punishment for illicit sex, but they have alternative explanations available if the woman's reputation is "above reproach." In Dinka culture, birth establishes a spiritual tie between the child and the midwife who helps deliver it. This woman is called *geem,* meaning 'receiver, accepter,' one who accepts God's gift to the tribe (the child). According to Francis Deng, "As soon as the baby is born, the midwife sucks out the mucus from its nostrils to enable it to breathe. Because this necessity is so repulsive, it dramatizes the midwife's intense . . . devotion to the child and justifies her spiritual power over it" (1972:39).

Immediately after birth, infants may be subjected to a wide variety of experiences. They may be nursed or fed immediately, or left without food for hours or days. They may be isolated or kept close to their mothers continuously. They may be prayed over, anointed, admired, or even killed. The custom of *infanticide* (child killing) is found in many societies. In areas where economic resources are strictly limited, as on a small Pacific island, infanticide is a crude but effective method of population control. In such settings, it is usually accompanied by a belief that a child does not become fully human until it has received a name or had some other ritual performed for it; infanticide may be regrettable, but it is not considered murder. Other types of infanticide relate to supernatural beliefs. In a few African societies, twins were considered so unlucky for the group as a whole that one or both of them were always killed. One need not approve of this custom to be an anthropologist, but it is necessary to suspend moral judgment while investigating such a practice and its consequences. Even within a single society, opinion concerning such practices may differ; compare the debates in contemporary American society on the moral and legal status of abortion at various stages of fetal development.

Newborn children may simply be wiped off with leaves or pieces of fabric, but in most societies they are soon bathed. American culture explicitly prescribes that the temperature of the bath water be close to the baby's body temperature to avoid a shock to the system, but other societies believe quite differently. In many places, children a few hours or days old are plunged into ice-cold water as a matter of course. Whether this practice "hardens" the children to discomfort or simply eliminates those who cannot endure it is unclear. One recent study came to the surprising conclusion that in societies where such cold baths are administered, the average height of adults is considerably above what would be expected by chance. The shock to the system seems to be related to increased growth, at least for those who survive (Landauer and Whiting 1964).

At the other extreme is the Dinka custom of administering extremely hot baths to infants. Every morning and evening the Dinka child receives a hot bath, even in the most scorching weather. This "bathing period" continues throughout the child's first year of life. The procedure is quite elaborate. A huge pot of water is boiled, and the mother or some other woman of the household sits on a wooden stool, holding a gourd, which she uses to dip out the water and cool it to the correct temperature. "As the mother pours the water onto the baby . . . she turns it from side to side, massaging and exercising its arms, buttocks, genitals, thighs, legs, and even its toes. During all this, the baby continues to cry in terror, but that is expected and bothers no one." The purpose of this bath is not cleanliness, which the

Dinka recognize could be achieved with milder water, but rather to increase the child's circulation and to help it adapt to post-natal life. It is also considered essential to the proper development of the child: "It helps the baby to grow up healthy, well-built, and well-poised. A child who grows up crooked, or clumsy in build or poise, is believed to be—at least in part—the product of improper bathing. This is why there is such emphasis on the techniques of massaging and exercising during the bath" (Deng 1972:41–42).

Child Training and Culture

The question "What does a newborn baby need?" is answered not by any innate parental instincts but rather by the cultural traditions of the community into which the baby is born. Society, in the persons of those adults responsible for the well-being of the newborn, satisfies the infant's most urgent (or at least most obvious) needs, but only as these needs are defined by the culture and only according to conventional plans for their satisfaction.

Every society recognizes that infants cannot feed themselves and that they need assistance from adults in satisfying their need for nourishment. But since human beings lack built-in or instinctive feeding patterns, the what, how, where, and when of infant nourishment are left up to the beliefs of the responsible adults, and these beliefs are part of the group culture. As Dorothy Lee has observed:

> The first experience of solid food will differ according to the culture. If he is a Tikopia, he will get premasticated food, warmed with the mother's body warmth and partly digested through her salivary juices; his mother will put it directly into his mouth with her lips. If he is in our society, he will get this food with a hard metal spoon, introduced into a mouth which has never experienced anything so solid or hard, into which not even teeth have yet erupted. In all this, the culture enters into the food experiences, shaping, emphasizing, even choosing the significant factors for defining the experience [Lee 1959:154–155].

Some constraints on infant feeding are the result of situational factors: Eskimo babies would not be raised on mashed bananas or Arabian nomads on whale blubber. Aside from such obvious restrictions, the context and content of infant feeding depend on learned ideas, and thus vary from culture to culture. One cannot satisfy a child's hunger with food in the abstract—

some particular substance must be provided, by some particular person(s), at a given place and time, and in a particular manner. Gardner Murphy has suggested the term *canalization* to denote the psychological process whereby "needs tend to become more specific in consequence of being satisfied in specific ways" (1947:161ff.). That is, as the need for nourishment is satisfied with a particular substance and in a particular manner, the child becomes accustomed to these things. The infant who needed liquid becomes a child who wants a Coke.

As a result of repeated interactions with persons and objects, children begin to form more and more stable notions of what their world is like. They learn, in a vague, wordless way, what they can expect from the people around them. They learn how to control and coordinate their bodies, and that when they act in certain ways they can expect to evoke certain regular responses from others. When they cry, they are picked up or nursed or punished or rocked; when they reach for a shiny object, they are helped or encouraged or slapped or scolded. Equally important is the *emotional tone* of interactions with adults, for children can tell whether their parents are relaxed and self-assured or tense, anxious, and uncertain.

To summarize, culture first influences behavior by the ways in which an infant's needs are met (or ignored). By responding to babies' needs for food, affection, sleep, activity, sexual stimulation, or elimination in *culturally patterned ways,* the significant adults in their lives shape their behavior in accordance with the expectations of the society. Children learn where and when they are expected to eat, sleep, or empty their bowels, and in what ways they can satisfy their cravings for muscular activity and exploration, for protection and warmth. The late William Caudill once said, "By three to four months of age, babies are very much cultural beings."

These generalizations about the effects of culture on child development are illustrated by a careful study of mother-child interaction in America and Japan, performed by Caudill and Helen Weinstein. In each country, thirty urban, middle-class, intact families were observed. In each, the parents had only one child, between three and four months of age. Mother-child interactions were recorded by trained observers, who noted what took place during 800 one-second time samples. Significant differences were found between the two societies. Caudill and Weinstein reported that

> the Japanese baby seems passive, and he lies quietly with occasional unhappy vocalizations, while his mother . . . does more lulling,

RENE BURRI/MAGNUM

The Japanese child learns patterns unique to his culture.

carrying, and rocking of her baby. She seems to try to soothe and quiet the child, and to communicate with him physically rather than verbally. On the other hand, the American infant is more active, happily vocal, and exploring of his environment, and his mother in her care does more looking at and chatting to her baby. She seems to stimulate the baby to activity and to vocal response. It is as if the American mother wanted to have a vocal, active baby, and the Japanese mother wanted to have a quiet, contented baby . . . they seem to get what they apparently want [1969:31].

They point out that these patterns of behavior "are in line with the differing expectations for later behavior in the two cultures as the child grows to be an adult." This is particularly true in the areas of family life and general interpersonal relations, where, according to many studies, Japanese tend to be more group-oriented, more passive, and more sensitive to nonverbal forms of communication than are Americans, who tend to be relatively individual-oriented, assertive, and reliant upon verbal communication in a context of physical separation. These differences are expressed in differing cultural conceptions of what an infant needs:

> In Japan, the infant is seen more as a separate biological organism who from the beginning, in order to develop, needs to be drawn into increasingly interdependent relations with others. In America, the infant is seen more as a dependent biological organism who, in order to develop, needs to be made increasingly independent of others [1969:15].

Careful comparative studies such as this one have shown that cultural differences are real and potent influences early in life (but cf. Freedman 1974).

The Social Functions of Child Care

Because human infants are so helpless, and because adults have few (if any) parental instincts, each culture must provide conventional plans for dealing with young children. These customary practices instruct adults in the way they are expected to act, and, to the extent that they are followed, they provide similar patterns of stimulation for each child born into the society. A society lacking such customs could not survive for long with its youngest generation starving, falling into fires, or being consumed by predators. Anthropologists use the term *social function* to refer to the *contribution that a custom makes to the working and survival of the society in which it is found.* In general, child-care customs have two kinds of social functions: they ensure the physical survival of the young by satisfying their basic biological needs, and they help to produce the kind of person (personality type) who will fit into the society and maintain its values.

Some system of child-care customs is found in every society. It is a *cultural universal* that satisfies a clear set of social functions. But there can be a great variation in *how* a child is cared for. Even the question "Who should care for the young?" may be answered very differently in different parts of the world. Let us consider some of the major alternatives.

1. Mother and/or father: There are several obvious biological reasons for assigning care of infants to the female parent, but cultures differ in the extent to which they make the mother solely responsible for various aspects of child care. At one extreme we find the type of household in which the male parent is frequently (or always) absent; less common is the other extreme type in which, owing to the mother's absence, the father has complete responsibility for the children. Most societies fall between these extremes, but few strike such an even balance

as do the Mountain Arapesh of New Guinea. According to Margaret Mead, the Arapesh

> regard both men and women as inherently gentle, responsive, and cooperative, able and willing to subordinate the self to the needs of those who are younger or weaker, and to derive a major satisfaction from doing so. They have surrounded with delight that part of parenthood which we consider to be specially maternal.... Their dominant conception of men and women may be said to be that of regarding men, even as we regard women, as gentle, carefully parental in their aims [Mead 1935:100].

During recent recessions many American fathers have found themselves out of jobs and in charge of children and households while their wives worked. Many of these men have felt their masculinity threatened by the enforced performance of maternal tasks, but such feelings would be incomprehensible to an Arapesh father.

2. Parents and/or other relatives: In modern-day, mobile American society, it is unusual for several generations of the same family to live close together or for adult *siblings* (brothers and sisters) to maintain close ties. The American household generally consists of the husband, his wife, and their young offspring. In more settled societies, however, the household often includes members of several generations and/or siblings of one or both parents, any or all of whom may customarily care for the young. Many groups rely heavily on the child's elder siblings to provide care. Margaret Mead has commented that in Samoa, for example, "no mother will ever exert herself to discipline a younger child if an older one can be made responsible." Samoan girls of six or seven are generally entrusted with the care of their younger siblings.

> Relatives in other households also play a role in the children's lives. Any older relative has a right to demand personal service from younger relatives, a right to criticize their conduct and to interfere in their affairs.... So closely is the daily life bound up with this universal servitude and so numerous are the acknowledged relationships in the name of which service can be exacted, that for the children an hour's escape from surveillance is almost impossible [Mead 1949a:25].

3. Relatives and/or nonrelatives: In most societies, children are cared for by their relatives (though a "relative" may be defined quite differently in different societies). It is customary among the wealthier classes of many societies, however, to em-

ploy unrelated persons, usually of inferior status, to care for the young. Working parents in our own society often rely on a series of baby-sitters or child-care centers during a child's preschool years.

4. Individuals and/or group: In most societies, primary responsibility for a child's welfare rests upon a few individuals, but the social group also takes an interest in this matter. Through the force of public opinion or through legal action, the group may intervene if its expectations are not met. In some societies, the community or the state may take primary responsibility for child welfare. For example, in the most widely known type of Israeli kibbutz (a kind of communal farming community), children are raised from birth through adolescence in community-run nurseries, dormitories, and schools. They visit their parents for several hours each week. In such a society, the parent-child relationship is quite different from what we may think of as natural, but there certainly are some advantages, such as the relative absence of intra-family conflict (see Endleman 1967:127–178).

Like all cultural patterns, the alternatives outlined here are *conventional.* None of them can be predicted from knowledge of human biology alone. This does not mean that they are unrelated to other aspects of the cultures in which they occur. The pattern for the Israeli kibbutz was deliberately developed as part of a conscious attempt to equalize the status of men and women by freeing most of the women in the community from child care. Care performed by unrelated baby-sitters or by the unemployed parent is linked to the economic structure of the society, while the Samoan and Arapesh systems of child care are intimately connected with the major values of their societies. To say that a cultural pattern is conventional means only that it *could be otherwise* under different circumstances, not that it is random or that it bears no relationship to human biology or to the rest of the culture.

LATER STAGES OF ENCULTURATION

As children grow older, their range of experience broadens. This broadening depends on increased bodily control and acquisition of language. When children can be relied upon to behave in minimally acceptable ways, they are "taken into society," and as they come into contact with persons outside the immediate family, the pressures to conform to the expectations of the community are increased. Infants can be more or less self-centered. As they grow older they must learn to communicate with others and must become aware that different kinds of persons and situations call for different behaviors. They must begin to learn the categories of social life and the verbal and nonverbal plans associated with these categories.

Social Functions of Language Learning

Parents often lose patience with children who are going through what we call the "why stage." Their constant questioning can be extremely and sometimes deliberately annoying. However, children's questions provide excellent evidence of the conventionality of culture. Children have so much to learn. The ideas and relationships, categories and plans that adults take for granted are all new to children, and language is a marvelous key that can help unlock the mysteries.

Cultures differ in the amount of emphasis they put on formal education as opposed to informal learning, and on verbal instruction as opposed to observation or imitation. In some American Indian societies, people are embarrassed to ask how to do a job. Among the Indians of Guatemala, even complex tasks such as operating a machine or driving a car are learned by observation and imitation. Learners simply watch until they feel they are ready to try on their own; they then take over, often with surprising success (Nash 1958:26). On the other hand, the people of Guadalcanal rely heavily on direct verbal instruction; in most situations children are subjected to a steady stream of verbal admonitions from responsible adults, telling them what to do and inculcating the primary values of generosity and respect for property (Hogbin 1964:33). In most nonliterate societies, informal education is supplied by watching and questioning one's elders, while the more abstract traditions of the group are transmitted through legends, myths, and songs. Formal educational institutions appear only in more complex societies, but they are always supplemented by informal education within the family and peer group (see Chapter 5).

Sooner or later, all normal people learn to behave in ways that are appropriate to the situations characteristic of their societies. Appropriate behavior includes the use of language in ways that others consider correct.

Words are labels for categories of experience. They enable us to group quite diverse events and sensations under a single heading and to discriminate them from other events and sensations. Categories that are named by different words also tend to have different plans for the actions associated with them. For example, in certain situations the color categories that we call "red" and "green" also carry the meanings "stop" and "go." To call a clear liquid "nitroglycerin" and an animal a "rattlesnake" is also to call forth certain modes of behavior toward them.

A language implies a way of looking at the world, a way of dividing continuous or variable phenomena into discrete and stable categories to which we learn to attach different kinds of responses. A beginner in a culture—whether a child or an anthropologist—must learn the names of thousands of categories of things and also the kinds of responses to each category that the society considers appropriate.

Social Careers

Within the social world, the maturing individual enters upon a social career. We learn that our society values certain kinds of behavior, and that our families and peers expect us to become certain kinds of people. Most of us strive to fulfill their expectations. Exactly what we will strive for depends primarily on the values of our culture. We may seek to accumulate material goods of a certain kind, or we may spend our lives earning spiritual merit by a life of prayer or by philanthropy. We may seek intellectual attainments, mystical experiences, or the glories of war. We may hope to have many children or remain celibate. Once we have begun a social career, many social and psychological forces operate upon us to maintain our conformity to group expectations.

Every known human society has somewhat different expectations for men than for women. The sexual division of labor is universal. Anthropology has demonstrated, however, that the association of particular tasks with one sex rather than the other is largely a matter of cultural convention. Things that are considered "men's work" in one society (e.g., gardening, fishing, weaving, cooking, or curing) may be considered "women's work" elsewhere, or may be assigned indifferently to both sexes. And these conventions may change in a relatively brief period in response to new opportunities or problems.

In a society with *only* sexual division of labor, every man would expect a career like that of every other man, and every woman like that of every other woman. All men would expect to hunt and fish in order to provide meat for their families, to make the tools they needed, to construct shelters, and to defend the group. All women would expect to care for children, gather plant food, prepare food and clothing, make baskets, and so forth. Because of personal preference or particular abilities, some people might specialize or take the lead in one of these activities, but they would still participate in all the others considered appropriate for their sex. Activities expected of persons would naturally be different at different times in their careers, but this variation too would be part of the pattern.

Actually, even the simplest known societies provide some alternatives besides the standard sexual careers. Nearly everywhere, part-time religious specialists take the lead in ceremonies, often involving curing. Such persons (*shamans*) are recognized by their fellows as being different, even though they may perform the usual tasks expected of their sex at other times. Some societies have separate careers for men who cannot fit into the usual pattern. Among the Crow Indians, a male who was unsuited for the life of a hunter and warrior was able to become a *berdache.* According to Robert Lowie, such "men-women" wore female clothing and performed the usual female tasks, often excelling in them (1956:48).

In more complex societies, the division of labor is much more elaborate, and a number of different careers may be available to each individual. The development of full-time specializations within a society depends primarily on the degree of technological development of the society, particularly the production of an economic surplus. When people exist at a bare subsistence level, there is little room for specialization. In areas of unusual natural abundance, however, or in societies that have mastered the techniques of food production, the existence of a surplus makes it possible to release some members of the population from subsistence activities. They may then devote much of their time to the production of specialized goods and services, and exchange them for necessities.

Typical careers found in societies with an assured food surplus include:

1. *Ritual specialists*—priests, diviners, curers
2. *Technical specialists*—warriors, traders, craftworkers (potters, weavers, metalworkers)
3. *Political specialists*—chiefs, judges, tax collectors

These careers may not be open to all members of the society, but the existence of such alternatives and the interactions among persons pursuing different careers increases social and cultural complexity.

One important effect of the division of labor upon society is the *creation of interdependence* among its members. French sociologist Emile Durkheim (1947) emphasized this social function of the division of labor: if men and women perform different but complementary tasks, each sex will tend to be bound to the other. Similarly, craftworkers and their customers, curers and their patients, industrialists and their suppliers depend on each other for goods and services.

Education and Social Control

The multiplication of careers calls for a variety of forms of enculturation. Even in societies where the number of careers is small, particular persons or groups must be made responsible for the continuing education of the young. Most often, this social function is fulfilled by a relative of the same sex as the child. The mother will instruct her daughters in the womanly duties, and the father will be responsible for seeing that his sons know what they need to know and behave as they should. Other relatives may supplement or replace the parents as teachers of certain topics. Among the Apache, the mother's brother is the one whom a boy must strive to excel in hunting and running. A special relationship is also found between a child and the father's sister. Among the Hopi Indians, this relative names the child; a girl goes to her father's sister for the important corn-grinding ceremony, while a boy is sponsored by her when he enters the warrior society.

The force of *public opinion* is very great in all small-scale societies (whether in Africa or Arkansas). A child's behavior reflects back upon the parents and other kinspeople. People everywhere are concerned about what the neighbors will say, and this concern provides an important motive for educating and disciplining the young. The forms of social control vary widely from culture to culture, but they are always present.

It is really only in large urban centers that the individual can to some extent attain anonymity and relative freedom from group pressures. But in a little community where everyone knows everyone else and where daily interaction and interdependence are to be expected, one does not violate custom lightly. In such societies, the threat of gossip or of the informal withdrawal of approval and cooperation is sufficient to keep most people in line. This point is stressed because of a widely accepted fallacy concerning primitive peoples: it is sometimes claimed that primitive people adhere to the customs of the group and obey its laws instinctively and without thought. But primitive peoples no more have law-abiding instincts than they have inborn senses of direction. It is true that in small, isolated societies, people do tend to have great respect for tradition per se, but in every society, the content of the traditions must be *learned,* and its members (if not visitors or ethnographers) are aware of the various social forces that constrain their behavior as well as the punishments that follow misbehavior.

At the same time, the egalitarian organization of social life makes it difficult for one individual to discipline another directly. Many observers have commented on the relative absence of physical punishment administered by primitive parents. Among the North American Indians, the mother's brother or an eminent tribal elder may be called on to admonish youngsters and to

COURTESY OF THE MUSEUM OF NATURAL HISTORY

Ritual specialists (shamans) of the Haida Indians underwent long, arduous training to cope with the supernatural.

instruct them concerning their duties, but it is unusual for a parent to use force in dealing with a child. Tribal peoples are often shocked by the "brutality" of civilized parents.

Threat of supernatural punishment is another means of controlling behavior. Stories of a mysterious owl that pecks out the eyes of naughty children or of giants and cannibal spirits who carry off offenders are widespread means of obtaining obedience. The occasional appearance of a stranger disguised as such a bogeyman contributes to the effectiveness of these beliefs. Among the Pueblo Indians, the various gods (or *kachinas*) are impersonated in elaborate and impressive ceremonies; some of these rituals include beating the boys with special whips. In this way, the parents are relieved of the odious task of direct discipline.

Beliefs in supernatural punishment, whether in this or another life, are particularly effective means of social control, since they may deter violations that would otherwise go undetected and unpunished. The belief that one's future position depends on proper behavior and merit earned in one's present life (reincarnation) is a strong force for conformity and performance of social obligations. Similarly, belief in *taboo,* which brings automatic punishment for an offense, is a deterrent to misbehavior. No reasonable man would steal a tabooed object if he believed that the action would bring illness or some other retribution.

Such beliefs also have the advantage of being *self-validating.* If a person is born into a low social position it is because of sins in a previous life; who can disprove it? If sinners are punished, it is because they violated a taboo. If innocent people suffer, they must have unknowingly offended some spirit or human sorcerer. If someone behaves in an unconventional manner, this behavior may be evidence that the person is practicing witchcraft. Accusation (or even the threat of accusation) may bring confession and conformity. Such an incident reinforces belief in witchcraft, and even the accused person may be impressed, for many groups believe that one can become a witch without knowing it.

In many societies, the strongest source of social control is the *peer group.* In our own society we recognize the high degree of conformity to codes of dress, speech, and behavior found among teen-agers. David Reisman (1950) has suggested that this "other-directedness" is a general feature of American middle-class culture. But peer-group influence is by no means limited to American society. Among the Red Xhosa, a traditionally militaristic tribe of South Africa, neighborhood groups of young men meet together regularly for parties and "cudgel games" (fighting with sticks). As Philip and Iona Mayer have shown, these meetings—which provide opportunities for sexual encounters, fights, and the development of intense local loyalties—are also the means by which Xhosa boys learn to canalize their sexual and aggressive drives into the restrained forms approved of by the youth group.

> These groups also provide a forum where male youth acquire politico-judicial skills and develop a concern with "law"—both highly valued in Red Xhosa culture. In these groups, too, social contacts with peers are progressively widened, in a way that makes for eventual self-identification as a Xhosa, over and above kinship and community identifications [1970:160].

In every society, then, conformity is brought about by means of education and social control. Ultimately, conformity is maintained by physical force (including prison or the firing squad). But primary controls on behavior are built into the individual in the early and later stages of enculturation, and they are maintained by informal pressure from family, peers, and local authorities.

Formal education in primitive society seldom involves going to a school. More often, elaborate instruction is given as part of a personal relationship between tutor and student or between craftmaster and apprentices. In societies where the only truly specialized career is that of shaman, a long and arduous preparation may be necessary before novices are allowed to practice their new skills. Among the Tapirapé, an Indian tribe of central Brazil, the shamans have many important functions and very high prestige. As described by Charles Wagley, the road to shamanism is difficult and often frightening. Tapirapé shamans exercise their powers primarily by *dreaming,* at which time they are believed to visit the spirit world. Young people of either sex may be recognized as future shamans because of their tendency to dream a great deal. The apprentice shaman may not bathe, indulge in sexual intercourse, or eat certain foods. Many novices do not continue after the first few nights, but

> other novices, more successful and more persistent, do dream. At first they see smoky forms of ghosts and sometimes forest demons; they as yet do not know how to talk with such spirits. . . . After several seasons the novice may see dangerous forest demons in his

unconscious state and he may talk with ghosts. . . . The mere fact that the young shaman has several dangerous dreams does not make him a proved shaman. He must take part in the "fight" against the beings of Thunder, and by the side of his mentor he may attempt cures. If successful, he may be called now and again by people for cures. With a reputation for several cures and with continual dreaming, during which he has supernatural encounters, he builds up his reputation as a shaman over a period of many years [Wagley 1959:421–422].

Most of the formal education found in primitive societies has to do with esoteric matters: curing, ritual, tribal mythology, and so forth. In the absence of writing, complex traditions must be communicated orally and stored in the memory. This is one of the few characteristics shared by all primitive societies. The detailed memory cultivated by shamans and storytellers is indeed astounding. For example, among the Navajo Indians, the "singers" (one type of curer) must memorize and perform complex rituals sometimes lasting for several days and nights. Memorization of these Navajo rites, which include complicated gestures, manipulation of ritual objects, and construction of sand paintings, has been estimated to require as much effort as would be required to memorize the entire score of a Wagnerian opera. Such comparisons are difficult to validate, but the memory displayed by the Navajo singers, particularly in the absence of any written model, is most impressive.

In other societies the transmission of ritual and practical knowledge may be made the responsibility of particular groups, often secret societies. Among the Pueblo Indians, a person who has been cured by members of one of the curing societies is required to join that group and participate in its activities. Other such groups carry on activities in connection with warfare or agriculture, just as experts in various fields of knowledge in our own society (military officers, agronomists, doctors, and so on) are made responsible for the practice and transmission of their own specialized skills and knowledge.

In many parts of Africa and India, blacksmiths form a distinct and usually hereditary group. To an outsider, there is something uncanny and mysterious about their ability to bend and shape metals. Within the group the skills are often surrounded with legendary and magical associations. Thus, although blacksmiths may be very low in the social hierarchy, they are also accorded a special kind of respect because of their reputation for sorcery. A similar attitude has been found in eastern Europe

toward the gypsies—another group with metalworking and al-
legedly magical skills.

Initiation Ceremonies

The initiation ceremony is a widespread custom that in many
societies constitutes the most significant educational experience of an individual. It is one of a number of ceremonies to
which Arnold van Gennep (1960) gave the name *rites of passage.* Other rites of passage include ceremonies connected with
pregnancy and childbirth, betrothal and marriage, death and
funerals, and even journeys. All of these ceremonies have to do
with the movement of individuals from one social position or
status to another. The change may involve physical locality,
group affiliation, or progression within a social career (from
childhood to adulthood, maidenhood to marriage, life to death).
In each case the ceremonies contain three ordered stages that
dramatize the change of status. Van Gennep called these stages
(1) separation, (2) transition, and (3) incorporation.

When moving from one social status to another, the individual first is physically or symbolically separated from his or her
present position, then passes through a transitional state, and
finally is reincorporated into society in a different status. The
individual cannot go directly from Status A to Status B, but must
proceed indirectly, as shown in Figure 2.1. The symbolic enact-
ment of death and rebirth, which plays such an important part
in Christian theology and ritual, is an extremely common form
of the rite of passage.

Anthropologists have placed emphasis on different parts of
this process. In his studies of male puberty rites, John Whiting
has emphasized the violent separation of adolescent boys from
maternal influence (the cutting of the apron strings) and their

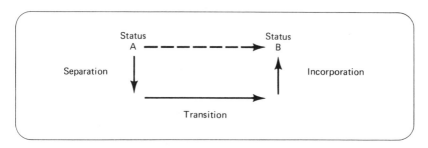

FIGURE 2.1 A Rite of Passage

incorporation into the world of adult males. His work indicates that in societies where young boys are particularly close to their mothers (to the point of sleeping for years in the same bed), initiation rites at puberty will be particularly traumatic, often involving circumcision or other genital mutilations (Whiting et al. 1967).

In many parts of the world, initiation rites have an obvious educational function. During the stage of transition, initiates must learn the behavior appropriate to their new status and/or demonstrate that they have mastered the necessary knowledge and skills. This process resembles basic training in the military: the boy initiate or recruit is torn away from his family and familiar surroundings; he is forced to undergo exhausting, intensive, and often humiliating tests of courage and stamina; he learns a new (esoteric) vocabulary and mythology, and behavior appropriate to his new status. When he successfully completes the initiation, he returns to society as a new kind of person, a real "man"—perhaps a Marine.

Initiation rites may last from a few hours to several years, and the emphasis may be placed upon any or all of the educational elements described above. In some groups technical skills may be communicated (including some very practical sex education), while in others the emphasis is on learning songs and legends. This is the time when distinctive tribal marks may be tattooed on or cut into the body; the latter practice is known as *scarification.* Among the aborigines of Australia, initiation was a long and extremely important ceremony, often involving circumcision, scarification, knocking out of teeth, and intensive training in group traditions and legends. Among the Tiwi of Australia

> small boys picked up the techniques of making spears and throwing sticks by spending time with older boys who in turn improved their skill both in making and using hunting weapons by spending time with the local men.
>
> Although much of this learning was fairly random, other instruction was not. During his initiation period a youth spent long intervals isolated in the bush with a couple of older teachers from whom he received training in religious and ritual matters. At the same time, of course, it was inevitable that the novice absorb some of the older men's experience in bushcraft. There was no corresponding initiation period for girls. What they learned, they learned first from the older women of their childhood household and later from the older women of the husband's household into which they moved as child-brides after puberty [Hart and Pilling 1964:49].

Tiwi initiations were climaxed by the *kolema* phase, held during the wet season, when the *kolema* yam provided abundant food. The *kolema* ceremony was a two-week festival that always attracted many people. It was quite a contrast with the initiates' isolation in the bush (separation and transition), as well as with the usual conditions of Tiwi life, since for most of the year the Tiwi (like most food-gathering peoples) lived in small, nomadic groups composed of a few families. The *kolema* festival was the main religious event of the year, "full of dancing, singing, wailing, and excitement. The excitement was the psychological result of so many people being together at the same time, a rare experience in the life of any Tiwi" (Hart and Pilling 1964:40).

Rites of passage play an important part in the social life of every group. They provide standardized ways of dealing with the life crises that occur in every society, and dramatize (for both the individual and the group) a person's social progression. The ceremonies serve important psychological and social functions. Without them, people feel unsure about their social positions, while the group does not know what to expect of them. Some experimental evidence from social psychology indicates that the more painful a rite of passage, the more a person values the new status (Aronson and Mills 1959:177–181).

Despite the many ways in which a society ensures obedience to tradition, enculturation is *not* primarily a punishing or restricting process. Children actively seek to master the culture of their group: they want to speak and to be understood, to be accepted, and to become real men and women. The learning of useful skills and the assumption of adult responsibilities are rewarding in and of themselves. Most societies try to help their members through their life crises, recognizing and rewarding their new-found abilities. There may be a feast to honor a young man who kills his first deer or enemy warrior, a story in the newspaper when a young woman passes her bar examination, or simply encouragement and approval when a student does well. Ernest G. Schachtel has written:

> Being born and growing up in a concrete society and culture drastically narrows the patterns of relatedness to the world offered to the growing child. On the other hand, it makes it possible for him not to get lost in the infinite possibilities of his world-openness, but to find, within the framework of his culture and tradition, his particular structure of relatedness to the world [1959:71].

We shall return to this important paradox in the Epilogue of this book.

Nacirema Initiation

The Nacirema live in the general area between the territories of the Cree of central Canada and the Tarahumara of northern Mexico. Some of their customs have been described by Ralph Linton (1936), Horace Miner (1956), and Thomas Gladwin (1962). The following description of their major initiation ceremony is based on several years of personal observation.

During the late spring, large gatherings are held in all *setats* to celebrate the passage of the members of an age-grade into adulthood. Initiation begins at an early age, for members of both sexes, and continues for twelve or more years, until the elders are satisfied that a young person has acquired the necessary knowledge to permit him or her to compete in the prestige system. Persons who do not complete this basic initiation are known as *drabawts* and are condemned, at least in theory, to menial occupations and low-status marriages. Many such men become warriors and attempt to acquire status and property by deeds of valor.

A striking fact about the preparation for Nacirema initiation is that, though sexual division of labor is strongly marked for adults, both sexes usually receive the same basic instruction in tribal mythology, folk science, and the manipulation of esoteric symbols. Females sometimes receive training in sewing or cooking and males in woodcraft, but these activities take little time compared with the many hours spent in rote learning of ideology, magical number combinations, and the representations of words by conventional junctions of signs. The Nacirema are very fussy about accuracy in the archaic representations of words, particularly when these signs bear no phonetic resemblance to the sounds they represent. It is not surprising that some successful people who have never been able to master the system employ scribes to ensure the ritual accuracy of their messages, since a single error in a message is enough to discredit the sender.

In the final initiation ceremony the young initiates are marched to some high place, while younger persons blow and beat on musical instruments. Kinspeople of the initiates watch with pride, sometimes calling encouraging remarks. The initiates are doubtless uncomfortable, but they smile bravely, for their ordeal is finally coming to an end. Often they are accorded certain adult privileges just before the final ceremony, such as the face-scraping rite described by Linton (for males) and the head-baking rite described by Miner (for females). Both sexes are dressed in their finest clothes, but the finery is covered by black robelike garments, which indicate the sacred nature of the ceremony. Initiates wear a peculiar black headdress, designed for its symbolic value.

The leaders of the initiation school, who have been responsible for discipline during the last four years of training, stand with the initiates, as do some local chiefs. When all have assembled, a leader of some local cult invokes the blessing of the gods upon the initiates and the main part of the ceremony begins. This stage consists, first, of a number of orations by the leaders, the visiting chiefs, and certain members of the group being initiated. The chosen initiates are expected to praise their instructors and to thank them for the great benefits conferred upon them and for allowing them to be initiated—despite the fact that the restless Nacirema youth have complained unceasingly during their preparation about the constraints and discipline of the instructors. The longest oration is then delivered by the highest ranking chief present. It is notable for its lack of relevance.

The climax of the ceremony is reached when each of the initiates is called forward to receive the blessing of the leaders and the mark of adulthood. Until now, the initiates have been treated as a group, but at last their individuality is recognized. The classic pattern of a rite of passage is enacted. The initiate leaves her age-group (separation). She humbly approaches the leader, who touches her right hand and presents her with a magical scroll with her name inscribed in archaic script (transition). She then returns to the group of initiates, having adjusted her headdress to indicate her new status (incorporation). Another blessing is recited, this time by the leader of a rival local cult, and the initiates (now known as *grádjuits*) march off to the sound of drums and horns, to join their families and friends.

The values expressed in the orations and in the ceremony itself contribute to the perpetuation of the initiation system and the adult society. Some parents have been known to take up residence in particular villages so that their children will be initiated by respected leaders and instructors. Initiates who show particular promise are encouraged to go through further ceremonies, acquire esoteric knowledge available only at special cult centers, and become instructors themselves. Although the financial sacrifices required to adopt such a life are considerable, many young people (presumably those who are most tradition-oriented) do so, and perpetuate the very system against which they had rebelled. Thus does the weighty hand of tradition press down upon each succeeding generation, molding its members to the ideals and expectations of the society.

RECOMMENDED READING

Mary Ellen Goodman, *The Culture of Childhood*. New York: Teachers College Press, 1970. A brief but enlightening account of the ways in which children in different cultures see themselves and are seen by adults, including material on learning, identity, values, and play.

Daniel G. Freedman, *Human Infancy: An Evolutionary Perspective*. Hillsdale, N.J.: Lawrence Erlbaum Associates, 1974. A challenging, sociobiological approach to the behavior of human infants and the genetic basis of individual, sexual, and population differences.

Robert L. Munroe and Ruth H. Munroe, *Cross-Cultural Human Development*. Monterey, Calif.: Brooks/Cole, 1975. A useful summary of cross-cultural research on human development, emphasizing the influence of culture on physical and psychological changes through the life cycle.

James P. Spradley and Michael A. Rynkiewich, eds., *The Nacirema: Readings on American Culture*. Boston: Little, Brown, 1975. A variety of writings on the remarkable culture of this North American group, including material on enculturation and schooling.

CHAPTER THREE
LEARNING A LANGUAGE

The genetic heritage of every normal child includes the capacity to learn one or more languages. *Which* language (or languages) we learn depends on the speech community in which we grow up. Usually this will be the home community of our biological parents, but there is no *necessary* connection between genetic heredity and speaking any particular language. If a child born in Germany, to German parents, is brought up among only native speakers of Japanese, he will learn to speak Japanese as his mother tongue; furthermore, in learning to speak or understand German, he will have *no advantage* over other Japanese speakers.

What does it mean to "learn a language"? To begin with, imagine entering a room where several people are conversing in a tongue completely unfamiliar to you. Instead of rapidly retreating, listen to them and try to understand what is going on. Your first impression—that which tells you that the language being spoken is one you don't know—is that the sounds are very different from those of English. Quite a few of the individual sounds may be familiar, but there will be some sounds and many combinations of sounds that you have never heard and that you can imitate only with difficulty.

Not only are these people making strange sounds, they also

Australian aborigine children (Pitjantjatjara) learn the sound system and meanings of a new language.

appear to understand one another—the sounds they are making are transmitting messages and provoking responses in the form of further messages, actions, laughter, or tears. Since you do not know the code, you have no way of understanding these messages, nor can you respond to them appropriately if they are addressed to you. This is a frustrating experience.

Consider the case of a child born into an English-speaking community. She has, in a sense, come into a room full of people speaking a language she does not understand. Unlike adults learning a second language, the child does not know there *is* such a thing as language, nor does she have any habits of speech that could interfere with her acquisition of English. How, then, does acquisition of language take place?

The general primate characteristics of curiosity, vocalization, and imitation certainly play some part in children's language learning. Unlike apes and monkeys, human children also seem to be born with a special capacity to learn the language of their community quickly and effectively. The mere imitation of sounds, though important, is only a small part of what the child must do.

Starting at about six months, children begin to "babble"— that is, spontaneously to produce sounds such as *ta, nu,* or *gee,* and commonly to reduplicate syllables (*tata, nunu, mama,* and so forth). By the time they are a year to eighteen months old, they usually have about twenty "words"; they follow simple commands and respond to "no." At this point, their comprehension of language is not much more advanced than that of well-trained dogs, but by twenty-one months of age a major advance usually takes place: vocabulary increases tenfold, they understand simple questions, and they speak two-word phrases of a few characteristic forms, for example, "dada go," "baby up," "see ball."

By two years of age most children have vocabularies of 300 to 400 words, and they use prepositions and pronouns in constructing two- and three-word phrases. The most rapid increase in vocabulary takes place during the following year: by age three many children know a thousand words.. During this period children learn to compose a wide variety of sentence types; more and more of their utterances are *free from grammatical errors,* even though they are *unlike anything an adult might say.* Child language is *not* just an imitation of adult language with mistakes.

At each stage, the child's verbal productions show patterning and system. It is as if the child is forming rules about how to speak and then systematically testing them, modifying them, and adding new ones until he achieves (unconsciously, of course) a set of rules that adequately guide his speaking and understanding. The rules have to do with categories of sounds, sound combinations, and the association of sound combinations with different meanings. The members of a speech community have equivalent sets of rules—plans for speaking— which make it possible for them to communicate complex and novel messages. Children must discover these rules for themselves with only occasional instruction from adults and peers. Parental attempts to teach children to speak have relatively little effect upon the speed with which these basic abilities appear. The child learns primarily by listening for recurrent *patterns of sound* and by inferring rules for their use.

Let us take one familiar example. In speech and in writing, most English speakers use the words "a" and "an" in regular and predictable ways. Literate adults are able consciously to formulate the rule that determines which of these forms of the indefinite article should be used. Most four-year-old children, however, use these forms correctly, even though they cannot read or write, are seldom instructed on this point, and do not consciously understand the distinction between a vowel and a consonant. Furthermore, our pronunciation of the word "a" is quite variable: in ordinary fast speech most Americans say it as a kind of grunted *uh,* but in more careful speech many people pronounce it as they do the vowel in *hay.* The sound of the vowel in the word "an" is like neither of these, but rather like the vowel in *hat.*

Children (or adults) learning English must learn to distinguish these sounds and to use them in correct combinations. They could, of course, adopt a gambler's strategy: noticing that "a" occurs far more often than "an," they could just say "a" all the time, figuring that they are more likely to be right than wrong. But, interestingly, children do not seem to do this: they seek the *pattern,* and despite mistakes, eventually learn the rule. Without being consciously aware of any reasons, they learn to antic- ipate the initial sound of the following word (even if it is one they are saying for the first time) and to use the appropriate form of the article. It should be emphasized that there is nothing in human anatomy that makes it *necessary* for English speakers to say "an" before a vowel. This rule is purely conventional, the result of a long process of language history. In fact, a thousand years ago, Old English had only the form *ān,* 'one,' which was rarely used as an article. This is why we say that linguistic rules are "conventional understandings" and a part of culture.

SOUND SYSTEMS

In trying to understand the sound system of a language, we must not be misled by written forms. In English (and in many other written languages) a letter may correspond to more than one sound. The converse is also true: a sound may be repre- sented by more than one letter. The important thing to learn is which *differences among sounds* always signal *differences of meaning.*

Some of these contrasts are clearly represented in traditional spelling: "pat" is different from "bat" in its initial sound, while "bat" and "bet" differ in their vowels, and "bet" differs from "bed" in its final consonant. Since these pairs of words differ only in the quality of a single sound, they are called *minimal pairs.* All English speakers agree that these differences are significant, and that such phrases as "bat boy" and "bad boy" have different meanings. A few technical terms will make the point clearer. Both *t* and *d* are pronounced by *stopping* (and then releasing) the flow of air from the lungs by placing the tip of the tongue just above the teeth. These sounds are both called "front stops." They differ in the quality known as *voicing*: the *d* is said to be "voiced" because the vocal cords are allowed to vibrate as it is pronounced (you can feel the vibration if you place your fingers lightly upon your larynx); the *t* is "voiceless" because the vocal cords do not vibrate when it is pronounced. (Another minimal pair that differs only in voicing is contained in the word "downtown.") The distinction between voiced and voiceless sounds, together with other differences produced by altering the position and muscular tension of the lips and tongue and by changing the shape of the vocal cavities, is the basis of all significant sounds in the English language. For example, the sound represented by the letter *k* is a voiceless stop, but it differs from the *t* sound in being pronounced with the back of the tongue against the back part of the mouth. The voiced stop produced with the tongue in the back position is *g*. These four sounds are distinguished from one another as shown in Figure 3.1.

Phonemes

The four stops discussed above are actually four *categories of sound,* defined by the two attributes of tongue position (front or back) and voicing (voiced or voiceless). In English, if all other sounds are held constant, these attributes consistently make a

	Position of Tongue	
	Front	*Back*
Voiceless	*t*	*k*
Voiced	*d*	*g*

FIGURE 3.1 Four English Stops

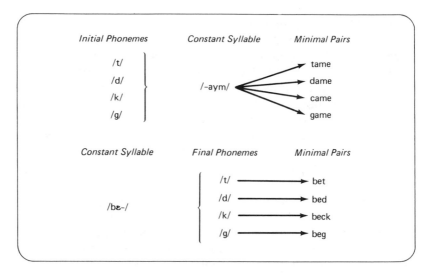

FIGURE 3.2 Four English Consonant Phonemes

difference in the meaning of words. We can show this by taking the four stops and placing each one at the beginning or end of certain syllables to produce different words. (See Figure 3.2.)

Sound categories that can be shown consistently to make a difference in meaning are known as *phonemes.* By convention, the symbols for phonemes are enclosed between slashes (/t/, /d/, /k/, /g/) to distinguish them from the letters of the alphabet.

A similar method can be used to show that our English letter *a* represents no fewer than five different *vowel phonemes.* If we take the initial sounds in the words "Africa," "Asia," "Australia," "America," and "Arctic," and insert them between the phonemes /t/ and /k/, we find that each change of vowel produces a word with a different meaning. (See Figure 3.3.)

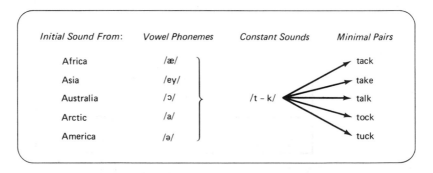

FIGURE 3.3 Five English Vowel Phonemes

The study of sound systems is called *phonology.* The phonemes of a language, like the dots and dashes of a code, communicate specific meanings only when arranged in conventional patterns. *Although phonemes signal differences of meaning, they are not in themselves meaningful.* The phoneme /t/ has no more meaning than the phoneme /p/ or /æ/, but they may be put together into units that do communicate meanings, for example, "tap," "pat," "apt." What is important about a phoneme such as English /d/ is that it is different from all other English phonemes: Because English speakers have *learned to pay attention* to differences in voicing and tongue position, we are able to attach different meanings to patterns of phonemes such as /bed/ versus /bet/ and /dot/ versus /tot/. But /d/ and /t/ do not, in themselves, mean anything.

In many languages of Asia, Africa, and Middle America, the *tone* or pitch with which parts of a word are pronounced affects its meaning. In Navajo, for example, there are four tones (low, high, rising, and falling). The Navajo word for "war" differs from the word for "eye" only by the presence of a high tone on the final vowel of the latter. Pitch is also used in English to indicate some differences of meaning (for example, in the command "Go home" versus the question "Go home?"). But English does not use tone to signal differences of meaning between minimal pairs of words.

The consistent voicing of consonants is so fundamental to the English sound system that it is hard for us to believe that other languages might not make use of this quality. Many American Indian languages get along quite well without it. In such languages, if a consonant phoneme is pronounced with the lips it will sometimes sound to English speakers like a *p* and at other times like a *b,* but no consistent difference in meaning will be attached to this variation.

On the other hand, many languages employ distinctions that are unimportant in English. For example, in English words that start with /t/ followed by a vowel, the /t/ is always accompanied by a little extra puff of air, called *aspiration*: you can detect it by holding a piece of tissue near your mouth as you say the word "till." When the /t/ is preceded by an /s/, however, the aspiration automatically disappears. The /t/ in "still" is said to be *unaspirated.* This distinction is never used to signal differences of meaning in English. In many other languages, however, aspiration is extremely important.

What does this mean in practice? Let us take four distinct sounds and see how they are classified in two hypothetical languages. All four sounds are frontal stops produced with the tip of the tongue, but two are voiced and two are aspirated:

t unvoiced; unaspirated
t' unvoiced; aspirated
d voiced; unaspirated
d' voiced, aspirated

In Language I, *voicing is phonemic* but aspiration is not (as in English). In Language II, however, *aspiration is phonemic* while voicing is not. As can be seen in Figure 3.4, each of these two languages will categorize these same four sounds into two phonemes, but each will do it in a different way. It should be obvious that speakers of Language I who try to learn Language II will have some trouble learning to hear the difference in aspiration while learning not to pay attention to the irrelevant difference in voicing. On the other hand, native speakers of Language II who attempt to learn Language I will have to learn to hear and control their pronunciation of voiced and unvoiced stops—a feature that signals nothing in their own language.

The grouping of sounds into phonemes is a process of categorization in which certain attributes (qualities) of the sounds are used and others ignored. The example above is identical in principle to the alternative ways of grouping pairs of objects on the basis of their formal attributes, as shown in Figure 3.5. Each of these ways of categorizing is *equally arbitrary* and *equally valid,* for there is nothing natural about the decision to use shape and ignore shading (Classification I) or to use shading and ignore shape (Classification II). Nor is it more natural to use

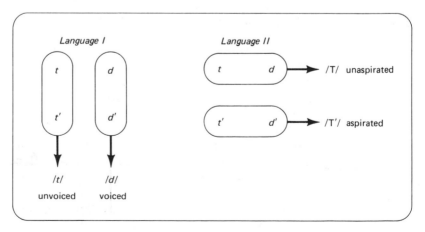

FIGURE 3.4 Phoneme Categories in Two Hypothetical Languages

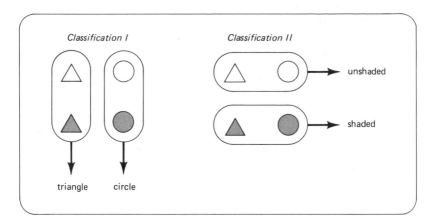

FIGURE 3.5 Alternative Categories

both shape and shading, though these two attributes together would give a four-way classification of objects equivalent to the classification of English stops in Figure 3.1.

Combinations of Phonemes

The number of phonemes in a natural language is usually between twenty and sixty. (English has about thirty-five). The phoneme categories are only one part of the sound system of a language. Along with the system of categories, there must also be a set of *plans*—instructions as to how the phonemes may be put together into larger units. These plans must be learned in the same way as the categories, for languages that have very similar phonemes do not necessarily allow them to be combined in the same ways. In some languages, sequential clusters of vowels are never allowed; in others, long strings of consonants (unpronounceable to an English speaker) are characteristic of most words. Some consonant clusters that occur at the ends of English words are never found at the beginnings: for example, the /skt/ found at the end of "asked."

The linguist Benjamin Lee Whorf constructed an involved formula that shows exactly which combinations of phonemes are allowed to occur in English words of one syllable (1956:223f.). This formula can be shown to predict all English monosyllabic words, except for some recent loans from foreign languages that are still pronounced (by some people) in the foreign way. Whorf's formula also predicts many words that do not now form part of the English language. Some happen to be archaic forms that are no longer used; others are "combining forms" that appear only as parts of larger words; but most of them must be regarded as "potential syllables" that the English sound system would allow to occur alone but which do not at present happen to have accepted meanings. Proof of this assertion may be seen in the fact that recently coined monosyllabic words, whether trade names ("Fab") or slang ("mods"), are all predicted by Whorf's formula, which was originally devised in 1940. It is unlikely that a product designed for English-speaking consumers would be named "Zbulft."

The sound system of a language, then, does two important things: (1) It *selects* from the range of possible human sounds a limited number of qualities (for example, voicing) which are systematically used to define differences among a somewhat larger number of signaling units (phonemes). This selection defines the categories (of sounds) that a speaker of the language must learn to recognize and to produce. (2) It *limits* the ways in which these categories may be combined by providing rules to govern the construction of larger units. These plans for speaking help to make human behavior predictable. While they limit what we may say, they also provide patterns for the creation of new forms.

Language and Speech

The discussion of the nature of sound systems has dealt with abstract categories and plans that are characteristic of language as opposed to speech. The units of language (phonemes and so forth) are *inferred* from observations of actual speech, and speech is astonishingly variable. Careful measurements show that it is impossible to pronounce a word twice in exactly the same way. When we say that two pronunciations of "bat" are the same word, we mean that we recognize the recurrence of three phonemes, /b/ /æ/ and /t/, in the same sequence; at the same time we are ignoring all kinds of differences in voice qualities such as pitch, loudness, breathiness, and speed. These non-phonemic differences are in the realm of *speech*. By speech we mean that concrete and observable behavior which manifests the abstract categories and plans of the language. The relationship between speech and language is a special case of the relationship between behavior and culture.

In trying to understand the regularities in speech behavior, the linguist distinguishes two kinds of variation. *Free variation* refers to differences in pronunciation for which no rules can be discovered, including the uncontrollable variations that creep in even when we try to speak consistently as well as audible variations that seem to have no significance (such as the two equally acceptable pronunciations of the word "economics").

Conditioned variation refers to differences in pronunciation for which some kind of rule can be found, though the speaker may not be aware of them. The linguist tries to explain as much variation as possible by showing that it is conditioned (regularly caused) by something else in the language system. For example, we have seen that English speakers produce an unaspirated /t/ when this sound follows an /s/ (as in "still"), while in most other positions the /t/ is aspirated. This is an automatic and thus conditioned variation in the phoneme, and so we say that /t/ has two phonetic *allophones,* audibly different sounds that "belong to" the same phoneme category. We can go on to state the rule that the allophone t follows /s/ and the allophone t' is found elsewhere. Another example is seen in the variation of /k/ in the words "keen"—/kin/—and "cool"—/kul/. One type of /k/ is pronounced farther back in the mouth than is the other. There is a rule that relates the type of /k/ to the vowel that follows it. (You might experiment a little and discover this rule, which you have been following all your life, but be careful not to be fooled by the traditional spelling of the words. Hint: the name "King Kong" also has both types of /k/.)

Speech is the actual behavior, whereas language is the set of rules (categories and plans) which explains the regularities observed in speech. Each person who learns a language, whether a two-year-old child or a sixty-year-old linguist, must infer the rules of the language from a sample of actual speech.

Some regularities in speech behaviors can be understood only by going outside the language system itself to examine the social context and its influence upon speech. The new field of *sociolinguistics* is concerned with the interaction between language and society. It deals with topics such as speech variation related to social class, bilingualism, attitudes toward language, switching from one dialect to another, and the social context of linguistic change. More and more variation in speech behavior has been shown to be conditioned by sociolinguistic factors. (Hymes 1973.)

GRAMMAR

We turn now from the study of sound systems, or phonology, to the topic of *grammar.* Few subjects are duller when poorly taught, but grammar can be fascinating if taught in such a way as to make us aware of the categories and plans that have been shaping our unconscious speech behavior for years. Grammar is generally divided into two related parts. The first, *morphology,* deals with the construction of words. The second, *syntax,* deals with the construction of phrases, clauses, sentences, and other types of structures larger than words.

Morphology

A word such as "bad" is a single unit and can be divided only into its three meaningless phonemes: /b/, /æ/, /d/. A word such as "unthinkingly" has four distinct parts, known as *morphemes;* each of these parts is found in many other words and each carries a particular meaning, so that even if you had never heard the word "unthinkingly" before, you could form a pretty good idea of its meaning from the respective meanings of {un-}, {think}, {-ing}, and {-ly}. (The braces indicate morphemes.) Furthermore, the parts of a word are not simply thrown together, for other combinations of these same parts such as "lythinkuning" or "ingthinklyun" are unacceptable (ungrammatical) in the judgment of all English speakers.

Morphology is concerned with the smallest meaningful parts of a language, the morphemes, and with the ways in which these simple morphemes may be combined to form complex words. The number of morphemes in any given language is finite but still large enough to make learning vocabulary a chore. As we have seen, morphemes are composed of one or more phonemes *in a conventional order* (/pæt/, /tæp/, and /æpt/ are not the same, and /ptæ/ is not even an English morpheme). Since the association between sound and meaning is also conventional, the usual way of learning the morphemes and their meanings is by memorizing them. The plans for putting morphemes together are much more general, however, and, once learned, can be applied to many groups of morphemes to produce words.

Linguists divide the morphemes of a language into *roots* and *affixes.* The root is the part of a word that carries the basic meaning, while the affixes modify this meaning. For example, the comparative and superlative degrees of English are usually formed by adding the affixes *-er* and *-est* to an adjective root. Since these affixes follow the root, they are called *suffixes.* Affixes that precede the root, such as English *non-,* and *mini-,* are called *prefixes.*

The *infix,* a type of affix that appears in the middle of a root, is not found in English, though it is common in the morphology of other languages such as Hebrew and Arabic. Most Arabic roots are made up of three consonants and require one or more vowel infixes to complete them: for example, the root *k-l-b* may be completed by infixes such as -*a*- to yield *kalb*, 'heart,' or *u-uu* to yield *kuluub*, 'hearts.' Other languages, such as Turkish, make extensive use of suffixes (as many as ten affixes may *follow* a Turkish verb root) but make little or no use of prefixes or infixes. English makes much use of suffixes and limited use of prefixes.

Languages may differ in the extent to which they permit *compounding*: the combining of two or more *roots* into a single word. English allows some (for example, "blackbird," "blockhead"), and German is famous for its long compounds, which may contain half a dozen roots (for example, *das Lebensversicherungsgesellschaftsfräulein*, 'the unmarried female insurance-company receptionist'). Some languages never use this plan for word-building.

Languages also differ in the amount and kinds of information that can (or must) be expressed by a single word. In English, most nouns are marked as singular or plural, but only a few indicate gender. Even our pronouns indicate gender only in the third person singular forms (he/she, him/her, his/hers). This arrangement seems quite natural to us, and only comparisons with other languages show how conventional English morphology really is. For example, in French every noun is either masculine or feminine, and French pronouns distinguish between *ils*, 'they' (masc.) and *elles*, 'they' (fem.).

In Spanish the number and gender of most nouns must be indicated twice: first in the article, which agrees with the noun, and again in a suffix added to the noun root, which shows whether it is singular or plural, masculine or feminine. For example, *los gatos* indicates 'the [masc. plural] cats [masc. plural],' as opposed to *las gatas*, 'the [fem. plural] cats [fem. plural].' Furthermore, since the grammatical category of person is clearly indicated by the verb, subject pronouns are rarely used: *Salió sin sombrero*, '[He, she, or it] went out [third person subject] without [a] hat [masc. sing.].' At the same time, object pronouns are often incorporated into the verb as suffixes: *Están escribiéndosela*, "[They] are [plural subject] writing-to-him/her-it."

These last examples have been taken from languages related to English, which the reader may have studied. In non-Indo-European languages, the differences are still more striking. Some languages, such as Chinese, allow no modification of a root, so that each word consists of a single morpheme. Others, such as Turkish, string a great many affixes onto a root, but all of these parts of the word remain quite distinct. In some languages (including many American Indian tongues), the word is immensely complex: roots and affixes have a variety of forms. When the parts of a word are put together, they modify one another so that sounds are changed in quality or completely lost. Subtle nuances of meaning are expressed in a bewildering variety of ways, and single words carry meanings that English speakers would have to express in quite lengthy phrases. In Navajo there is a single word, *baadeesh?áát*, which translates as "I will give him one [solid] object [which is roundish in shape]." The root of this Navajo word is *?áát,* meaning something like "to handle a single roundish solid object."

In analyzing and describing the morphology of a language, linguists attempt to discover and clearly set forth some of the rules that govern speech behavior. From the apparently chaotic variability of a spoken language, they infer categories of morphemes and plans for word-building. Since the morphology of every language, whether simple or complex, is systematic, they are able to demonstrate regularities and describe rules. For example, how are plural nouns formed in English? If you answer, "By adding an *-s* to the singular," you are too much influenced by the written form of the language. There are obvious exceptions (ox : oxen, deer : deer), but they are few and can simply be listed in a grammar. Listen, however, to your pronunciation of the following words: hats, bags, taps, lads, racks, roses. Actually, English nouns take one of three plural suffixes: /-z/, /-s/, /-əz/. There is a simple rule that tells you which of these sounds to add, depending on the final sound of the singular form. You have been following this rule all your life without being consciously aware of it!

Creating plural forms by suffixation seems to us the most natural thing in the world; again, only comparison can show how much a matter of convention this particular morphological device is. Hebrew creates most plurals by adding the suffix *-im* or *-ot,* but which of these suffixes is chosen depends on the inherent gender of the root, not its final sound. Many languages get along very nicely without any plural affix, and their speakers think it rather silly to insist on saying "two books" when "two book" would presumably do as well. Other languages may designate plurality by prefixes or by change of tone or of vowels (as we do in "man : men"). Still others, such as Homeric Greek, distinguish other types of number, for example, singular, dual (two), and plural (more than two). Is one of these systems better than the others? No. All of them communicate quite clearly in their own terms. Each morphological system *selects* from the possible ways of combining morphemes and *limits* the ways in which various concepts may be expressed in speech.

Morphemes are contrasted with one another in two general ways. As formal categories, they may be contrasted in terms of the phonemes of which they are composed. Thus the phoneme sequences /big/ and /pig/ represent different morphemes, the difference being manifested in the phonemic distinction between /p/ and /b/. But morphemes may also be contrasted in terms of their *distribution,* that is, their occurrence with other morphemes.

The concept of distribution is difficult to grasp, but it is important both in linguistics and in the general theory underlying this book. The distribution of a morpheme means, most simply, the other categories of morphemes with which it is found. For example, the past tense morpheme {-ed} occurs only as a suffix with verbs; conversely, any word that takes this suffix must be a verb. Similarly, the prefix {mini-} occurs only before a noun. When we study the distribution of any kind of cultural form we want to know its context: where it is found in relation to other forms, including its geographic location and its occurrence in time. (See Chapter 11.)

Syntax

The next higher level of language structure is *syntax*: the arrangement of words into larger grammatical structures—phrases, clauses, and sentences—in such a way as to show their relationship to each other. It has been demonstrated that although the number of morphemes in any language is finite, the number of possible grammatical sentences is *infinite* (Chomsky 1957). In learning a language we do not simply memorize a large number of sentences; rather, we learn patterns or plans for speaking. These plans enable us to combine categories of morphemes in such a way that we can understand (and be understood) even if a particular sentence has never before been produced by a speaker of English.

The syntactic rules of human languages are just as conventional and vary just as much as the morphological or phonological rules. In English we rely quite heavily on *word order* to tell us, for example, who did what to whom. In the sentence

"The girl hit the boy," we know that the aggressor is female and the victim male because "girl" precedes the verb; the meaning is clearly different from "The boy hit the girl." In many languages the *grammatical relations* of subject and object are indicated by affixes, so that word order is less relevant to syntactic meaning. In Latin, for example, the relations of subject and object are indicated by suffixes, so that the order in which they are mentioned makes little difference.

Syntactic rules govern *agreement* among the parts of a sentence. We know that the English verb must agree in person and number with its subject (for example, I am, you are, he is, they are). In Hebrew, the verb must also agree in *gender* with its subject, so there are different verb forms for "he says" and "she says." In Navajo, there must be agreement between the verb and the *shape of its object*: a different verb stem must be selected if one is talking about long and thin or flat or round objects. For example, ?at means 'to lose or toss something,' but only if the something is a flat, flexible object; if it is round or bulky, one must use the verb stem "niit." Finally, in French both articles and adjectives must agree with the gender (and number) of the noun they modify: thus, since "book" is considered a masculine noun and "table" a feminine one, one must say *un livre blanc,* 'a [masc.] book white [masc.],' and *une table blanche,* 'a [fem.] table white [fem.].'

Syntax also provides patterns for changing verbs into nouns ("hit" to "the hitter"; "burn" to "the burning"), and for making questions out of statements and negatives out of positives. Such rules may be simple or complex. For example, in Spanish most negatives are formed by simply putting the word *no* in front of a positive statement, and questions have the same word order as non-questions. In English we must often rearrange the wording of a statement to make it into a question or a negative: *"He went* to the game" becomes *"Did he go* to the game?" or *"He didn't go* to the game." To form a negative in the Micmac Indian language, one must use both a negative word (*mo*) before the verb and one of several negative suffixes after the verb root, as if to say: "No, he went-not."

With a great deal of hard, careful work, it is possible to establish a set of syntactic rules that will account for the regularities in a long list of English (or Spanish, or Navajo) sentences. But most linguists today have an even more difficult goal: they would like to discover rules that would represent the *knowledge* of native speakers, including their ability to produce and interpret sentences they have never heard before. Such a "generative grammar" would do for the sentences of a language what Whorf's formula does for the syllables of English: it would predict all the grammatical sentences of a language. This goal is important because it calls attention to the most remarkable property of human languages: their productivity. *Productivity* refers to the fact that, given a few dozen phonemes, a few thousand morphemes, and a set of morphological and syntactic rules, *an infinite number of grammatical sentences* can be constructed, and people who share this abstract language will be able to interpret correctly all of these sentences, including those they have never heard before.

The problem of how linguistic productivity can be best represented by syntactic rules is a highly complicated one that need not concern us here. This problem is similar to other important problems in ethnography and social anthropology. Much of human behavior, in addition to speech, is governed by conventional rules; this does not mean, however, that we endlessly repeat the same actions. Social rules are also productive. We are constantly engaged in interpreting the novel actions of our fellows and judging them as socially appropriate or inappropriate, just as we understand novel utterances and judge them as grammatical or ungrammatical. Productivity is a property of all cultural systems, for in language, technology, or social structure, the rules that limit behavior also provide patterns for new responses (see Epilogue: Culture and Freedom).

SEMANTICS

Semantics deals with all of the questions that are implicit in the phrase "Morphemes carry meaning." What is meaning? What does it mean to say something carries meaning? How can meaning be described, except by the use of morphemes whose meanings are already known? And how can we best describe and understand changes in the meaning of a morpheme? These and many other semantic questions are among the most difficult problems of modern linguistics.

Anthropologists must constantly deal with semantic questions, both in trying to understand the meaning of words and actions in an alien culture and in trying to communicate to other scientists what they have learned. This is a process of translation, and it calls for a sensitive appreciation of *both* languages and cultures. Even within the English language there are ample opportunities for misunderstanding. For example, most Americans use the term "breakfast" to refer to a light meal eaten early in the morning. On the island of Jamaica, however, this term has several different meanings. Middle-class Jamaicans eat "breakfast" in the morning, but it is a much more substantial meal than in the United States. Their lightest meal (called "supper") is eaten in the late evening—sometimes after ten. Poor Jamaican farmers eat their lightest meal early in the morning, but they call it "tea"; for them, "breakfast" is a medium-to-heavy meal eaten at midday!

When even familiar words may have so many different meanings, how can anthropologists or linguists get at the meanings of words in an unfamiliar language and culture? They learn in the same general way as the little child who must learn how to speak not only grammatically but also *appropriately.* The sentences "That is my dog" and "That is my father" are both grammatical, but normally only one will be appropriate to a given situation. Children learn the correct use (the meanings) of words by observing speech acts in their social environments, by trying to understand and make themselves understood, and by being corrected (or ignored) when they speak incorrectly.

Words that refer to concrete objects are probably the easiest to learn, and young children show great fascination with the names of things—to the point of driving their parents crazy. The anthropologist can soon learn to ask, "What's this?" or "What's that?" but it is much more difficult to ask the right questions about objects or events that are not physically present. Also, many words do not refer to anything concrete (consider the many meanings of the word "on" in English phrases such as "on time," "on the air," "put on," "on the table," and "on your own"). Fortunately, in all languages words fall into classes (categories) that share certain meanings (plans for use), and the learner can try to discover the systematic contrasts within and among these classes. Semantic classes consist of morphemes that have similar *meanings.* Such classes are sometimes called *domains,* and linguists speak of the "domain of kinship terms" ("father," "brother," "aunt," and so on) and the "domain of animal names."

Some of the most interesting work in anthropological semantics has been done in the domain of color terminology. Every known language has a group of semantically related words dealing with color. These words divide up the visible spectrum into a limited number of categories; but since the color spectrum is continuous, any division of it into discrete parts must be partly conventional. (According to the Optical Society of America, under laboratory conditions human beings are able to distinguish as many as ten million different "colors," so the need for *some* sort of classification is apparent.) One method developed for studying the domain of color terms is to present a speaker of Language X with a large number of standard color chips, and to ask him to sort them into piles of the same color. He is then asked, "What do you call this color [category] in Language X?" Finally, for each color term he is asked to pick the one color chip that is most characteristic of that color, called the "focus" of the term (Berlin and Kay 1969).

Application of this method to dozens of languages from all over the world has revealed several surprising points. First of all, the number of *basic color terms* (such as our "red," "green," and "blue," but not "scarlet" or "lavender") ranges from two to eleven. In languages with only two terms, one term labels the whole range of "light" colors and the other term the "dark" colors. The boundaries of the two color terms may vary from language to language, as do the words used to label the categories, but the *focus* of each term is always the same—respectively, "white" and "black." This last statement may be generalized to more complex systems of terms: for any two systems with the same number of color categories, the boundaries between categories may vary considerably, and the words associated with each category are conventional, but the focus of each of the corresponding categories will be very similar.

Furthermore, if we arrange these systems in order of increasing complexity, it turns out that each additional category appears in a *regular order*. That is, a three-term system always adds red to the light/dark contrast; four-term systems have the first three plus either yellow or green, and five-term systems include all of these. In sixth place comes a blue term, which distinguishes a range of colors that five-term systems include in their green and dark ranges, while the seventh term added is always some variety of brown. Except for the varying order of appearance of yellow and green, this sequence seems to be *universal*. That is, any language that has a term for blue will also have terms for (at least) the five earlier colors. (Beyond seven terms, the order of appearance of basic terms for gray, pink, orange, or purple appears to be quite irregular.)

Let us look at one specific terminological system—that of the Hanunóo, a tribal people of the Philippines, whose culture has been carefully described by Harold C. Conklin. The Hanunóo are a horticultural people who make extensive use of the plants in their tropical environment. They have dozens of specific color

Color Term	Translation	Range of Colors in English
1. mabi: ru	relative darkness, blackness	black, violet, indigo, blue, dark green, dark gray, and deep shades of other colors and mixtures
2. malagti?	relative lightness, whiteness	white and very light tints of other colors and mixtures
3. marara?	relative presence of red, redness	maroon, red, orange, yellow, and mixtures in which these colors are seen to predominate
4. malatuy	relative presence of light greenness, greenness	light green and mixtures of green, yellow, and light brown

FIGURE 3.6 Hanunóo Color Categories (after Conklin)

terms, but each of these terms fits into one of the categories labeled by four basic color terms (Figure 3.6).

Clearly this is a system of color categories very different from our own. Conklin was able to show that their system is based on a number of distinctive attributes that are very important to the Hanunóo. For example, the contrast between *marara?* and *malatuy* is of particular significance in terms of the plants upon which these people depend for most of their food: *malatuy* means not only greenness but also something like succulence, and to a Hanunóo it is opposed to *marara?* not only as a range of colors, but also as indicating fresh as opposed to dried-up organic material (Conklin 1955:339–344).

Body Parts and Componential Analysis

Like the color spectrum, the human body is a continuous unit; for some purposes, however, it is essential to think of it as composed of parts. Since there are few clear-cut natural divisions, these parts must be conventionally bounded and labeled. Where does the neck end and the head begin? Every culture provides a conventional way of categorizing parts of the body, together with plans for the use or display of those body parts. Rules of modesty, for example, are plans for showing or covering particular body parts under various circumstances. The terms used for body parts in various cultures can be used to illustrate the technique of semantic analysis called *componential analysis.*

The goal of this approach is to divide a semantic domain into its component parts by showing the systematic relationships among terms. For example, the Kewa of eastern New Guinea speak of the upper trunk of the body as consisting of three parts—the back, chest, and arms; the nape of the neck and the shoulders are thought of as linking areas. Each of these body parts has its proper function. The Kewa terms can be arranged to show the *part–whole relationship* of back, chest, and arms to the upper trunk, as in Figure 3.7. Each of the parts can be divided into its components, showing the systematic relation- ships among the terms: ribs are part of the back, which is part of the upper trunk, and so forth. Terms that are on the same level in such a diagram are said to *contrast* with one another; terms on the higher levels are more *abstract* than the specific terms below them.

Semantic domains may also be structured by the *species–genus relationship,* in which subordinate categories are thought of as kinds of the larger category to which they belong. For example, the English terms "elm," "maple," and "cedar" refer to kinds of trees; "hammer," "ax," and "pliers" are kinds of tools. Componential analysis is useful for under- standing the ways in which plants, animals, relatives, tools, colors, and many other kinds of objects or events are catego- rized in a given culture. Our own biologists have developed a system of Latin names (a scientific taxonomy) for classifying the

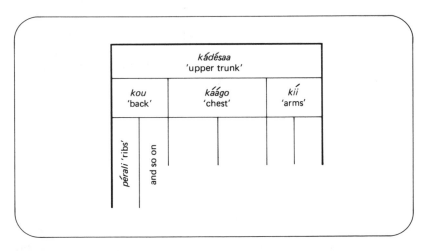

FIGURE 3.7 Part–Whole Relationship of Some Kewa Terms for Body Parts

millions of known life forms into species, genus, family, order, and so forth. But every human society, no matter how small, has a way of classifying living things that enables its members to identify and communicate about important plants and animals. Such systems are known as *folk taxonomies.*

Folk taxonomies are much more practically oriented than are scientific ones. Their categories are closely associated with plans for action. The biologist usually arranges plants in categories according to their evolutionary relationships, but the average person in any society is more interested in what can be done with a given plant: whether it is edible or poisonous; whether it can be used to make string, baskets, or cloth; if it can be used to make medicine; whether its bark is suitable for covering a shelter or a canoe.

Folk taxonomies are most elaborate in the areas of greatest concern to the people who use them; for example, the Eskimo have several words for specific types of snow, as do most skiing fanatics. The ethnographer who wishes fully to understand a culture must carefully explore its crucial semantic domains. This scrutiny will frequently lead to other areas of inquiry, as, for example, Harold Conklin's study of the Hanunóo's plant classification led him to analyze their color categories.

By learning a language, people acquire ways of categorizing sounds and plans for putting these sound categories together into more and more complex structures: morphemes, words, sentences, conversations, orations, and so forth. Language helps us to make discriminations and to formulate complicated plans. Through language, people learn the traditions of their society, including what will be expected of them in circumstances they have not yet met. They learn of past events (which may or may not have happened) and of supernatural forces (which may or may not exist). Enculturation, including language learning, transforms a promising primate into a unique human animal with a sense of history and an awareness of the possibilities of the future.

RECOMMENDED READING

Ronald W. Langacker, *Language and Its Structure,* 2d ed. New York: Harcourt Brace Jovanovich, 1973. A clear and up-to-date introduction to fundamental concepts of linguistic analysis, including material on language history and linguistic universals.

Roger Brown, *A First Language.* Cambridge: Harvard University Press, 1973. A fascinating account of recent research on the way children learn and use language in the first years of life. Most of the information is based on intensive studies of English-speaking children, but comparative data on other languages are also presented.

Keith H. Basso and Henry A. Selby, eds., *Meaning in Anthropology.* Albuquerque: University of New Mexico Press, 1976. A collection of rather advanced studies showing how anthropologists are using semantic concepts and techniques to understand the creation of meaning in culture.

Pier Paolo Giglioli, ed., *Language and Social Context.* Baltimore: Penguin Books, 1972. An excellent and highly readable collection of articles on all aspects of sociolinguistics.

Dell Hymes, ed., *Language in Culture and Society*. New York: Harper & Row, 1964. A fine collection of classic articles on all the areas in which linguistics and anthropology have common interests.

PART TWO
SOCIAL SYSTEMS

In the last chapter a distinction was drawn between an abstract language system and the observable speech behavior that manifests that system, that is, between the language conceived of as learned categories of sound associated with plans for speaking and the actual speech movements of the vocal organs that produce sound waves. In this section the distinction between behavior and the shared categories and plans that account for regularities in that behavior will be expanded and applied to other parts of human culture.

When they encounter relatives, friends, or strangers, craftworkers, priests, or chiefs, members of every society act *as if* their behavior were regulated by rules governing who should do/say what to whom. Like the language system, a social system both influences and is inferred from the observable actions of individuals. And like language, it consists of categories (of persons) associated with plans (for interaction). *The rules of a social system apply not to single individuals but to categories of persons.* For example, when Private Smith salutes Captain Black and Captain Black salutes Colonel Green, the observable salute manifests a general rule governing interaction between *any* military persons of these ranks: one "salutes the uniform, not the man."

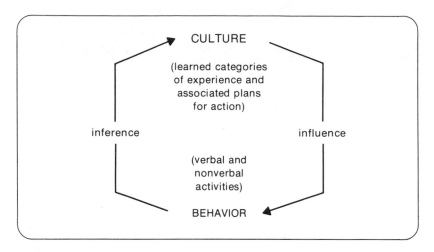

The Relationship between Culture and Behavior

   Social rules are statements of customary or expected behavior. If we represent the saluting rule by the formula *a → b,*
the meaning is: "Persons of rank *a* are expected to salute
persons of rank *b* (and will be punished for failure to do so
unless there are extenuating circumstances)." This rule has
two parts: the categories of persons to whom it applies (*a, b*)
and the plan for interaction associated with their approaching
one another (→).
   Since they are conventional, social rules may be violated
for any number of reasons. Ignorance of the rule is sometimes
a very good excuse, at least for children and for strangers to a
society. A violation may also result from *confusion of
categories.* In the military subculture this sort of violation is
unlikely because uniforms and insignia are designed to make
an individual's rank immediately apparent. But in other
situations one cannot always be so sure of what kind of
person one is dealing with. Most people have had the
experience of approaching someone for assistance in a store
only to discover that the "salesperson" is really a fellow
shopper.
   Even when the category is correctly identified there may be
confusion as to the appropriate plan for interaction or conflict
among alternative plans. (Should you offer a cigar to a lady?
Or a tip to a headwaiter?) On the whole, however, social life
proceeds quite smoothly. When anthropologists speak of a
highly *integrated* social system they mean one in which
confusions and conflicts have been reduced to a minimum

through common understandings and explicit social rules. This is always a matter of degree, for no society is completely integrated. But no social group can exist without considerable sharing of common (or at least equivalent) categories and plans for action.

Because social and linguistic rules can be violated, we speak of culture *influencing* behavior rather than determining it. Some kinds of violations are rapidly and severely punished, but nothing can prevent those violations from sometimes occurring. If I choose to say "an dog," to drive on the wrong side of the road, or to omit saluting my commanding officer, I am free to do so, for these rules are conventional. Some violations rarely occur because we are not aware of the cultural patterns that are influencing our behavior in these areas, and it is hard to break a rule that you do not know you have been obeying. For example, of the three violations noted above, the linguistic one is the least likely to occur, even though its consequences would be the mildest, because very few English speakers are conscious of the grammatical patterns they regularly follow.

Culture influences behavior in regular ways because people who have been enculturated in the same society share (consciously and unconsciously) many beliefs and expectations. Behavior is predictable to the extent that people live up to one another's expectations. Of course, a culture cannot provide precise rules for every possible occurrence. A social system, like a language system, must be *productive:* from a limited number of categories and plans, a very large, and possibly infinite, number of socially appropriate actions may follow. Productivity involves the application of quite general principles to novel problems and situations.

Understanding how social systems work is a genuine scientific problem. In every society, people learn, store, and use a limited number of conventional plans that enable them to act appropriately and to judge behavior (their own and that of others) as either acceptable or unacceptable. The discovery of these plans and of the ways in which they may be productively combined is one task of the ethnographer. (See Part Five.)

Another example will clarify the meaning of "plans." An automobile driver in the United States must pay close attention to many features of her environment, but as she approaches an intersection the presence of a traffic light becomes particularly important. Out of her whole field of vision, she must selectively attend to a small lighted disk, judge whether it is red, yellow, or green; and respond appropriately. These three *color categories* (each of which includes a wide range of hues) are conventionally associated with standardized *plans for driving*—in this case, respectively, stopping, slowing, and passing through the intersection. There is nothing "natural" about either color or its association with a particular plan: blue could be substituted for green and red could indicate "go."

George Miller, Eugene Galanter, and Karl Pribram define a *plan* as *"any hierarchical process in the organism that can control the order in which a sequence of operations is to be performed"* (1960:17). Like computer programs, behavioral plans consist of a series of steps toward a predetermined goal, together with a way of testing whether one step has been properly completed before going on to the next.

People are not computers, though. No two American drivers respond to a yellow light with exactly the same combinations of muscular responses. Drivers may slow by shifting into a lower gear, by braking (with either foot), by lifting a foot from the accelerator, or by any combination of these steps. What all drivers share is a hierarchy of plans that leaves the details of execution up to the individual. It is these expectations—not the behaviors—that are learned in the process of enculturation. Similarly, in performing our parts in the drama of social life we are seldom taught what our exact lines should be. Rather, we learn an outline that each individual fills in, with greater or lesser skill. (See Goffman 1959:73.) This process of dramatic realization will be discussed further in Chapter 6 under the heading "Social Organization." We begin with the abstract categories and plans that comprise the social structure.

CHAPTER FOUR
KINDS OF PERSONS

SOCIAL ROLES

In describing social systems, we must deal with categories rather than individuals and with general plans for action rather than specific acts, even when the categories are normally represented by only one individual at a time (e.g., the Pope or the President of the United States). That is to say, we are interested primarily in social roles rather than the individuals who perform the roles, except insofar as their behavior provides material for a description.

We may define a *social role* as any category of persons that in a given society is associated with a conventional plan for interaction with at least one other category of person. When we focus on the role as a category, we are interested in how one role *contrasts* with another. (How is a President different from a Congressman?) When we focus on the role as a plan for interaction, we are interested in the total *content* of the role. (What kinds of behavior are appropriate to a President?) These two aspects of a social role are closely related.

The role of President of the United States has many complex plans associated with it. Some are explicitly stated in the Constitution (for example, commanding the armed forces, appointing officials, signing or vetoing bills). Others have developed and changed as the American social system has grown (for example, delivery of a State of the Union address). We shall use the term *role attribute* to designate each of the different *kinds of behavior expected of a person who performs a given social role.* The role of President consists of hundreds of attributes, some of them unique to the presidency. It is the particular combination of attributes that makes one role contrast with all others, just as it is the selection and arrangement of phonemes that makes one morpheme different from another.

Most social roles have among their attributes a *role label.* The label is a word or phrase used by members of a society to address or refer to a particular kind of person. Role labels and other types of insignia help both members of a society and ethnographers to recognize roles being performed.

Unfortunately for the ethnographer, some roles do not have labels, some have several labels, and some labels are associated with a number of roles. Familiar examples are the sequence "janitor–custodian–sanitary superintendent" and the many possible meanings of the label "doctor." A label may be used, then, as *evidence* for the existence of a distinct role, but only with the greatest caution, just as a linguist uses the traditional spelling of a written language in determining its phonemes.

Each social role also has one or more criteria for *recruitment* to the role. Recruitment is the process by which individuals become entitled to perform social roles. Recruitment criteria are the prerequisites for legitimate performance of a role: for example, to become President, a person must be a natural-born citizen of the United States, be at least thirty-five years of age, receive a majority of the electoral votes in a national election, and so forth. Individuals who perform roles (such as "medical doctor") without possessing the associated recruitment criteria are guilty of *fraud:* they represent themselves as persons with rights to which they are not entitled. Considerable light is shed on the nature of social systems by the study of such frauds. Our society even has role labels that are applied to persons who specialize in fraudulent performances: "quack," "impostor," "con man," "bigamist."

Ralph Linton introduced the concept of social role into anthropology in *The Study of Man* (1930:113–131). He distinguished between two general types of recruitment. Recruitment by *achievement* involves something one must do in order legitimately to perform a role (be elected, ordained, commissioned, and so on). Recruitment by *ascription* takes place when a role is ascribed to an individual with little or no deliberate effort on his part (as when one reaches legal majority or is born into a family, caste, or nationality). The distinction between ascribed and achieved roles is not always easy to make, for many roles are filled by a combination of both types of recruitment (e.g., the President must have been born a citizen but he achieves election).

Each type of recruitment has advantages and disadvantages. Since ascribed roles are usually determined at birth, those who are going to perform them can begin their training early. They know what kinds of persons they will be, whether queens, warriors, or shoemakers; and since their future careers are determined by forces beyond their control they have little choice but to prepare themselves as best they can. In the caste system of India, theoretically all roles were filled by ascription. Such systems have the advantages of stability and individual security.

Americans tend to consider ascription undemocratic, and believe that encouraging individual achievement is the most efficient way to ensure good performance. Unfortunately, recruitment by achievement does not automatically guarantee the "best person for the best job," and it may sometimes reward the most unscrupulous. When the number of opportunities is limited, some frustration of ambitions is inevitable. This leaves many persons angry, insecure, and without acceptable rationalizations for their failure to succeed.

KINSHIP ROLES

Modern genetic theory is only a hundred years old, but culture has provided us with theories of kinship for tens of thousands of years. Kinship usually involves some recognition of *organic continuity,* that is, physical relatedness; but although kinship is generally based on biology, it is biology *as interpreted by culture.* In our society, for example, paternity is assigned with some uncertainty in a large proportion of births. This fact, together with the custom of adoption, means that we must distinguish among three kinds of fathers: (1) the true *physiological father,* whose sperm fertilized the ovum from which the child in question developed; (2) the *genitor,* who is believed by members of his community (according to their culturally derived theory of reproduction) to have impregnated the child's mother; and (3) the *pater,* or socially recognized father, through whom the child may claim linkage with other kin.

The facts of mammalian biology make it possible to identify the maternal parent (though even here questions do occasionally arise; babies are probably mixed up in hospital nurseries more frequently than we should like to believe). Nevertheless, it is useful to distinguish between the *genetrix,* the woman who presumably gave birth to the child, and the *mater,* the socially recognized mother through whom the child may claim kinship with other members of the society.

To be considered legitimate in most societies, a child must have both a mater and a pater through whom he derives his social position. A person lacking the pater at birth is generally placed at a social disadvantage, even though his genitor may be known or suspected. Although the genitor and the pater are usually the same individual, the widespread custom of adoption regularly disrupts this connection. In a number of societies, alternative arrangements are fairly common, as in the following examples.

1. *Toda polyandry:* Among the Toda of southern India it was customary for a woman to marry several brothers. The socially recognized pater of her children was the one who performed a certain ritual before the birth of her first child. Any of the brothers might be the genitor, but the one who performed this ritual was the pater, even if he died before the conception of subsequent children.
2. *Nuer ghost fathers:* Among the Nuer of East Africa, if a man died before having offspring, his brother might marry his widow (or some other woman) and father children in the name of the deceased. The pater of these children was considered to be the ghost of the first brother.
3. *Female fathers:* In certain African societies, usually where wealth can be transmitted only from father to child, a noblewoman who has accumulated considerable wealth may marry a female slave; the slave then has children by an authorized lover, and these children may inherit wealth and social position from their socially recognized pater (the noblewoman).

A *kinship system* consists of a number of social roles, resting on a biological basis, but elaborated by the culture in a conventional way. In the words of Robert Lowie, "Biological relationships merely serve as a starting point for the development of sociological conceptions of kinships" (1948:57).

Analyzing Kinship Roles

A few symbols will be useful and sufficient for the analysis of kinship roles:

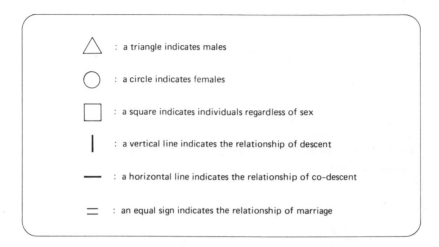

The following symbol cluster designates a parent/child relationship, ignoring the sex of the individuals:

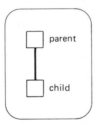

When the sex of the related persons is considered, there are four possibilities:

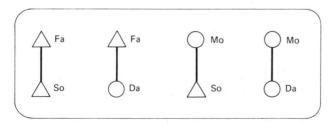

Individuals descended from the same mater or pater (co-descent) are known as siblings. Without consideration of the sex of the individuals, this relationship is represented:

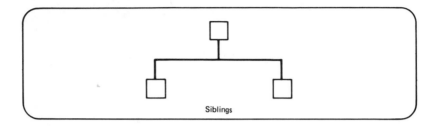

Siblings

When the sex of any two siblings is considered, there are three logical possibilities:

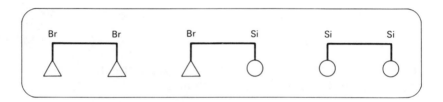

Persons whose kinship linkage to one another may be traced through ties of descent or co-descent alone are called *consanguineal kin,* what we would call "blood relatives." Anthropologists use the name "ego" for the person from whose point of view a relationship is regarded. Thus the next diagram shows the linkage (by two ties of descent and one of co-descent) between ego and a consanguineal kinsman, his father's sister's son:

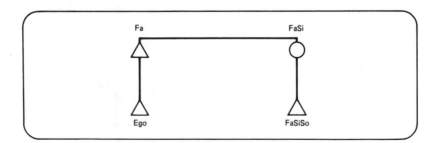

A married pair with their joint offspring, descendants of this relationship, is symbolized by the cluster:

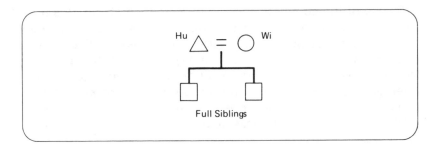

Full Siblings

When more than one spouse is permitted to a person, the relationship of co-marriage becomes possible. The most common form is known as polygyny and may be symbolized as:

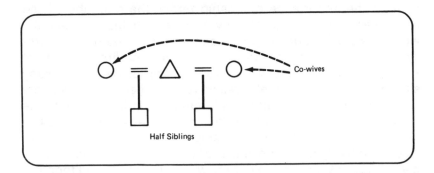

Half Siblings

Persons who are linked to one another by ties of marriage rather than (or in addition to) ties of descent are known as *affinal kin.* Thus ego's affinal kin includes his wife and in-laws as well as the spouses and in-laws of all his consanguineal kin. As shown in the next diagram, ego is an affinal kinsman of his brother's son's wife, being linked to her through three kinds of relationships: co-descent, descent, and marriage:

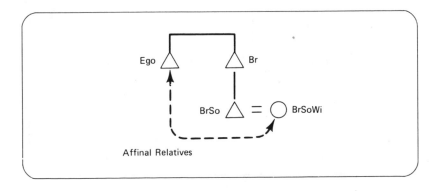

Affinal Relatives

By use of the concepts and symbols defined above, it is possible to describe quite precisely the relationship between ego and any of his or her consanguineal or affinal relatives, living or dead, in ascending or descending generations. It is possible to distinguish several hundred kinds of relatives, going only three generations from ego in both directions. No kinship system can provide a different role label for each of these kinds of relatives. Therefore, the classification of kin into categories is essential.

Kinship Terminology

The American lawyer and ethnologist Lewis H. Morgan first recognized the importance of kinship terms, the role labels used in different societies to classify kinsmen. In his monumental work, *Systems of Consanguinity and Affinity of the Human Family* (1871), Morgan compiled and compared hundreds of sets of kinship terms from many parts of the world. He found many similarities in the ways relatives were classified in widely separated groups speaking different languages. In keeping with the dominant anthropological theories of his day, Morgan tried to demonstrate an evolution of kinship systems from the primitive classificatory type to the more advanced descriptive type. A *classificatory kinship terminology* was one that lumped together certain relatives under a single term, so that, for example, ego would apply the same kin term to both Fa and FaBr or to both Mo and MoSi. This system was contrasted with the *descriptive kinship terminology,* which provided separate terms for such relatives and which referred to more distant relatives by combinations of the primary terms.

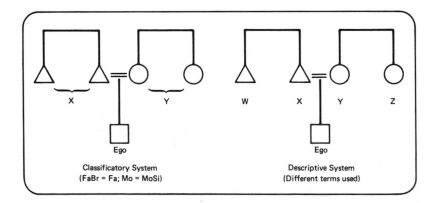

Classificatory System
(FaBr = Fa; Mo = MoSi)

Descriptive System
(Different terms used)

A purely descriptive system would have to provide separate terms for each of several hundred kinspeople. All known kinship systems, however, have fewer than fifty terms. Thus *every* system of kinship terminology is classificatory to some degree. The English system distinguishes between father and father's brother, but the term applied to the latter relative (uncle) lumps him together with the mother's brother, and is to this extent classificatory. From the point of view of a society in which mother's brother and father's brother are labeled by different terms—and there are many such societies—our term "uncle" classifies together two different kinds of relatives.

A more fruitful approach to kinship terminology was first suggested by A. L. Kroeber in a brilliant paper first published in 1909. Kroeber outlined an approach to the analysis of kin terms that was elaborated forty years later by George Peter Murdock in his book *Social Structure* (1949). The Kroeber-Murdock approach suggests that in each society a limited number of criteria are used to define contrasting categories of relatives. For example, when the criterion of *relative age* is applied to all of ego's kinsmen, it sorts them into two classes: those older than ego and those younger. Kinship systems differ in the criteria they use and the extent to which each criterion is applied. Thus, in analyzing a set of kinship terms, we ask which criteria are being used and which are being ignored.

1. Generation

The first criterion, as defined by Murdock, is that of *generation.* The question to be asked is whether a given term indicates the generation of the person to whom it is applied (relative to ego). Thus the English terms "mother" and "grandson" indicate persons who must be respectively one generation above and two generations below ego. In fact, with the exception of our "cousin" term, all English kinship terms use this criterion. A system of kin terms that recognized *only* the criterion of generation would require only as many terms as there were generations: ego could use one term for all members of her own generation (siblings and cousins, regardless of sex), another term for all members of her parents' generation, and so on. No such kinship systems are actually known, but the criterion of generation appears in all kinship systems. "Hawaiian type" kinship terminology classes cousins of ego's generation together with her siblings. The "Crow type" and "Omaha type," however, sometimes ignore the criterion of generation, grouping certain relatives in ego's generation under a single term with relatives in higher or lower generations.

2. Sex

The criterion of sex is also common in kinship terminologies. Some systems of kinship terms ignore the criterion of sex in alternate generations: a single term may be used by ego for father's father and father's mother, while they may use a single term for ego and his sister. The English system includes words with these meanings (grandparent and grandchild), but the usual terms do express the sex of the relative. Conversely, the term "cousin" does not indicate the relative's sex. Every language has ways of indicating some particular relative by a descriptive combination of terms, but in the study of kinship terminology we are concerned with the simple role labels usually employed in address or in reference.

3. Affinity

The criterion of *affinity* appears when a kinship term is applied to either consaguineal relatives or affinal relatives (in-laws), but not to both. It is ignored when a term lumps together both types of relatives, as does the English term "aunt," which may designate a parent's sister or a parent's brother's wife. As Murdock points out, terms that ignore this criterion are often found in societies that encourage or insist upon marriage with a particular relative. For example, when ego is *expected* to marry his father's sister's daughter, he may use a single term for this relative and for "wife," while the term for father's sister may resemble that for "mother-in-law." Compare the Micmac terms: *nsugwis,* "parent's sister," and *nsugwijič,* "wife's mother" (the suffix *-jič* is an affectionate diminutive).

4. Collaterality

The criterion of *collaterality* involves a distinction between two kinds of consanguineal relatives. *Lineal* relatives are those with whom ego is linked solely by direct ties of descent (not by co-descent): ego's parents, her parents' parents, and so on; his children, her children's children, and so on. Ego's parents' siblings and their offspring are called *collateral* relatives.

Kinship terms that ignore the criterion of collaterality merge lineal with collateral relatives, as in the earlier example of a single term applied to both father (lineal) and father's brother (collateral), or to both mother and mother's sister. A common type of merging within ego's own generation involves siblings and certain cousins; for example, sister and her mother's sister's daughter may be called by a single kinship term. (Actually, one's siblings are neither lineal nor collateral relatives. The term *ablineal* has been suggested for this relationship.)

5. Bifurcation

The criterion of *bifurcation* (forking) is unfamiliar to English speakers, although most societies use it at least occasionally. When bifurcation is recognized, ego uses different terms for relatives, depending on the sex of the linking relative. English speakers usually lump together analogous relatives from both sides of a family: an "uncle" may be a father's brother or a mother's brother. We use bifurcation in a roundabout way when we speak of "a cousin on my mother's side" or "my paternal grandfather." Many societies that merge father and father's brother (ignoring the criterion of collaterality), however, carefully separate the father's brother from the mother's brother (using the criterion of bifurcation). In such a society, ego would have two different terms (X, Y) for the men of his or her father's generation, applied as follows:

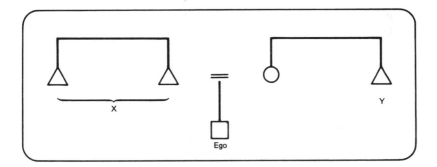

In general, kinship systems make *systematic* use of the criteria they use. If, for example, collaterality is recognized in the labeling of one pair of relatives, so that father and father's brother are called by different terms, it is likely that this criterion will be used to distinguish other pairs of relatives (for example, son and brother's son). In this respect, kinship systems are similar to phonemic systems in which, as we have seen, a limited number of qualitative criteria (voicing, tongue position, and so on) are systematically used to classify sounds into a few significant categories (the phonemes of a language). In language systems and in kinship systems we find a selection of and an emphasis on certain attributes of sounds or of persons, and a systematic tendency to ignore other attributes and the categories that could be based on them.

The criteria discussed above (generation, sex, affinity, collaterality, and bifurcation) constitute Murdock's "major criteria" of kinship. Figure 4.1 illustrates some of the possible combinations of these five criteria. They are supplemented by three "minor criteria," which, when used, tend to be restricted to only a few relationships.

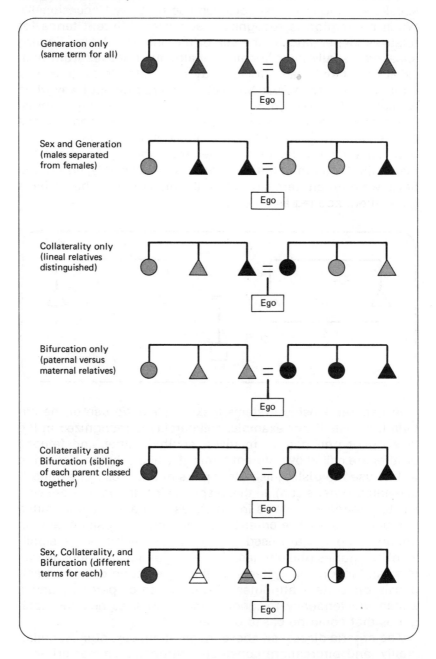

FIGURE 4.1 Classification of Relatives with Recognition of Various Combinations of Criteria (same shading indicates use of same term)

6. Relative Age

In kinship systems where the criterion of relative age is recognized, ego may use different terms for elder and younger siblings, both her own and those of her parents. Relative-age terminology is generally found in societies where people's seniority gives them some privilege or authority over their kin.

7. Speaker's Sex

In general, ego and his siblings use the same kinship term for each type of relative. But when the speaker's sex is recognized, ego and his sister must use different terms. Among the Haida Indians of the Queen Charlotte Islands, a boy and his sister refer to their male parent by different terms. From the Haida point of view, the English term "father" is a classificatory term covering two quite distinct relationships.

8. Decedence

Murdock's final criterion, decedence, applies when a kinship term changes upon the death of a connecting relative. It is not too difficult to imagine social customs that would impel ego to use a different kinship term toward, say, her father's brother, after her own father's death. Use of this criterion, however, is quite rare.

A few other criteria are also used with some regularity in kinship terminologies, but those already considered are sufficient to illustrate this approach to the study of kinship structure. One reason for the study of kinship is practical. In the kinds of societies studied by anthropologists, kinship is frequently the key to understanding all kinds of social actions, from marriage to inheritance, from witchcraft to political power.

Kinship Terminology and Behavior

Anthropological studies have made it abundantly clear that terminology is an important clue to expected behavior. We must beware, however, of the fallacy of deducing rules of behavior (past or present) from terminology. Like other kinds of role labels, kinship terms are generally applied to categories of persons toward whom ego is expected to act in the same way; each kinship category is associated with a set of plans. If ego uses a single kin term for both his father and his father's brother, it is probable that he is expected to treat them alike and that he has similar expectations of both. The use of one term for two persons who are related to him in different ways does *not* mean that ego cannot tell the difference between them, or that he cannot somehow state his specific relationship to each. Nor does it mean that ego calls his father's brother "father." It does mean that for certain social purposes, the criterion of collaterality that separates them may be ignored; their common label is best translated as "male relative of the next higher generation on the paternal side." Since different social arrangements might encourage this type of classification, however, we must always investigate the actual behavior as well as the terms.

Among the social customs that affect kinship terminology are the *marriage regulations* of a society. Many societies have regulations that permit or encourage ego to marry a cross-cousin (a daughter of his mother's brother or father's sister; see Figure 4.2). In such a society, ego would probably use different terms to refer to cross- and parallel cousins, since his anticipated behavior toward them is so different.

Another example of marriage regulations that influence kinship terminology can be seen in societies where a man who takes a second wife is expected to marry his first wife's sister. This practice is known as *sororal polygyny* (see Figure 4.3). In such societies, ego might use the same kinship term for his mother's sister's daughter as he does for his own sister, since his father will probably be married to his mother's sister.

Murdock found that in sixteen out of eighteen societies practicing sororal polygyny, the same term was applied to both sister and mother's sister's daughter, whether ego's father was married to both sisters or not. This kind of terminology is also found in some societies that do not permit sororal polygyny. Therefore, although marriage regulations can help us understand certain

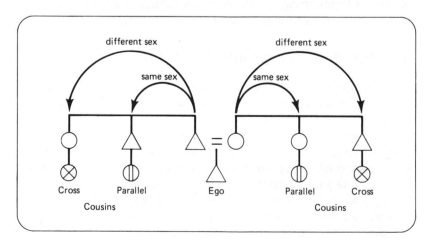

FIGURE 4.2 Parallel and Cross-Cousins

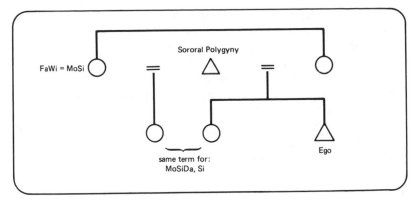

FIGURE 4.3 Sororal Polygyny and Terminology

features of kinship terminology, it would be wrong to infer the existence of a marriage rule simply from the presence of certain kinship terms. Kin terms are labels for categories of relatives, but the plans associated with each category must be determined separately for each society.

Marriage Regulations

The major types of marriage regulations found in the world's societies are listed and defined below:

I. monogamy—one spouse at a time
  a. strict—no remarriage
  b. serial—remarriage permitted

II. polygamy—plural spouses permitted
  a. polygyny—plural wives
    i. sororal—wives must be sisters
  b. polyandry—plural husbands
    i. fraternal—husbands must be brothers

III. preferential (or prescriptive) marriage
  a. cross-cousin marriage—should (or must) marry cross cousin
    i. patrilateral—man should marry father's sister's daughter
    ii. matrilateral—man should marry mother's brother's daughter
  b. parallel-cousin marriage—should (or must) marry parallel cousin
    i. patrilateral—man should marry father's brother's daughter
    ii. matrilateral—man should marry mother's sister's daughter (rare)
  c. levirate—man expected to marry widow of his deceased brother
  d. sororate—man expected to marry sister of his deceased wife
  e. mother/daughter marriage—man marries widow and her daughter(s)

IV. group-specific marriage—this includes a variety of rules falling into two major types
  a. exogamy—requiring marriage *outside of* a given social group
  b. endogamy—requiring marriage *within* a given social group
    i. social class or caste
    ii. locality
    iii. kinship group (lineage, clan, moiety, and so on)
    iv. religious group

Preferential marriage rules (such as IIIa and IIIb) may cause difficulties if ego simply does not have the right kind of cousin; for example, if a man's father's sister is childless or his mother has no brothers. The solution to this problem brings us back to the significance of kinship terminology. In a society with, say, preferential matrilineal cross-cousin marriage (IIIa-ix), the rule should be stated as follows: a man is expected to marry a woman whom he *calls* "mother's brother's daughter." Since all kinship terminologies are classificatory, ego's own mother's brother's daughter is only one of the women who fall into the category with this label. There will generally be several eligible women called by this term. If not, a compromise or exception can always be made.

Every culture defines certain categories of persons as suitable or unsuitable mates for other categories of persons, and almost every member of a society is influenced by these regulations in his or her choice of a spouse. In this way, marriage regulations serve as recruitment criteria for the social role of spouse. American society defines the category of suitable mates by a combination of racial, religious, ethnic, and social class factors, and the vast majority of marriages take place between persons who live in the same locality. Thus, before we wonder at kin-based marriage rules, we should realize that our own range of potential mates is severely limited.

Social Relationships

A kinship role exists only in relation to a reciprocal role: one can be a mother's brother only in relation to a sister's child, a husband only in relation to a wife. Each such role implies its reciprocal, and the pair of roles taken together compose the *social relationship.* Thus we may say that the marriage relationship is composed of the reciprocal roles husband/wife, the avuncular relationship of the roles parent's brother/sibling's child, and so on. This is true of nearly all types of roles and relationships: employer/employee, performer/audience, teacher/pupil, doctor/patient, friend/friend, and so on. The reciprocity of social relationships is a basic fact of social structure. Recognition of this fact should help us to see that social roles have an essential *function* to perform: they are cultural devices that smooth and coordinate interaction among the members of a society. They do so by enabling people to know what to expect of others and what others expect of them. By learning and performing their own roles, all persons contribute to the maintenance of their society and its traditions.

The reciprocal nature of social relationships requires a give-and-take such that both members of a relationship get something in return for their participation. Among the benefits given and received in many kinship relations are food, affection, protection, power, loyalty, labor, pleasure, property, service, and security. Exploitation occurs if one member of a relationship continually gives more than she receives. Exploitative relationships tend to be unstable, although when the exploiting member has a monopoly of power or other benefits they may persist for some time.

SEX ROLES AND AGE ROLES

One set of roles found in every society is the pair *male* and *female.* These are generally lifetime roles, ascribed to each person at birth, though some kind of intermediate role, such as the Crow *berdache* or the Cheyenne "half-man, half-woman" may be achieved later in life. The two basic sex roles allow three possible sexual relationships: male/male, female/female, and male/female. Although most social interaction is governed by more specific kinds of role attributes, sex roles provide an ever present background to social behavior. In an unfamiliar situation, one may have no other clue to the kind of person one is dealing with. In more clearly defined situations, the sex roles of the participants may *condition* their performances in various ways—for example, by prescribing different forms of dress or speech or posture for a man or a woman performing a given role.

Cultural anthropologists agree that *sex roles are learned* and that the content of sexual relationships depends primarily on culture. This is not to deny the biological basis of these roles. Rather, as with kinship roles, each culture interprets and elaborates the biological differences in a conventional and partly arbitrary manner. Margaret Mead, who has spent many years studying the relationship of sex to social customs, states that

> it is not enough for a child to decide simply and fully that it belongs to its own sex, is anatomically a male or a female, with a given reproductive role in the world. For growing children are faced with another problem: *"How male,* how female, am I?" He hears men

branded as feminine, women condemned as masculine, others ex-
tolled as real men, and as true women. He hears types of respon-
siveness, fastidiousness, sensitivity, guts, stoicism, and endurance
voted as belonging to one sex rather than the other [1949b:136].

Each society develops different sex roles that define the way
a man or a woman is expected to act. Margaret Mead's book
Male and Female shows that some societies elaborate very little
on physiological differences, viewing men and women as pretty
much the same, while others emphasize the differences between the sexes and call forth quite different behavior from
each.

The conventionality of the content of sex roles is most obvious in matters of superficial appearance. Most American Indian men had long hair and painted their faces, while among
most contemporary Americans these are attributes of the female
sex role. Conventional standards of beauty and sexual attractiveness had led, in various times and places, to styles of dress
that we would consider outlandish and forms of body mutilation
that seem to us grotesque. The styles of yesterday often amuse
people of today, just as the costumes of today will amuse our
descendants. Body mutilations are by no means restricted to
primitive peoples; alongside scarification, head-flattening, and
lip-stretching, we must place foot-binding, ear-piercing, and the
bustle. As Horace Miner says of the Nacirema:

> There are ritual fasts to make fat people thin and ceremonial feasts
> to make thin people fat. Still other rites are used to make women's
> breasts larger if they are small, and smaller if they are large. General
> dissatisfaction with breast shape is symbolized by the fact that the
> ideal form is virtually outside the range of human variation
> [1956:506].

Comparative studies have shown that traits thought of as typ-
ically masculine in one culture may be considered feminine in
another. This is true not only of appearance but also of psychological characteristics such as aggressiveness or curiosity and
alleged abilities such as physical endurance or spiritual powers.
The division of labor by sex is universal, but *which* tasks will be
assigned to *which* sex is largely a matter of arbitrary cultural
definition. In some societies only men perform agricultural
tasks, in some only women, and in others agriculture is the
responsibility of both sexes. Similarly, shamans in a given society may be primarily of either sex, just as most medical doctors
in the United States are men, while in the U.S.S.R. the vast ma-

jority are women. Cultures tend to rationalize their divisions of labor, but the beliefs that men or women make better shamans or doctors are just as conventional as the practices they justify.

Age roles are also universal, though the specific age categories and the plans for behavior associated with these categories are learned. The various stages of the human career are conventionally established, just as each culture divides up the light spectrum into color categories. In traditional Chinese culture, a child was considered one year old at birth, and advanced to age two at the New Year (when all members of the society added a year to their age), whether that came ten days or ten months after the child's actual birth. In American culture there are different ages at which a person may vote, marry, purchase liquor, drive an automobile, cease attending school, and retire with a pension. These categories, based upon chronological age, operate together to determine a person's *social age* and thus to define individual rights and obligations within the social group.

Most preliterate societies do not calculate a person's absolute age in years or months, but they often attach great importance to distinctions of seniority. Some primitive social systems use age to organize group relationships (see page 125). For example, among the Masai, a warlike people of East Africa, young men in their late teens and twenties lived apart from their families in a special camp for warriors, where they ate, slept, and were visited by their sweethearts. They left this camp on offensive or retaliatory raids against neighboring tribes, killing enemies, earning glory, and stealing cattle to bring back to their village. When a Masai man reached his early thirties, the warrior phase of his life would end; he was then an elder, and was expected to marry and settle down. This adjustment was as difficult for the Masai to make as is involuntary retirement for the still-active business executive in our society.

Each culture and subculture categorizes the "ages of man" in different ways, associates different plans for behavior with these ages, and *values* the various age roles differently. The age that is considered the best may be very revealing of the basic patterns of the culture. In some societies, childhood or youth is considered the best time of life. In others, old age is most highly valued, the role of elder being respected and desired. In still other societies, the vigorous young adult is considered to be at the height of his powers. For example, the Tarascan Indians of north-central Mexico associate vitality (*esfuerzo*) with the body heat of an individual, and according to their division of the life cycle:

a person goes through three "ages" in a lifetime. The first, from birth to puberty, is one of gradually increasing body heat—which spells health—and vigor. The second, from puberty to about 30 years of age, is that of maximum strength and vitality. After 30 a person gradually loses his esfuerzo as his body grows old and cold [Foster 1967:129].

Interpretations of American attitudes toward life stages are not in agreement, though all studies show that old age brings very little prestige. Some scholars emphasize the youth culture of the United States, pointing out the growing desire of Americans to think young as well as to look young. Others have suggested that the "prime of life" comes at a different point in the subculture of each social class. For the lower-class male, whose occupation is likely to involve little education and much manual labor, the prime of life comes in the twenties and early thirties. For the upper-middle-class person, these are likely to be years of continuing education and a struggle to get established, with professional and financial success coming later, in the forties and fifties. Such differences between group expectations create very different social problems. The conflict between the generations and the isolation of elderly people so common to our society may even be absent in groups with different ideas about age roles.

OCCUPATIONAL ROLES

As Everett Hughes has pointed out, "Careers in our society are thought of very much in terms of jobs, for these are the characteristic and crucial connections of the individual with the institutional structure" (1958:64). Social position is determined largely by occupation. In simpler societies, a person is much more likely to be identified with his or her kinship group or locality, for there are no true occupational roles, only the division of labor by age and sex, supplemented by a few part-time specialties. The part-time shaman, trader, or craftworker is the forerunner of the priest, merchant, or artisan. Even when such roles are ascribed to an individual on the basis of kinship, they enrich the social structure by making possible new kinds of relationships.

In many of the world's societies, recruitment to occupational roles is determined strictly by heredity. Where this is the case, occupational training can take place within a family setting: the daughter of a potter knows that she too will one day be a potter,

BLACK STAR

This boy has started to learn the appearance and behavior expected of the male role in his society.

and she begins at an early age to acquire the skills and knowledge that she will need.

In societies where personal preference enters into the choice of occupation, formal training is required. The Navajo Indian who wishes to become a ritual singer must persuade an experienced singer to teach him a chant; he must undergo weeks of concentrated training, for which the teacher receives considerable gifts. The training of the Tapirapé shamans, described in Chapter 2, also requires years of preparation and discipline.

To perform occupational roles, people must possess certain *skills* and *knowledge,* which they may display in the material objects they produce or in the services they perform for others. Whatever the task, the performer of a specialized role serves as a repository for some part of the group's total culture which not every member of the society understands. Thus the other members are dependent on specialists, and must assume that they do in fact possess the skills and knowledge they claim.

Most social relationships have a different meaning for each

of the participants. The obligations of one party to a social relationship are the rights of the other (for example, a worker's right to be paid for her labor implies the employer's obligation to pay her). Beyond this, a person's attitude toward a given relationship depends on his past experience in the role he must perform. For those specialties known as the "professions," Everett Hughes has summarized this dilemma in a pithy phrase: the client's *crisis* is the professional's *routine.* That is, the critical and unusual situation that brings a person to consult a specialist, whether curer, lawyer, undertaker, or dance coach, is exactly the kind of situation with which the specialist deals day after day. Thus the doctor deals constantly with sick and dying people, but each patient understandably thinks of his or her own illness as unique.

Specialists are faced with a peculiar dilemma of their own, which Erving Goffman refers to as the conflict between *action* and *expression.* To find clients, specialists must communicate the fact that they are prepared to do something for people, and this requirement for expression often gets in the way of their actions. As Goffman comments, if people wish to dramatize the character of their roles, they may have to expend a good deal of energy. The appearance of casual competence may require long and arduous preparation. The dilemma of action versus expression is that "those who have the time and talent to perform a task well may not, because of this, have the time or talent to make it apparent that they are performing well" (1959:32–33). But it is the *appearance* of competence that inspires confidence, since the fact of competence is usually unmeasurable. Learning a role is not enough; one must translate knowledge into action, and one's performance must be accepted by others as legitimate.

LEADERSHIP ROLES

A leadership role is a social role involving the legitimate exercise of *authority* over other persons. People with authority are socially entitled to command the actions of others, and their commands are backed up by *social sanctions:* rewards and punishments. Exercise of authority varies with the culture and the type of social group. It may consist of a casual suggestion or a decree, an opinion or a code of law. In any case, when they act within the limits of their leadership roles, leaders can expect their followers to obey. Leaders are specialists in decision-making. They are entitled to act for or in behalf of others. The leader/follower relationship is always characterized by this fundamental *asymmetry* of authority.

On the basis of the leader's source of authority, four general types of leadership role may be distinguished. The first is the *hereditary leader,* whose claim to authority is based on position in a kinship group—for example, the oldest living male in a royal lineage. Such a leadership role is thus ascribed, although when more than one individual has a claim to become leader, achievement may also enter into the picture. The history of disputed royal successions is filled with poisonings, assassinations, and rebellions, all of which eliminate the careless or trusting person from positions of authority. Hereditary leaders are socially recognized (their authority is considered legitimate) because of *who they are* rather than what they can do. This does not mean that their power is unlimited. The authority of most hereditary leaders is limited in many subtle ways. Although many hereditary African rulers have been referred to as absolute monarchs, Meyer Fortes and E. E. Evans-Pritchard observed:

> The forces that maintain the supremacy of the paramount ruler are opposed by the forces that act as a check on his powers. . . . Institutions like the king's council, sacerdotal officials who have a de-

A charismatic leader—John F. Kennedy campaigning in 1962.

cisive voice in the king's investiture, queen mothers' courts, and so forth . . . work for the protection of law and custom and the control of centralized power. . . . The balance between central authority and regional autonomy is a very important element in the political structure. If a king abuses his power, subordinate chiefs are liable to secede or to lead a revolt against him [1940:11].

A second type of leadership role is that of *bureaucratic leader.* Achieved attributes play the largest part in the recruitment of these leaders. They attain positions of authority by passing through positions of lesser authority. Their achievements involve *competence* (often judged by standardized tests) and *seniority* (number of years of service). Bureaucracies arise under rather special social conditions, and they both attract and develop the kind of person who has moderate ambitions and who desires a career filled with routine and security.

A third type of leader, which the great German sociologist Max Weber considered the direct opposite of the bureaucratic type, is the *charismatic leader.* Such leaders are unique persons who rise to authority in times of great social crisis; by force of personality they command enthusiastic followers who may bring about a genuine social revolution:

> Charisma, meaning literally "gift of grace," is used by Weber to characterize self-appointed leaders who are followed by those who are in distress and who . . . believe him to be extraordinarily qualified. The founders of world religions and the prophets as well as military and political heroes are the archetypes of the charismatic leader. Miracles and revelations, heroic feats of valor and baffling success are characteristic marks of their stature. Failure is their ruin [Gerth and Mills 1958:52].

The upheaval brought about by charismatic leaders is generally followed by what Weber called the "routinization of charisma." Rigid institutions of the bureaucratic type adapt the ideas of the leader, converting radical ideas into dogma that can be taught and followed routinely. Novel ideas are modified and made acceptable to a large following.

The fourth type of leadership role is the *representative leader.* The basis of these leaders' authority is the fact that they were chosen by a group of people and are *responsible to them.* Leaders of this type may possess attributes of the three other types; they may come from important families, may have attained high bureaucratic office, may possess considerable personal charisma. But these qualities are not the basis of their authority.

Representative leaders may continue to lead only so long as their followers are willing to obey; there are ways of depriving such leaders of authority without overturning the whole social system, as was seen in the resignation of Richard Nixon. Among the Iroquois tribes of New York State, members of the intertribal governing council were chosen by the leading women of certain lineages and could also be deposed by these women. Among the Plains Indians, a young war leader proved himself in battle, and his authority lasted only so long as he was successful. (Older men were expected to display quite different leadership qualities.)

In most small hunting and gathering societies (bands), the leader is simply the oldest or the most experienced man in the group. He may decide when and where to move camp, and what hunting techniques should be used; he may attempt to settle intraband disputes. Beyond these specific functions, he has no power over members of the band. Marshall D. Sahlins distinguishes "tribal societies" from the more complex "chiefdoms" on similar grounds:

> The typical leader in a tribal society is only the glorified counterpart of the influential elder in a hunting and gathering society. Like the latter . . . he builds a following on the basis of personally-established ties. He creates loyalties through generosity; fearful acquiescence through magic; inclination to accept his opinions through demonstration of wisdom, oratorical skill, and the like. Leadership here is a charismatic interpersonal relationship. Since it is based on personal ties and qualities, it is not hereditable. It is not an *office* within a definite group: it is not *chieftainship* [1961:327].

Since authority is always asymmetrical, roles can be ranked in accordance with the degree of authority they carry. Bureaucratic organizations such as the military require an elaborate and explicit *ranking* of roles so that all members know who is entitled to give orders to whom. The ranking of roles according to relative authority need not correspond to the *valuation* of roles according to their relative prestige. In some societies, positions of power are treated as necessary evils, and no one will admit to a craving for leadership. The Nuer of northeastern Africa, for example, place so little value on leadership that, in the words of Evans-Pritchard, they "have no government, and their state might be described as an ordered anarchy" (1940:5–6). Other peoples accord the highest honors to their leaders and are very uncomfortable in the absence of clear-cut authority. In our society, some roles are highly valued (for example, concert

pianist) but carry little or no authority, while others with considerable authority (for example, policeman) are low in prestige.
Thus authority and prestige, though they often go together, may
also diverge.

THE PERSONAL ROLE AND THE SOCIETAL ROLE

The personal role is a social category composed of a single
individual. Its attributes include a *label* (the personal name be-
stowed by some social group) and a set of *plans* (patterns of
behavior that define the kinds of actions which that person ex-
pects of himself, and which others expect of him). If George
acts in an unusual manner we may say that "he is not himself"—
he is not playing the personal role that we have come to expect
of him, even if identical behavior by another individual would
have passed unnoticed. Personal roles are built up out of all the
personal and social relationships into which an individual enters. The personal name is essential to one's sense of individuality. To refuse to use a person's name, or to assign her a
number, is to treat her as a member of a category (official, pris-
oner, student), rather than as an individual.

At the other extreme from the personal role is the *societal
role.* This is a category that applies to all the members of a
society. In a modern national state it is equivalent to the role of
citizen. Attributes of the citizen role include expectations of
being loyal to the state, obeying its laws, enjoying the rights of
citizenship, speaking the language of the country, and acting in
accordance with its unwritten customs. Such expectations apply to all members of the society, regardless of the kinship,
occupational, or other roles they may play. The citizen role contrasts primarily with the role of alien, a kind of person to whom
these expectations do not necessarily apply.

The attributes of a societal role are often so subtle that one
is quite unaware of them; this is one reason for the vague discomfort that many people feel in visiting foreign countries. Goffman has identified one of the general attributes of the American
societal role and contrasted it with the expectations found in
the Shetland Islands:

> In middle-class Anglo-American society, when in a public place, one
> is supposed to keep one's nose out of other people's activity and
> go about one's own business. It is only when a woman drops a
> package, or when a fellow motorist gets stalled in the middle of the
> road, or when a baby left alone in a carriage begins to scream, that

middle-class people feel it is all right to break down momentarily the walls which effectively insulate them. In Shetland Isle different rules obtained. If any man happened to find himself in the presence of others who were engaged in a task, it was expected that he would lend a hand, especially if the task was relatively brief and relatively strenuous. Such casual mutual aid was taken as a matter of course and was an expression of nothing closer than fellow-islander status [1959:230].

In tribal societies, the societal role includes all kinds of customary behavior that is characteristic of *us* as opposed to *them*. Such behavior includes speaking the tribal dialect and conforming to local customs. In such groups, the societal role contrasts with the role of stranger, outsider, or perhaps enemy. Quite commonly, the term used by tribal peoples to describe themselves may be translated as "real people" as opposed to inferior outsiders: the Micmac term is *elnu,* "person," while the Navajo call themselves *dene,* "the people." Tribal ways of thinking have also persisted into more complex societies, and a similar conception of the societal role may be studied in those who contrast "red-blooded Americans" with "dirty foreigners."

An understanding of social roles is essential to the analysis of social structure, but it is also helpful in combating ethnocentrism, racism, and sexism. Once we understand the degree to which human behavior is influenced by learned expectations about roles and relationships, we learn to see other social systems as alternative ways of organizing social life. Cross-cousin marriage, hereditary leadership, and contrasting sex roles are not "unnatural" or disgusting. They are simply adaptations that various groups have developed to solve universal human problems such as: Whom should I marry? Whom should I obey? What does it mean to be a woman (or a man)? We need not adopt any of these alternative solutions, but we can learn to appreciate their advantages and disadvantages as we gain a better perspective on our own way of life.

RECOMMENDED READING

Ralf Dahrendorf, *Essays in the Theory of Society*. Stanford: Stanford University Press, 1968. A series of provocative essays, one of which, "Homo Sociologicus," is the best available treatment of the concept of social role—its history, significance, limitations, and implications for modern life.

Robin Fox, *Kinship and Marriage*. Baltimore: Pelican Books, 1967. The most readable brief introduction to the complexities of anthropological studies of kinship and marriage. (Part of this book is actually more relevant to materials in the next chapter.)

Erving Goffman, *Relations in Public*. New York: Basic Books, 1971. In this book Goffman is concerned with the various verbal and non-verbal ways that we signal our relationships to others (and our attitudes toward ourselves) when we are in public places.

Stanley Milgram, *Obedience to Authority: An Experimental View*. New York: Harper & Row, 1974. An ingenious and frightening experiment is used to explore the conditions under which ordinary people will obey orders that appear to harm others.

David M. Schneider, *American Kinship: A Cultural Account*. Englewood Cliffs, N.J.: Prentice Hall, 1968. In this and his other writings on "kinship," Schneider argues that these phenomena can be understood only from a relativistic position that emphasizes the categories, symbols, and meanings found in each society.

CHAPTER FIVE
KINDS OF GROUPS

CATEGORIES AND GROUPS

A category of persons consists of individuals who share one or more of the characteristics that define the category. For example:

People who live in Boise, Idaho
Officers of the Tibetan Merchant Marine
Women with hair longer than fourteen inches
Migrant farm laborers
Students at Reed College in 1974–1975
Women married to Stephen J. Glutz of Cleveland
Living descendants of Thomas Jefferson
The Baltimore Colts

These are all categories of persons, though of clearly different types. One is a "null category"—that is, it has no members since there is no Tibetan merchant marine. Another has but a single member at any given time (unless Mr. Glutz is a bigamist). Still others (which?) are *merely* categories; that is, nothing can be said about their members beyond the fact that they happen to share the defining criteria; they do not form a *group*.

In this chapter the term *social group* refers to any definite category of persons associated with a plan for collective action. A group's members must display a "stable and embracing pattern of mutual interaction" (Goffman 1963:23). It may have any number of members, but the two-person (or *dyadic*) group is the limiting case, and is equivalent to a social relationship (see above).

Many types of groups may be distinguished. Groups may be classified according to the degree of *formality* of their structure. A highly formal group is one with clearly defined rules concerning recruitment, division of labor, rights and obligations of members, times and places of meeting, and so forth. A highly formal group in our society would be a trade union or a men's lodge such as the Masons. Informal groups, such as cooperative work parties or social gatherings, lack such explicit rules; the conduct of the members is regulated only by their personal relationships and the specific task at hand. Between these extremes fall all kinds of semiformal groups that have some but not all the characteristics of formal groups.

Notable group characteristics include *continuity through time* (relatively permanent though ephemeral), *mode of recruitment* (automatic or voluntary, corresponding to ascribed or achieved roles), and *corporacy* (presence or absence of property in which members have joint interest). These characteristics are not independent of one another. For example, a corporate group whose members share in the benefits of some valuable "estate" (for example, land, cattle, or capital equipment) will usually have a relatively formal structure and a high degree of continuity over time. Semiformal and formal groups usually have *names,* and one of the rights of membership may be the right to use the group name or to display its identifying insignia.

Group Integration

Groups also differ in the degree to which their members feel committed to one another and to continued membership in the group. Degree of *integration* of a group means the strength with which the parts of the group stick together.

Emile Durkheim (1947) pointed out two types of group integration: *mechanical solidarity* and *organic solidarity.* Mechanical solidarity is based on the similarity of the parts (segments) of a social group. They stick together because they are alike: their members have similar experiences, ideas, and emotions,

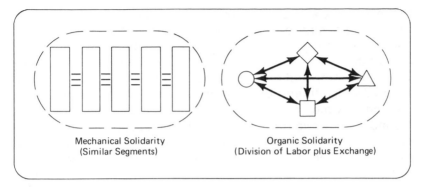

Mechanical Solidarity
(Similar Segments)

Organic Solidarity
(Division of Labor plus Exchange)

FIGURE 5.1 Two Types of Internal Social Integration

do the same kinds of things, and understand one another. All groups possess a certain degree of mechanical solidarity or they could not function as groups. As Durkheim pointed out, however, a group based solely on mechanical solidarity has a tendency to fall apart precisely because each of its segments is equivalent and thus functionally independent of the others.

Organic solidarity, on the other hand, is based on *differences* between the parts of a group. It is a consequence of the division of labor, which makes the segments unequal and interdependent. Durkheim drew an analogy to the organs of the body, each of which has its own task to perform, and cannot function without the others. Organic solidarity requires the constant exchange of valued goods and/or services among the segments of the group. No social group can continue without a certain degree of organic solidarity, even if the need for exchange must be artificially established and maintained. As Durkheim noted, much sexual division of labor is objectively unnecessary. By making men and women dependent upon one another, however, division of labor increases the organic solidarity of the sexes, which furthers the integration of society (see Figure 5.1).

Both kinds of solidarity are essential to group integration. The differences and exchanges that produce organic solidarity require a degree of trust that can come only from (mechanical) similarity. Georg Simmel (1955) pointed out that *even social conflict* requires a common basis of understanding and an agreement to abide by certain rules. Both conflict and cooperation are continuing social relationships. But total indifference will destroy a relationship, just as its counterpart, apathy, can destroy a group.

In addition to the internal integration (solidarity) of a social

group, we may also study the degree of its external integration—
that is, the extent to which it is bound up with other groups in
society. Some groups (for example, criminal gangs) exclusively
benefit their own members, whereas other groups perform services for clients and/or for the society as a whole (for example,
the Methodist church or the Coast Guard). The necessity of recruiting new members and maintaining vital services leads even
the most exclusive groups into some transactions with the outside world; and the larger society frequently takes an interest
in subgroup activities, even when the group is a dyad composed
of "consenting adults."

Group Functions and Specialization

The plans for collective activity associated with a given category
of persons may range from making war to making love, from
producing automobiles to consuming marijuana. Nevertheless,
it is useful to consider these purposes as examples of three
general social functions, which may be defined as follows:

1. *Task function:* the orientation of the group toward producing objective effects on its physical, biological, or social environment; for example, producing a product, exploiting or protecting a resource, winning a war or a game.
2. *Control function:* the orientation of the group toward
   maintaining its own internal structure (and growth)
   through conformity to behavioral and recruitment norms;
   for example, enculturating and disciplining group members and (when relevant) recruiting qualified new members.
3. *Expressive function:* the orientation of the group toward
   satisfying the psychological needs of its members, including those needs that result from individual participation in
   the task and control activities.

Every human group is primarily oriented toward one of these
functions, but all three functions are present to some degree—
if not explicitly, then implicitly. For example, each military unit
has a mission (explicit task function), but the leaders of these
groups are fully aware of the need to maintain military discipline
(implicit control function). Group morale depends on the satisfaction of the psychological needs of the members (implicit
expressive function). Some activities can fulfill a number of

functions at once; such activities tend to become a regular part of the group schedule.

The task function is usually explicit; in some cases, however, it may be implicit as compared with other functions. A classic example is Bronislaw Malinowski's analysis of the *kula* ring of the Trobriand Islanders. The Trobrianders and their neighbors in the Massim area of Melanesia carry on extensive inter-island trade, using outrigger canoes to carry goods over miles of open sea. From the Trobriand point of view, however, it is not the production of or trade in useful goods that justifies these dangerous expeditions. This task function is satisfied incidentally in the process of exchanging valuable but nonutilitarian articles (necklaces and armbands) with one's *kula* partners. These valuables must not be kept for long by any one person, but must be passed along around the circle of islands forming the *kula* ring, the armbands traveling in one direction and the necklaces in the other:

> the acts of exchange of the valuables have to conform to a definite code. . . . The ceremonial attached to the act of giving, the manner of carrying and handling the valuables shows distinctly that this is regarded as something else than mere merchandise. Indeed it is to the native something that confers dignity, that exalts him, and which he therefore treats with veneration and affection [Malinowski 1960:510–511].

As a result of the *kula* transactions (which Malinowski likens to a display of the British crown jewels), considerable wealth is created and distributed, but the explicit function of this group effort is to satisfy the psychological needs of the *kula* partners and their associates for prestige.

Many groups find it useful to assign the three functions to different individuals or subgroups. The differentiation of task, control, and expressive functions is particularly clear in complex societies. Occupational groups are primarily oriented toward the accomplishment of specific tasks, while the police and the courts specialize in social control. Expressive functions tend to be carried out by part- or full-time specialists in psychotherapy, religion, and the arts. In most societies the family remains unspecialized in function; this is one reason for its universal importance. Even within the family there is some tendency toward specialization, one parent acting as task leader and the other parent as leader for expressive and control purposes. Experimental studies of small, task-oriented groups have repeatedly shown a tendency for one person to specialize in task direction while another person becomes the socio-emotional leader. Groups with primarily expressive functions (such as many communes) eventually encounter difficulties with their environments that call forth specialized task leadership.

The remainder of this chapter will deal with the varieties of social groups that are found in human societies throughout the world. The groups will be classified according to the basis upon which their memberships are recruited (residence, kinship, occupation, and so on). Within each type, concrete examples will illustrate the characteristics of integration, formality, and continuity, and the group functions discussed above.

RESIDENTIAL GROUPS

Like most animals, human beings tend to cluster together rather than scatter. This clustering is both a cause and a result of group formation. In discussing the origin of the city, Lewis Mumford has suggested the twin metaphor of "the magnet and the container" (1961:3–15). He proposes that people are attracted to a place by some desirable quality of the area, and that after they have occupied it for a time, it comes to "contain" them and their works within permanent structures (walls, temples, granaries).

People do become emotionally attached to a place. They learn how to use its resources, and they come to value the alterations that they and their ancestors have made in the environment. These alterations include material items—paths, cleared fields, irrigation ditches, shrines, or secular buildings— and nonmaterial items—a belief in the presence of benevolent spirits, for example, or a feeling of loyalty to the home of one's ancestors.

Whatever their original reasons for coming together, those living in one place are likely to develop common patterns of experience, leading to mechanical solidarity, and a division of labor, leading to organic solidarity. A category of persons is initially defined solely on the basis of its spatial boundaries. It becomes a *residential group* with the development of a *plan* that specifies appropriate forms of intragroup behavior.

Households

Different types of households are built on different principles of recruitment. Social groups are formed by means of recruitment rules that specify the kinds of persons that are entitled to membership in the group. In the case of the household, the attributes that entitle one to take up residence generally have a basis in kinship and/or marriage. Paul Bohannan defines the *household* as "a group of people who live together and form a functioning domestic unit." Members of a household "may or may not constitute a family" (1963:86). Even in our society, where the ideal middle-class household is the *nuclear family* (husband and wife and their children), there are many deviations. In addition to the nuclear family, members of an American household may include grandparents, parents' siblings, children's spouses, and even nonrelatives (friends or servants), grouped around the married couple.

In other societies, the tie between spouses is less fundamental to the formation of households. For example, among the Hopi Indians of Arizona, the core of each household was a group of sisters together with their daughters (both single and married) and the daughters' children. The husbands of all these women were considered guests rather than regular household members. A Hopi man was truly at home only in his sisters' household, to which he retired on ritual occasions and whenever the tension in his wife's household was great. Unmarried males slept in their mothers' households only when they were very young; after they were six or seven years old, boys would sleep with brothers and friends at various places in the village.

Still elsewhere, the significant tie on which households are based is that between father and son. For example, among the Tanala of Madagascar, the typical household was composed of a man (the founder) together with his married and unmarried sons and their wives and offspring. Such households are found primarily in societies where the cooperation of persons of one sex is highly valued and economically important. Households containing three or more generations of males were not uncommon in rural areas of the United States during the nineteenth century. A common (though by no means universal) social change that accompanies the growth of cities and industry is the breakdown of such extended family households and their replacement by more mobile nuclear family groupings.

Sometimes consanguineal kinship determines residence, completely overriding the marriage tie. Among the Ashanti of Ghana, West Africa, the typical household consists of an old woman, her sons and daughters, and the daughters' children. The spouses of the married adults live in the nearby households of their own maternal kin. This logical arrangement does lead to some practical difficulties. Children are always running through the streets of an Ashanti village carrying food from their

A one-family compound of the Kassem tribe in northern Ghana. The round dwellings house the family head and his four wives.

mothers' cooking huts to their fathers' houses, and special arrangements must be made when spouses wish to sleep together.

Among the Tallensi, another tribe in Ghana, the core of the household is a group of men, but the practice of polygyny creates complex domestic units. A typical Tallensi dwelling consists of a number of circular buildings joined together in a circle by a mud wall. The buildings may include one or more cattle sheds, granaries, bedrooms, pantries, and kitchens for the wives of the head of the household, as well as rooms for the wives and young children of his married sons and frequently a separate sleeping room for adolescent boys (see page 291). A young Tallensi man is expected to bring his wife into his father's household; he is entitled to membership in this residential group by virtue of his ascribed role as son, whereas she enters in the achieved role of son's wife.

Anthropologists use a number of technical terms to label postmarital *residence rules,* which specify where a newly married couple is expected to live. These terms include:

    I. Unilocal—the couple is expected to live with the kin of one spouse
      a. Patrilocal—they live with the family of the groom (Tallensi)
      b. Matrilocal—they live with the family of the bride (Hopi)
      c. Avunculocal—they live with the groom's mother's brother (Trobriand Islands)
   II. Duolocal—each continues to live with his/her own kin (Ashanti)
  III. Ambilocal—the couple is expected to live with the kin of either spouse, depending on specific circumstances (Norwegian Lapps)
  IV. Neolocal—the couple is expected to establish a new residence independent of the family of either spouse (modern United States)

These terms are not entirely satisfactory. For instance, they have been used to refer to both residence *within* an established household and residence *near* a particular group of kin, and "near" may indicate any distance from an adjoining dwelling to the other side of the village. Nevertheless, these terms are widely used for comparative purposes, and a brief discussion should sensitize the student to the variety of possible social arrangements.

Various *combinations* of residence rules are also commonly found. For example, in societies that practice "bride service," the couple may first live with the bride's family for a number of years, with the groom under the authority of his wife's father; when the period of service is completed, he and his wife go to live with his family. This system is known as "matri-patrilocal residence." In many other societies, the initial period of residence (perhaps until the birth of the first child) may be with the groom's family, after which the couple may establish an independent residence. This system might be labeled "patri-neolocal" residence. It is probably much more common in the United States than is generally recognized.

Both the patrilocal Tallensi and the matrilocal Hopi have separate sleeping places for young boys. This custom is found in many parts of the world. It is most highly developed among certain East African tribes, such as the Nyakyusa: the young boys actually build a separate village of sleeping huts at some distance from their parents, although they continue to eat in their former households and to work in their fathers' fields. (The Nyakyusa case is particularly instructive, and will be considered further in the section on age groups). Elsewhere in Africa the male dormitory or settlement is associated with a *military* orientation of the society, and the young men who live there are often the warriors of the group; their segregation seems intended to keep them free of family ties and ready at all times for raiding or for defense. The men's house may also have a primarily religious function (as in New Guinea) or an economic one (as among the Indians of northern California). Even where residential groups are built upon similar principles of recruitment, the plans associated with these categories of persons may be quite different.

Young men who live apart from the rest of their society are not necessarily deprived of sexual contacts. As noted in Chapter 4, the Masai warriors who lived in a separate camp until about thirty years of age were visited there by their sweethearts. There is an entire book devoted to the men's dormitory (*ghotul*) of the Muria Gond of central India, and it is clear that this institution does *not* function to keep the sexes apart, though lovers are forbidden to marry each other later in life (Elwin 1947).

Coeducational dormitories have been established in many kibbutzim in the modern state of Israel as part of a deliberate attempt to bring about equality of the sexes and to encourage independence of children from their parents. In the kibbutz described by Melford Spiro, groups of age-mates of both sexes are raised together from birth by trained specialists (nurses and teachers), while married couples share rooms in another part of the community and are visited by their children only at certain times. Married women are thus freed from the usual tasks of child care and are able to take equal roles with men in the economic and political affairs of the community. Spiro explored the psychological effects of this child-raising system in his book *Children of the Kibbutz* (1958). One of his notable findings is that despite the extremely permissive attitudes of the adults, marriage or even sexual intercourse among the individuals who have been raised together in these groups is virtually unknown.

The so-called *matrifocal* household is a residential group having as its core a woman and her young offspring. The woman may be married or unmarried, but in any case the man who fathered her children is not a regular part of the household. Matrifocal households are found in large numbers in many parts of Latin America and also in the United States, primarily in urban areas and among impoverished members of minority groups. Just as the nuclear family household appears in industrial societies, the matrifocal household is produced by an interplay of economic and social forces.

Anthropologists have become increasingly aware that the structure of households cannot be understood by simply stating the typical residence rule or the average composition (for example, no American family really contains 2.5 children). We now pay greater attention to the *developmental cycle of the domestic group,* studying typical *changes* in composition and the socioeconomic factors responsible for them (Goody 1958). We also try to understand the *plans for household formation* that determine where an individual will live, and with whom (see Chapter 6).

The Structure of the Local Community

In most societies, the household is integrated into a larger, more inclusive residential grouping, the *local community.* In a few hunting and gathering societies the household is isolated and self-sufficient most of the time (for example, the Eskimo), but there is usually a period during which several households come together for social and ritual activities. The local community need not be sedentary, and it may have considerable turnover in its membership, but it is almost always associated with a definite range of territory. Despite fluctuations in its membership, the local community maintains its identity over time by recruiting new persons to membership and to leadership roles.

Where economic conditions permit the existence of very large local communities, residential groupings such as the *neighborhood* may subdivide the local community. These internal divisions of the local community may simply be a matter of convenience, but in primitive societies they often have a kinship basis. A division of the local community into two parts, with complementary functions, is also extremely widespread. Modern American communities tend to subdivide along social class lines (the right and wrong side of the tracks) with a neutral meeting ground in the downtown area.

All animal populations tend to grow as large as available resources allow. There are three alternative plans open to a growing human community: stabilization, fission, and aggregation. Which alternative is chosen depends on a complex interplay of natural and cultural forces.

Though human societies differ greatly in their abilities to exploit a given environment, every community eventually experiences the pressure of its numbers upon its food resources. Where access to land is strictly limited (as on a Pacific island), *stabilization* occurs: the population is limited either by the natural forces of famine or by some cultural practice such as birth control or infanticide.

Fission occurs when subgroups migrate to new territory and establish their own communities with access to further resources. This alternative depends on the availability of free land or on the power of the fissioning group to take what it needs by conquest. Population growth that results in community fission may cause a chain reaction in which expanding groups pressure neighbors who must in turn displace their neighbors. When fission takes place between parts of a descent group (see below), it is usually referred to as "segmentation."

In simple societies, newly established communities tend to be small-scale replicas of their parent communities; thus, although the communities have common origins and experiences, there is no specialization of function to bind them together, and their sense of common identity is eventually lost.

In complex societies, however, the bonds between communities are more organic. With the development of food production and of effective modes of communication (including transportation of goods), it becomes possible for some local communities to grow to considerable size. When fission does take place (peacefully or by conquest of new lands), the daughter communities remain tied to the parent community through bonds of mutual interest and need. This process is called *aggregation.* Under the right conditions of growth, fission, and integration it may lead to the development of chiefdoms and states (cf. Service 1975).

The local community is the usual focus of ethnological investigation because it is, at least in tribal societies, the smallest unit within which a total culture can be studied. As Conrad Arensberg has pointed out, the local community "is the minimal unit realizing the categories and offices of a culture's social organization. It is the minimal group capable of reenacting in the present and transmitting to the future the cultural and institutional inventory of their distinctive and historic tradition" (1955:1143).

In investigating the social structure of a local community, ethnographers try carefully to determine the kinds of groups that make up the community, the kinds of persons found in these groups, and the plans that regulate the interaction within and among these categories. They must also study relations between communities, particularly when exchange relations exist among communities that have become specialized within a larger system. For example, a peasant society, as Robert Redfield has defined it, is composed of rural communities that are involved in complex relationships with urban centers. Although the individual peasant community may resemble a tribal farming community, it also engages in political, economic, and cultural exchanges with an urban center. Such relationships that are unknown in tribal societies. To study a peasant community as an isolated unit would be to miss its most significant characteristics (Redfield 1956; cf. Bock 1968).

Residence is one of the great principles upon which social groups are organized. The residence rules of a society help people to answer the universal question "Where should I live?" at different times of their lives. The categorical contrast between "resident" and "nonresident" must be clearly defined if people are to know what is expected of them. On the state level of organization this contrast becomes transformed into the distinction between citizen and alien, and the relationship of these categories to actual physical residence is weakened. Citizens of a state may be born and live in other countries, where they are considered aliens. Nevertheless, while a state without resident aliens is conceivable, a state without resident citizens is unthinkable.

KINSHIP GROUPS

If residence is the first principle of group formation, kinship is the second. In both primitive and modern societies, ascribed social roles and group memberships are limited or determined by *where* one is born and *to whom*. Since each individual may be genealogically related to hundreds of others, most cultures provide *rules of recruitment* into the various kinship groups that compose a society. These rules involve a selection of criteria, recognizing some genealogical attributes and ignoring others. Within the group of relatives, descent rules may define several degrees of closeness. Associated with each group and subgroup are plans for group activity and interaction. These plans often call for economic, religious, or political cooperation among group members, and in every society kinship groups are concerned with the regulation of marriage, for it is through marriage that the continuity of a group is ensured. The most common rules of recruitment and the groups they result in are listed in Figure 5.2.

Recruitment Rule	Membership Criteria	Type of Kinship Groups
I. Bilateral (or "cognatic")	Affiliation traced through parents and linking relatives of either sex	Kindreds
a. ego-centered	Traced outward to known limits by each individual; overlapping	personal kindred or "great family"
b. not ego-centered	Traced outward from some prominent person in each generation	stem kindred
II. Unilineal	Affiliation traced from "founder" through linking relatives of one sex only	Descent Groups (lineages, clans, phratries, moieties)
a. patrilineal	Automatic affiliation through father and male linking relatives; bounded	patrilineage, and so on
b. matrilineal	Automatic affiliation through mother and female linking relatives; bounded	matrilineage, and so on
c. duolineal (or "double descent")	Combination of II-a and II-b	each person belongs to *both* a patrilineal and a matrilineal group
III. Ambilineal (or "multilineal")	Nonautomatic: individual has choice of affiliation with the (lineal) group of either parent (or with the group of a spouse's parent)	Nonunilinear Descent Groups (septs or rammages)

FIGURE 5.2 Rules of Recruitment and Types of Kinship Groups

The Kindred

American kinship organization leaps from its smallest unit, the nuclear family, to its largest category, the *personal kindred.* We do recognize different degrees of "closeness" among known relatives, but we have no clearly bounded groups that act as units. Compared with the vast majority of kinship systems known to social anthropology, this situation is very unusual.

Our system is, technically, *bilateral* and *ego-centered* (Type 1a), limited only by ego's knowledge of his or her genealogical connections. That is, individuals consider themselves equally related to kinspeople on both the mother's side and the father's side, regardless of the sex of the connecting relatives through whom the link is traced. A father's brother's child, a father's sister's child, and a mother's sibling's child are all called by the same kinship term and are all considered equally close relatives (cousins). Our plans for interacting with relatives become more vague and less obligatory, however, as their genealogical distance from us increases: many Americans neither know nor feel any obligations toward their third cousins. The American personal kindred may be visualized as a series of concentric circles with ego in the middle, surrounded by his or her nuclear family, and beyond them, successive circles of kin, decreasing in terms of knowledge and expected behavior (see Figure 5.3).

Bilateral kinship groups of this type have at least two considerable drawbacks: (1) they are only vaguely bounded, and because "close" and "distant" are relative terms, there is no clear-cut way of *excluding* any consanguine from the group; (2) being ego-centered, the circles of kin overlap but do not exactly coincide for most relatives, so that few individuals share the same kindred. Individuals share their total personal kindreds only with their full siblings. Any other relatives will have different sets of consanguines on at least one side.

These drawbacks do not normally trouble us because the American kindred seldom functions as a group. That is, although our bilateral relatives comprise a category and although we possess plans for dyadic interaction with particular kinds of

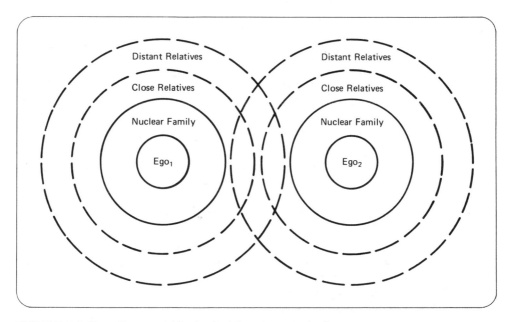

FIGURE 5.3 Two Personal Kindreds (showing overlap)

relatives, few if any plans apply to the group as a whole. In some parts of American society it is common for the kindred to gather occasionally for periodic reunions or for life-crisis celebrations (weddings, funerals, special birthdays), but attendance at these ceremonial occasions is determined as much by proximity in space as by closeness of relationship. The vague boundaries of the kindred become an inconvenience mainly at celebrations such as weddings, where the number of guests must be limited, because hurt feelings can arise. (Cf. Schneider 1968.)

When bilateral descent groups act together regularly, further structuring is required so that people may know exactly who is included and what is expected of them. In the Anglo-Saxon kindred, this structuring was accomplished by the assignment of specific responsibilities to different degrees of relationship. For example, if a person was murdered, all members of his or her kindred through third (but not including fourth) cousins were expected to participate in the blood feud (or to share proportionally in the indemnity paid by the murderer's kindred). Under these circumstances, it is understandable that the Angles and the Saxons were quite adept at calculating their degree of relationship to all other kin. The famous feuds of the southern Appalachian region in the United States and the vendettas of Sicily are familiar examples of entire kindreds taking responsibility for avenging the murder of a member.

There are other ways of structuring bilateral kinship groups. Robert Pehrson (1954) has shown that the Lapps (nomadic herders of northern Scandinavia) place strong emphasis on the sibling group as a point of reference, producing clear-cut kin-based groups. A number of male siblings, their wives, and their children form the core of such a group, and others affiliate with the group by virtue of some bilateral genealogical link with the sibling core. There is a good deal of shifting between local groups, and men sometimes join their wives' groups if there is a need for extra males. Thus Lapp groups are based on a combination of bilateral kinship and common residence.

Another type of structure is provided by what William Davenport calls the *stem kindred*—the personal kindred of a prominent individual. Such a group can have clear-cut boundaries, and continuity is achieved through a pattern of succession to group leadership such as primogeniture. An example is found in rural Ireland, where title to farmland is passed from a man to his first-born son. The titleholder in each generation has a small personal kindred whose members have definite rights and obligations even if they are not resident on the land (Davenport 1959:565).

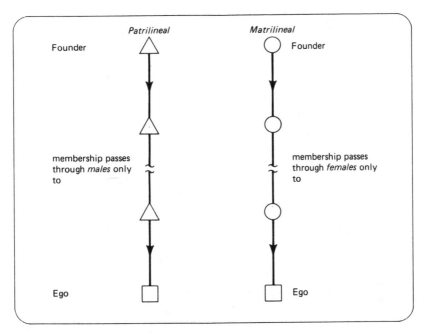

FIGURE 5.4 The Unilineal Descent Group

True Descent Groups

The unilineal descent group is best thought of as a line descending from some particular ancestor (the founder) to ego through a number of lineal relatives, all of the same sex (see Figure 5.4).

In a bilateral kindred, ego traces his or her relationship to other members through both males and females; but membership in a unilineal descent group is transmitted through linking relatives of *one sex only*. The effect of this difference is quite far-reaching.

To begin with, unilineal descent groups are strictly *bounded*. Although ego recognizes kinship with all consanguineal relatives, the unilineal principle *excludes* the majority of consanguines from ego's descent group. Because of this consistent exclusion, *the composition of the unilineal descent group is the same for every member of the group.* This is a great advantage when descent groups are to be mobilized for some kind of action, for each person belongs to one and only one such group; furthermore, when *corporate* descent groups are associated with the inheritance or maintenance of an estate, the unilineal principle makes possible greater continuity of management. These advantages may account for the fact that the majority of known societies make some use of the unilineal principle.

The Lineage

A *lineage* is a unilineal descent group all of whose members can trace actual genealogical connections to one another through linking relatives of one sex. Figure 5.5 shows a typical matrilineage: it is composed of the female founder, her children (both male and female), the children of her daughters (only), and of *their* daughters. Notice that, while the founder's son (X) is a member of this lineage, X's wife is *not* a member, nor are their children, for they belong to the lineage of their mother. Note carefully that a matrilineage consists of both males and females, but that membership in the lineage is transmitted through females only. Ego's sons and daughters will also be members of this lineage, but the children of her male sibling will not be members.

The patrilineage is the mirror image of the matrilineage; descent is traced through males only. Figure 5.6 shows a typical patrilineage stemming from a male founder through his sons and their sons. Americans can usually grasp the patrilineal principle if they think of the way in which family names are inherited in our society (although our practice of having a woman change her name at marriage somewhat complicates the situation). Again we see that both males and females are members of a patrilineage, but in this case membership is transmitted only in the male line.

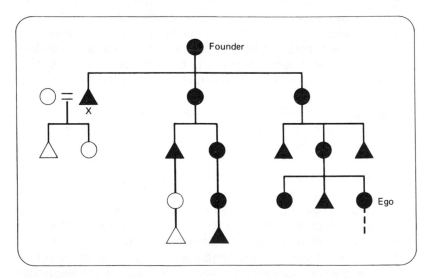

FIGURE 5.5 A Typical Matrilineage (black symbols are members)

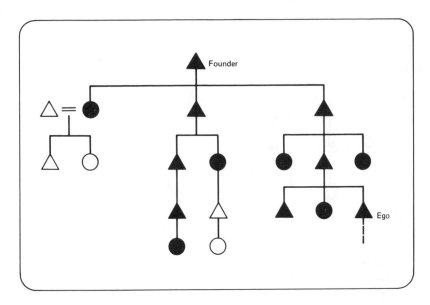

FIGURE 5.6 A Typical Patrilineage (black symbols are members)

In Figure 5.7 ego's siblings and cousins in his own generation are represented, as well as his lineal relatives back three generations. In a bilateral system, *all* people in this figure would be members of ego's kindred. Shading has been used to indicate which of these people are members of ego's matri- and patrilineages. As can be seen, only ego and his siblings are members of *both* of these groups. The numerous unshaded figures represent ego's consanguines who are *not members of either lineage;* please note that in ego's own generation all of his crosscousins fall into this category.

In a double-descent system (Type IIc) both matrilineal and patrilineal descent groups are present (though one may be more important than the other). Thus ego and his full siblings belong simultaneously to two lineages, one through their mother and the other through their father. Figure 5.7 shows that this is *not* the same as a bilateral group. Relatives represented by unshaded figures would not belong to either of ego's lineage groups. Even when applied twice, the unilineal principle still forms bounded groups from which some consanguines are excluded.

By virtue of membership in a unilineal descent group, ego acquires certain rights and obligations. He is usually able to call on his fellow members for goods and services, and they on him. He cannot do this with relatives outside of his group, even if we

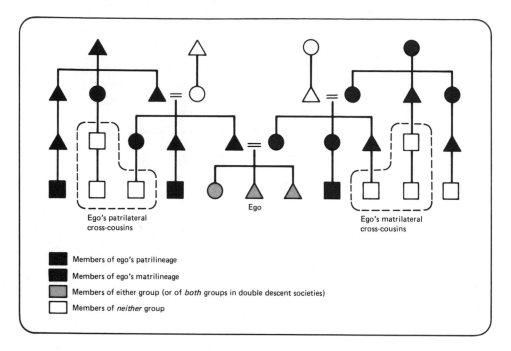

FIGURE 5.7 The Unilineal Principle

would consider them equally close under our bilateral principle. In double-descent systems, the rights and obligations that ego has in his patrilineage are generally quite different from those in his matrilineage. For example, ego may inherit land from his mother, his mother's brother, or some other matrilineal relative, and cattle from his father or his father's brother. Double-descent systems are not numerous. They are found most frequently in Africa and Oceania, but have also been reported from South Asia and South America.

Even in societies where only one type of unilineal descent group is found, ego has some rights in relation to descent groups other than his own. In a society with patrilineages, while ego is a *member* only of his father's lineage, he may have a standardized relationship with all the members of his mother's patrilineage (her siblings, her father and his siblings, and her father's brother's children). In matrilineal societies, even though a man does not usually inherit from his father, he may have benefits from and obligations toward the members of his father's matrilineage (his father's sister and her children, or his father's brother).

The concept of unilineal descent helps us to understand *avunculocal residence,* in which ego and his bride live in the household of ego's mother's brother. In a matrilineal society such as the Trobriand Islands, the mother's brother frequently has considerable authority over ego, because he is the closest adult male relative who is a member of ego's descent group (see Figure 5.8). Thus ego's father (who belongs to a matrilineage different from ego's) has as an heir his own sister's son, and it is this young man (rather than the father's offspring) who comes to live with him as an adult.

The unilineal principle, combined with the widespread rule against marriage within a lineage, helps to explain the prevalence of cross-cousin marriage. Ego's cross-cousins can *never* be members of his unilineal descent group, whether the rule of descent is patrilineal, matrilineal, or duolineal. Thus in a society with unilineal groups, a rule of lineage *exogamy* (out-marrying), and a preference for marriage with some consanguineal relative, the cross-cousin is an obvious choice.

Members of lineages do not necessarily live in the same areas, and it is important to separate principles of descent from principles of residence, even though they coincide in a large number of cases. Lineages grow and decline in size, and they are faced with the problem of what to do when they reach a minimum or maximum population level. Like residential groups, lineage groups can combine or undergo fission. Segmentation generally takes place along lines implicit in the lineage itself; for example, the patrilineage represented in Figure 5.6 would most likely split into two parts with the descendents of each of the founder's two sons forming a new lineage. When fission does take place, the new lineages may either go their separate ways or retain ties of some kind, just as residential groups may undergo complete fission or combine fission with aggregation.

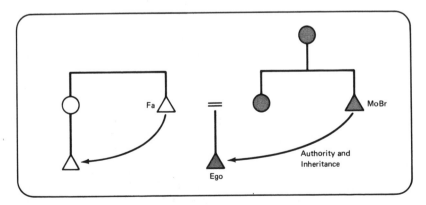

FIGURE 5.8 Avuncular Authority in a Matrilineal Society

Clans, Phratries, and Moieties

Even in societies where genealogies are carefully remembered, there comes a time when the exact connection between distantly related persons is lost or forgotten. Nevertheless, because of the long-standing relationship between their respective descent groups, such persons may still consider themselves to be relatives. This situation is a probable origin of the social group known as the *clan*.

Clans have the following characteristics in most societies where they are found:

1. They are unilineal descent groups, tracing descent in the male or female line from a remote and often mythical ancestor/ancestress.
2. Their members consider themselves to be relatives even though exact genealogical connections cannot be traced and perhaps never existed.
3. They are exogamous (marriage is forbidden among members) and sexual intercourse between members is considered incestuous.
4. Unity of the group is maintained by a clan name, a clan symbol, and/or ceremonies performed by all component lineages.
5. They may be composed of localized lineages, but the clan itself is not usually localized; rather, it crosscuts other types of residential groups.

As long as some awareness of membership is maintained, clans can grow to an immense size. In traditional Chinese society, some clans (such as the Wongs) numbered in the tens of millions. All people having a given family name considered themselves related. Members of these huge patrilineal clans were forbidden to marry, and they were obliged to help other clan members even if they were totally unacquainted.

Because clans are not localized, they perform a very important social function: by crosscutting residential groups, they tie together a society that might otherwise break up into numerous geographic subdivisions.

Component lineages in a clan may enjoy relative equality. When each of the lineages is considered equal to every other lineage, the clan tends to be relatively formless—a kind of federation of equivalent units with ceremonial or economic functions, and with equal opportunities for members from all lineages to participate. Under certain conditions, however, there may develop a system of ranked or stratified lineages within the clan. Such stratification may have important implications for further social development. (Cf. Fried 1967.)

Clans are also frequently grouped into larger units called *phratries.* Although a phratry is not in itself a unilineal descent group, it may be involved in the regulation of marriage. That is, in some societies phratries are exogamous (members of the same phratry may not marry), while in others they are endogamous (members of the same phratry are expected to marry so long as they do not belong to the same clan).

When the descent groups within a society are grouped into only two main divisions (whether or not phratries are also present), the two divisions of the society are known as *moieties* (halves). Figure 5.9 is a diagram of a society in which lineages are grouped into fourteen clans, clans are linked into five phratries, and phratries are divided into moieties. This hierarchy of groups binds a society together into an integrated whole. The clan type of social organization would clearly be impossible without the unilineal principle that defines bounded kinship groups. Of equal importance are the marriage rules, economic rights, and ritual obligations that create alliances among these groups, binding them together over many generations.

The versatility of unilineal descent groups, together with their power of social integration, accounts for their presence in so many societies. The clan, whether matrilineal or patrilineal, plays a variety of important roles. Given this category of persons

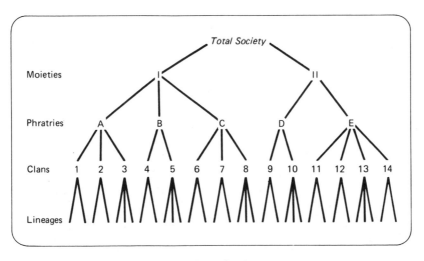

FIGURE 5.9 The Structure of a Clan Society

defined by the unilineal principle, any number of plans can be associated with it. In some societies (for example, Navajo) the clan is mainly related to the control of marriage; in others (Iroquois, Scotch Highlands, Roman) it has primarily political functions. In some cultures (Pueblo Indian) the control of marriage is mixed with various ceremonial and economic functions, while still elsewhere the primary functions of the clan seem to be either military, religious, or economic.

When clans are involved in warfare and feuding, it is quite common for the clan to be viewed as an undifferentiated unit and for vengeance to be taken in what we would consider an indiscriminate manner. "A life for a life" sometimes means that if a member of Clan A kills a member of Clan B, *any* member of Clan A may be slain in reprisal. This type of revenge often leads to a vicious circle of act and counter-act. It also has the effect of making the members of a clan feel responsible for their hot-blooded members. (Interracial and interethnic strife in the United States often have some of these characteristics, as do rivalries among schools and colleges, on a somewhat more innocent level.)

Unilineal descent groups may be named or unnamed. Many clans take the name of some plant or animal. Among the Iroquois Indians of New York State, the following clan names are still in use: Turtle, Wolf, Beaver, Deer, Ball, Eel, Hawk, Heron, Snipe, and Bear. All of these clans (and their subdivisions) are grouped together into moieties known as Wolf and Turtle. (Clan names help to maintain the unity of a descent group after its members have lost track of their genealogical connections to one another.)

In some societies clan names (or symbols) have more far-reaching significance. These are the so-called *totemic clans,* unilineal descent groups named after some natural species. The clan members are believed to stand in some special relationship to that species, often one of descent. Members of a totemic clan may trace the ultimate origin of their group back to a mythical totem ancestor who actually was an animal. Whether this belief is held or not, members of a totemic clan commonly share certain responsibilities toward the species for which their group is named; for example, they may be required to carry out certain rituals in connection with it, which are not required of the members of other clans.

Among the aborigines of Australia, totemic clans were extremely important. Food-gathering activities were a matter of life or death, and each clan was responsible for carrying out *increase ceremonies* for its particular totem in order to ensure an adequate supply of food for the entire tribe. The origins of the clans were related in complicated myths, and the lengthy ritual performed at initiations and increase ceremonies involved acting out portions of the myths.

The phenomenon of *totemism* (totemic clans together with their myths and rituals) has long fascinated students of human behavior. Dozens of theories have been advanced to account for the origin of totemic beliefs and practices. Most recent work on totemism, however, emphasizes the categories used in classifying, social groups and, the relation of, these categories to the natural world. Claude Lévi-Strauss has stated that "totemic ideas appear to provide a code enabling man to express iso-morphic properties between nature and culture. Obviously, there exists here some kind of similarity with linguistics, since language is also a code which, through oppositions between differences, permits us to convey meanings" (1963a:2). Just as language makes use of selected natural vocal qualities (voiced/voiceless, front/back, and so forth) by systematically organizing them into a conventional code that conveys meanings, a totemic social system makes use of the natural differences among selected species (Turtle/Wolf, Bear/Eagle) to convey notions of social relatedness. When a member of such a society says, "I am a Bear," he is making a statement about the clan to which he belongs, the social (and sometimes psychological or physical) attributes of its members, *and* his relationship as a clan member to members of other groups. (See Chapter 9, Belief Systems.)

Castes

The totemic clan can be compared and contrasted with another type of kinship group—the *caste*. Castes are most highly developed in India. They are large unilineal descent groups (usually patrilineal) and differ from clans in that (1) they are *endogamous* and (2) they are named for traditional *occupations* rather than natural species. Two further characteristics of caste societies are: (3) the *ranking* of castes relative to one another and (4) the *interdependence* of caste groups, brought about by strict occupational specialization within a complex division of labor.

The endogamy (required in-marriage) of Hindu castes means that these groups must be fairly large, for in most of India, marriage with close relatives and within the local community is forbidden. Although a woman who marries into a lower-ranking caste brings disgrace upon herself and her group, the custom of *hypergamy* allows a man to take a wife from a slightly lower-ranking group without prejudice, and their children belong to the father's caste. For this reason, Indian castes may be considered patrilineal descent groups. Unlike clan societies, where integration is achieved through the exchange of women, caste societies must achieve organic solidarity by the exchange of goods and services.

In many parts of modern India the association between caste and occupation is breaking down. In the traditional system, however, there were such castes as the Brahmins (priests), the Merchants, the Farmers, the Weavers, the Barbers, the Potters, and the Sweepers; each had its own role to play in the community, and each jealously guarded its rights. The caste system, with its complex interdependence of parts, so permeated Hindu society that even members of other religions (Christians and Muslims) were incorporated into it. Special relationships were set up between individual members of these castes. For example, a farmer would receive the services of a particular priest or barber throughout the year and then, at harvesttime, he would present him with a sizable gift of grain.

The strict ranking of castes gave a distinct flavor to the traditional Indian social system. This ranking, based on "ritual purity" and justified by scriptures and legends, created a hierarchy of groups within which all persons had their place, their privileges, and their duties. At the top of the hierarchy were the Brahmins, below them the Warriors, Merchants, Farmers, and most craftworkers; at the bottom of the hierarchy were the "outcastes," groups whose impure occupations (such as working leather or otherwise handling dead animals) made them unworthy of consideration. This hierarchy was maintained by a complex series of prohibitions on social contact among members of different castes. It was morally justified by a theology that promised reincarnation of a good person into a higher caste. An individual's caste was fixed (ascribed) by birth. (It was possible for an entire caste to raise its relative position within the hierarchy by adopting a less polluting mode of life. This process took much effort and several generations to complete; though rare, it provided the caste system with some flexibility.)

In summary, descent groups are conventional categories of kin associated with plans for common action. These plans may regulate only a few activities (marriage, access to land, or economic cooperation); or, as in the case of Hindu castes, they may affect every area of a person's life (religious, economic, and social), leaving individuals with no opportunity to alter their positions. The descent groups that are dominant in a society generally try to justify their relative positions and privileges by myths and legends that tell of the origin of the group and explain its right to superiority. Since actual relationships among social groups change with time and circumstance, however, it is not surprising that the myths that serve to validate one state of affairs undergo constant alterations to bring them in line with changing situations.

PEER GROUPS AND ASSOCIATIONS

People who share some interests or social characteristics other than those based on common residence or descent are called peers. The term *peer group* is used to designate a category of individuals who share such interests and/or characteristics, and who have developed a sense of solidarity and shared expectations about behavior.

Age and Sex Groups

Sexual division of labor is universal in human society, and all peoples recognize that individuals' abilities vary with age. These two facts, culturally elaborated, give rise to the differing social careers of men and women. In simpler societies, age and sex are the primary characteristics determining peer group membership. They remain important in more complex societies, although they are supplemented by a variety of other career-based criteria. We are concerned here with the formation of groups that act as units under certain circumstances, and which may acquire corporate functions. One example of this type of group is the age-set.

An *age-set* is a group of persons of one sex (usually male) who have been born or initiated during the same period of time. Age-sets are most commonly found in Africa, though they are also known from North America. Among the Nandi, a pastoral tribe of Kenya, every male belongs to an age-set from birth. The age-sets are groups of males who are circumcised at the same time. Huntingford reports that there are

> seven sets, and at any given time one of these is that of the warriors, two are those of boys, and four are sets of old men. The warrior set is referred to as "the set in power," because during its period of

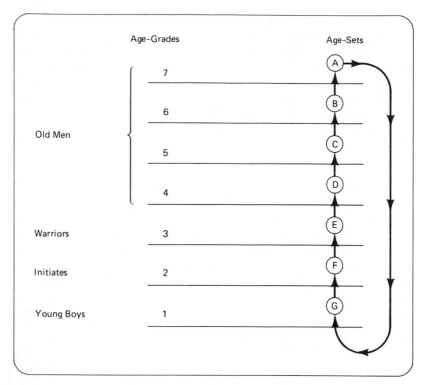

FIGURE 5.10 Nandi Age-Sets and Age-Grades

office it is responsible for all military operations, and has in addition certain privileges; it is in power for a period of about fifteen years, at the end of which it retires, and the set next below it, which during this period has been circumcised, takes its place . . . the retiring warriors becoming elders. . . . At the same time the set of the oldest men, who by that time are all dead, passes out of existence as an old men's set and its name is transferred to the set of the small boys, the most junior set. The sets thus work in a recurring cycle, and the names appear again and again [1960:215].

The Nandi age-sets move through a series of *age-grades*—social categories of "small boys," "initiates," "warriors," and "elders." These age-sets have military and political functions (see Figure 5.10). Nandi women have no age-sets, but they go through the grades of *tipik* (girls) and *osotik* (married women), the transition taking place at marriage. (Another type of age association with mainly control functions—that of the Red Xhosa—was described in Chapter 2.)

Throughout most of East Africa, age-sets cut across the local divisions of tribal societies and tie together segments that would otherwise lack integration. Among the Nyakyusa of Tanzania, however, age is the basis of territorial divisions, producing groups called *age-villages.* Up to the age of ten or eleven, boys live with their parents and herd their fathers' cattle. As they approach puberty, "they leave the herding of cows to their younger brothers, and themselves begin the business of hoeing the fields which will occupy them until they die; secondly, they no longer sleep in the houses of their fathers but join an age-village of boys" (Wilson 1963:19). At first, several young boys sleep together in a crudely made hut, but later, as the age-village grows, they build more substantial, individual houses to which they will eventually bring their wives. The personal bonds forged during these early years are very important, for Nyakyusa men value above all the "good company" of their contemporaries—eating and talking together with other men of their own age group.

After a certain period of time, political authority is officially transferred to the younger generation and permanent village leaders (headmen) are chosen: "Eight or ten years after the young men of the senior boys' village of the chiefdom have begun to marry, their fathers hand over the government of the country to them. This transfer of authority is effected in an elaborate ceremony called the 'coming out' " (1963:22).

Fission into two equal parts is the fundamental mechanism of social growth and change in Nyakyusa society. At the time of the coming out, ideally the chiefdom is split into two sides under the rule of the old chief's two eldest sons. At the same time, two age-villages of men are established in each side under the leadership of appointed headmen, and soon thereafter boys' villages split off from each village of men. Among the Nyakyusa, "age and locality coincide, while kinship cuts across local groupings, fathers and sons, and very often brothers, being in different villages. But kinsmen tend to be established in the same side of a country, and so to remain within one chiefdom" (1963:33).

In contemporary American society, age and sex are used as criteria for recruitment to a wide variety of roles: educational, occupational, and political. The feminist movement has made us aware of just how extensively and irrationally the criterion of sex is used, and it has also given us instances of the "mere category" *female* becoming the basis for genuine social groups.

Although age is used together with other criteria for recruitment to various American groups, it is seldom the primary basis of group formation. There are, of course, some exceptions. Voluntary organizations of senior citizens have common age as their main qualification for membership, and the arbitrary age grades for driving, drinking, and voting are also familiar.

The closest things to true age-sets in American society are probably the neighborhood gang and its formal equivalents, the college fraternity and sorority. The neighborhood gang is a small, homogeneous group. Its members find companionship and self-expression through conformity with their variety of the American youth culture. Pressures toward conformity are especially strong. Unlike the Red Xhosa group organization, in which peers teach one another the traditional values of the larger society, gangs are frequently opposed to "adult expectations and discipline," and are oriented toward athletic competition and sexual conquest, fast cars, drugs, and excitement (Parsons 1949:221).

Prestige in the neighborhood gang is often achieved by means that the larger society considers irresponsible or illegal. Indeed, this particular type of youth culture may be seen as a reaction against dominant cultural patterns. American society stresses adult responsibility, and the individual's place in society is determined by competence in a rather narrow occupational area. In the gang, one's whole personality is important, and opportunities are found for display of admired qualities, if only on Saturday nights. The adult attitude toward this youth culture is an ambivalent combination of hostility ("those darn kids") and imitation of youthful styles and behavior.

Occupational Groups and Associations

Primitive societies have few full-time occupational specialties, and those that do exist do not usually give rise to associations. It is only in civilized societies (and particularly in industrial ones) that occupational organizations become important. Craft guilds, business and professional associations, and labor unions are examples of *occupational groups* that may be based upon such a criterion. The functions of such groups are primarily economic. They may also take on social or political functions as far as the interests and solidarity of the members allow.

In the small societies studied by anthropologists, we often find groups of men or women cooperating on some common task, but such groups are better treated as voluntary associations, since their composition changes as new members join and others leave. A *voluntary association* is any group of persons who act together by choice to attain a particular end. Voluntary groups may be classified in two ways: (1) by their *degree of continuity*—transient or semipermanent; and (2) by the major *explicit function of the group*—task performance, social control, or expressivity.

The work party is a typical transient, task-oriented group. It may be devoted to nearly any type of task: hunting, fishing, gathering of resources, preparation of food, transport of heavy or bulky objects, warfare, defense, and so on. Such groups are formed in response to particular short-term social needs, and in many societies constitute the most highly organized groups present. In the Great Basin area, Paiute Indian families came together annually for a communal hunt of rabbits or antelope, but when this small surplus was exhausted, the families would have to disperse to their respective gathering territories.

Although we say that membership in such groups is voluntary, close analysis often shows that affiliation is based on the activation of preexistent ties of kinship, locality, age-set, or some other common interest. Leadership is usually informal if the work to be done benefits all the members of the group. If the benefits are unequally distributed, some kind of task leadership will have to be exercised. Thus, cooperative groups may join in harvesting one another's crops with little overt direction, but if a work party comes to the assistance of one person with particularly large holdings, he will generally have to feast the members of the work party or reward them in some other way.

The explicit function of a work party may be incidental to a more important implicit function. For example, among the Siuai of the Solomon Islands, a local leader who wants to increase his own prestige will hire a slit-gong maker to fashion one at some distance from the village. When it is ready, the leader will call together a work party to transport the heavy instrument to the men's ceremonial house. The larger the work party, the more prestige the leader receives when he generously feasts them upon completion of the task. Thereafter, whenever the slit-gong is sounded, people remember the feast and speak of the gong as "sounding the renown" of the leader (Oliver 1955:379–386).

Task-oriented voluntary groups become important when continuing social demands cannot be met by the regular groups in a society. Such situations arise particularly at times of rapid cultural change, when the family or the local community is unable to adapt to new requirements. For example, when a society that has been producing food on a subsistence basis becomes involved in the production of a cash crop for a national or world market, voluntary associations of growers that cut across kinship and local groups are often formed. When tribal peoples migrate into urban centers, voluntary organizations often help newcomers adapt to unfamiliar conditions. These organizations are the functional equivalents of the immigrant societies formed by various ethnic groups in the United States; their aims were to help new arrivals to learn English, get jobs, and otherwise adapt to American culture.

Some voluntary groups have the explicit function of giving their members opportunities for display, activity, or other forms of self-expression. They range from transient play groups to fairly permanent organized athletic or artistic associations. To say that such expressive groups are voluntary does not mean that no other relationships exist among the participants. The author studied a Canadian Indian reserve where, on one occasion, the entire membership of the baseball team was drawn from the personal kindred of the team manager; but the members of a voluntary group *need not* have such ties.

Expressive groups may also serve other functions. Anthropologists have not always considered the formation and structure of voluntary expressive groups to be important, and the careful reporting of such information is a fairly recent development. A good example of what can be learned about such groups is Charles Frake's work with the Philippine Subanun. In Subanun gatherings, the drinking of native beer plays an important part. By careful analysis, Frake was able to show standard stages of interaction involved in beer-drinking and to demonstrate that "the Subanun drinking encounter . . . provides a structured setting within which one's social relationships beyond his everyday associates can be extended, defined, and manipulated through the use of speech" (1964:131). Legal disputes are often resolved in such informal gatherings. In American society it is standard practice for political activities to be carried on in the context of a cocktail party or a golf game.

Social control and education are often implicit functions, but some voluntary groups have these functions as primary aims. For example, the cooperative ethnic groups formed by American immigrants were described above as task-oriented. After their tasks had been accomplished, however, may of them lingered on as recreational groups with the explicit aim of preserving ethnic customs or languages, to give the American-born generations a sense of their cultural heritage. In simple cultures, the closest thing to a voluntary control-oriented group is the secret society (discussed earlier in Chapter 2). Secret societies perform their control and educational functions by indoctrinating new members (teaching them certain esoteric parts of their culture) and by presenting periodic ritual performances in which the myths and values of the group are symbolically enacted. An example is the Buswezi, a widespread secret society of Tanzania. The activities of this group include ritual, spirit possession, dancing, and curing; members are obligated to keep the group secrets and to assist one another. After several years, one is eligible for initiation into the inner circle, where more esoteric doctrine is learned.

> The Buswezi is a rare example of a society, consisting of numerous small units which are independent of each other, which flourishes without any organization but the acknowledgment of authority based on erudition and efficiency in spheres connected with the ideological purpose of the society. The organization is strong because it takes no cognizance of the rank or ability of members in any field outside the society [Cory 1955:925].

Secret societies and fraternal organizations flourish in modern American communities. Groups such as the Masons and the Elks may carry on civic programs and extensive recreational activities, and they take occupational or totemic names, but the primary function of all such groups has to do with social integration. The taking over of task, control, and expressive functions by public and voluntary organizations is a general pattern of change in American culture. It is related, above all, to the decline of the family as a multifunctional group.

Racial and Ethnic Groups

Within a complex society, racial and subcultural differences may also give rise to organized social groups. These differences can usually be understood as consequences of the varied histories of subgroups, but whether they are biological, cultural, or a mixture of the two, the important anthropological question is: How do these differences *function* within the larger society, separating people and binding others together? The functions of racial and cultural differences are not automatic; they depend on conventional ways of classifying people and traditional attitudes toward the categories. In the United States, persons with one or more African ancestors are generally classified as black, but in Haiti, persons with one or more European ancestors are classified as white. In Brazil there are dozens of terms referring to different racial categories, but most of them are overlapping and are used in highly ambiguous ways. Each of these sets of categories and plans can be understood in terms of the cultural context in which they function, but none of them makes much sense in purely biological terms.

We have already noted that recent migrants to an urban center or to a new country often form voluntary associations to assist one another in coping with new problems. It makes a big difference, of course, whether one's migration was voluntary or forced, and whether members of one's racial or ethnic groups are admired, ignored, or despised in the new setting. Even if they do not develop formal groups, people who speak the same dialect and practice the same customs will, when placed among strangers, become aware of their ethnic identity. In the United States, the doctrine of the melting pot assumed that ethnic differences would gradually disappear. But they have not done so, and a great many people now question whether this goal is even desirable. (cf. Bennett 1975.)

Many ethnic groups have been completely destroyed—their languages no longer spoken, their cultures preserved only in museums. It would be a mistake, however, to assume that the world is inevitably moving in the direction of cultural homogeneity, or that groups that insist on their ethnic distinctiveness are being irrationally stubborn. Anthropologists are often accused of being romantics or of wanting to preserve tribal peoples as "living museums." More important is our awareness of the *positive value of cultural diversity.* Just as biological adaptation is always relative to the particular environmental situation, cultural adaptation is also a relative matter: a society (or a species) that becomes overspecialized is in serious danger when the environmental conditions change. Diversity in ethnic groups can be an important source of innovation and creativity for the total society.

Some minority ethnic groups, such as American Indians, are the remnants of a once large and diverse aboriginal population. The ancestors of these surviving groups were victims of European expansion and colonial empires from the sixteenth century to the present. Defeated by the superior military power of Spain, England, or the United States, they were often enslaved or confined to "reservations" where they could no longer practice their traditional culture. This is not the place to review the evils of imperialism, the greed of entrepreneurs, or the unhappy consequences of most missionary efforts. What is truly remarkable is the survival of some of these groups despite centuries of war, plague, confinement, and exploitation. Furthermore, the mid–twentieth century has seen a reawakening of racial pride and a sense of ethnic identity among many oppressed peoples— from Black Power to the Pan-Indian Movement in the United States, and elsewhere from African nationalism to the state of Israel.

Anthropologists have only recently begun to understand the major factors involved in the development, maintenance, and loss of ethnic identity. These factors include: (1) the presence or absence of differing ecological adaptations; (2) the nature of contact situations and exchange relations among ethnic groups; and (3) the ways in which ethnic identity affects political partic- ipation and recruitment to valued social roles. Studies of ethnic groups are particularly important to our understanding of the dynamics of social change and the relations between individuals and the groups they belong to (Barth 1969).

SOCIAL CLASSES

Complex societies tend to become stratified into a number of *social classes*, divisions of the total society whose members differ in their prestige in accordance with their access to valued resources and positions of power. Social classes are more like categories than groups in that they share certain attributes but seldom act together—their members do not usually share plans for action. Marxist theory deals with the conditions under which the members of a social class become conscious of their joint interests and act accordingly.

Complex systems of social classes have existed ever since the empires of the Old and New Worlds were established. Con- temporary classes are based on descent, ethnic identity, wealth, and formal education. Social classes tend to be quite stable, although in class systems, in contrast to caste systems, some movement of individuals from one class to another is possible. Social classes develop their own subcultures and are charac- terized by their differing life-styles within the larger social sys- tem.

Social classes and castes are examples of groups that are ranked in accordance with their relative value. In a society where the groups are nobles, commoners, and slaves, there is no prob- lem in arranging the groups according to power and prestige. We may then inquire into the size of each group, and investigate the possibility of an individual's moving from one group to an- other: the phenomenon of *social mobility*.

The American social class system is difficult to describe, because class membership is based on a combination of social, economic, and cultural factors, and because the system varies considerably from region to region within the country. Most students of the American class system agree on the following points:

1. There is much less mobility between classes than is generally believed, particularly into the highest and out of the lowest strata.
2. Families tend to be classed together, and the most sensitive indicator of a nuclear family's rank is the occupation of the male family head.
3. The most important channel for social mobility today is the system of formal education.
4. Members of racial and ethnic minorities have much lower chances for mobility than do others.

Aside from these points, there is considerable disagreement about the importance of social classes and the degree to which people identify with their own class or emulate the values of higher ranking groups. (See Veblen 1953; Bottomore 1966.) But it is clear that social classes influence their members' behavior significantly in all complex societies.

SOCIETAL GROUPS

It is now time to ask: What is a society? To begin with, a society is a group. It has members. It is composed of people, and its size can be determined with reasonable accuracy. This point is stressed to clarify the difference between society and culture, for a culture is *not* a group. It has no members. Culture is composed of shared categories and plans. Whether they are shared by two persons or two hundred persons makes little difference. Furthermore, separate societies may have highly similar cultures, while within one large society there may be found a great deal of subcultural variability.

A *societal group* (a total society) is composed of kinship groups, residential groups, social classes, and so on. The nature, size, and composition of these groups, and the plans with which they are associated, are the factors that distinguish one social system from another. These groups are the carriers of culture, for the division of labor assigns the responsibility for mastering and transmitting various aspects of the culture to various groups within the society.

The men's secret society clubhouse in New Guinea, which women and uninitiated boys are forbidden to enter.

There are some things that every member of a society is expected to know—the attributes of the *societal role* (see the last section of Chapter 4). The most inclusive category with which individuals identify themselves will generally be the societal group to which they belong, and this identification will influence their behavior in regular and important ways. Just how much the societal role influences a person's behavior depends on the homogeneity and integration of the society. When the societal group is small and relatively isolated—what Robert Redfield called a "folk society"—all members of the group share much of their culture, so many regularities in their behavior can be attributed to the societal role: "He acts like that because he is a Tiwi." When the societal group is large, complex, and open to cultural influences from many sources—typical characteristics of an urban society—it is harder to define the attributes of the societal role. In all societies, however, this role includes recognition of legitimate political leadership and acceptance of shared plans for settling disputes, making decisions, and coordinating activities.

The folk/urban distinction is one means of classifying societies for the purpose of comparing their cultural characteristics. On the basis of his work in several Mexican communities, Robert Redfield (1941) suggested three general differences. He found urban societies to be secularized, individualized, and disorganized, whereas folk societies were more pious, group-oriented, and culturally integrated. Some scholars have taken issue with one or more of these points, but Redfield's ideas have provided a valuable framework for the investigation of social and cultural change.

Institutions

One general characteristic of complex societies is the development of *institutions*—relatively self-contained social groups that organize a variety of social careers into a system. The term "institution" here refers to actual social groups (such as governments, churches, and military organizations) which play important parts in the structure of large-scale societies. They tend to be at least semipermanent; they are quite formally organized, often in a hierarchical manner. Within the institution a large variety of social roles are linked into careers and authority relationships.

Some institutions, such as prisons, mental hospitals, army barracks, and monasteries, have special characteristics that make them useful objects of study. Erving Goffman calls this type of establishment a *total institution,* "a place of residence and work where a large number of like-situated individuals, cut off from the wider society for an appreciable period of time, together lead an enclosed, formally administered round of life" (1961:xiii). These relatively isolated social systems provide a type of laboratory for the ethnographer. They may be studied for their own sake, in an attempt to understand their structure and function; but they may also be studied so that the subcultures of these total institutions may be compared with the culture of the larger society, and thus shed light on the categories and plans that we take for granted.

The major institutions in a society provide evidence of the dominant interests and values of the members of that society. At various times in the history of Western civilization, religious, military, political, or commercial institutions have risen to positions of dominance within particular societies; at other times, two or more institutions have arrived at a balance of power. In the third and fourth centuries A.D., political and military institutions struggled for power. During the Middle Ages, the Roman Catholic Church attained a position of dominance, partly because of the fragmentation of political institutions under feudalism. During the Renaissance, national states and commercial institutions rose hand in hand, overthrowing feudal institutions at different times in different nations. Today, in most countries there is a balance between military, political, and commercial institutions. This balance is complicated by the formation of vast power blocs representing opposing ideologies. Some notable scholars such as Pitirim A. Sorokin and Arnold Toynbee predict an eventual return to dominance by religious institutions. This text offers no prophecies, but suggests that our imaginative writers and poets have often anticipated future trends with far greater wit and accuracy than most social scientists.

We have now surveyed the major kinds of groups found in human societies. The emphasis has been upon kinship and residential groups because they account for much of the structure of simple societies and continue to be important in complex societies. We have also discussed the major types of peer groups, associations, and institutions that provide alternative types of structure.

To summarize: a social group is a category of persons, defined by conventional criteria, associated with plans for activity and for interaction with other groups. All social groups face the same problems: adaptation to the environment, recruitment and enculturation of personnel, and maintenance of conformity to group norms. The functions of a social group are responses to these problems; in every group, the functions of task performance, expression, and social control are present, explicitly or implicitly. The anthropological study of social systems involves description and analysis of the groups that make up a society and the ways in which they function.

We are by nature social animals, but the social groups in

which we live are determined culturally as well as naturally. Every societal group constitutes a subdivision of the human species on the basis of linguistic, geographic, historical, and/or religious factors. Within a society, separate subgroups develop which stress some attributes of kinship, locality, or common interest, and ignore others. The principles of group formation *limit* the range of human interaction and understanding, by assigning each person to a specific community, family, clan, caste, or peer group. It is only through the selective limitation of behavior that people are able to communicate and to know what is expected of them.

Once again we face the basic *paradox of human culture:* without selectivity there can be no language and no social system; but this same selectivity means that people must live in different groups and speak different languages. Translation of every human language into every other human language is possible because of the basic similarities among all persons. It is on this common humanity that we must pin our hopes for peace and understanding among human groups. But anthropology also argues for the value of *pluralism*—the coexistence within complex societies of ethnic groups carrying diverse subcultures. Such diversity is valuable both because it adds richness to our social life and because it provides the material for innovation and adaptive change (see Chapter 6).

RECOMMENDED READING

Roger M. Keesing, *Kin Groups and Social Structure*. New York: Holt, Rinehart & Winston, 1975. An excellent brief account of the kinds of social groups that are based on kinship and their typical functions, illustrated with clear case studies.

J. A. Barnes, *Three Styles in the Study of Kinship*. Berkeley: University of California Press, 1971. An advanced analysis and critique of three ways of analyzing kinship—American, French, and British.

Monica Wilson, *Good Company: A Study of Nyakyusa Age—Villages*. Boston: Beacon Press, 1963. A well-written description of an East African society in which groupings based on age are important parts of the social structure. Also deals with politics, witchcraft, and economic organization.

Louise Lamphere, *To Run after Them*. Tucson: University of Arizona Press, 1977. An account of cooperating groups in a Navajo community which clarifies the relationships among kinship, marriage, and residence in this Native American society.

T. B. Bottomore, *Classes in Modern Society*. New York: Vintage Books, 1966. A good, brief introduction to concepts of social class and theories about their functioning in the social structure of modern states.

Louis Dumont, *Homo Hierarchicus*. Chicago: University of Chicago Press, 1970. An in-depth study of the caste system of India and its implications for social theory. Difficult but rewarding.

CHAPTER SIX
STABILITY AND CHANGE

u ntil now this book has emphasized the categories and plans that influence interpersonal behavior in a society. But, people do not just sit around carefully categorizing phenomena and planning what they should do: they act. They put the rules of their culture into operation by making decisions, anticipating the actions of others, developing skills, seeking useful alliances, avoiding unpleasantness, and pursuing positive satisfactions. This chapter will be concerned with the way social structures are put into action, and the way they change.

SOCIAL ORGANIZATION

As the British social anthropologist Raymond Firth has insisted, "to see a social structure in sets of ideals and expectations alone is too aloof.... It is equally important ... to stress the way in which the social standards, the ideal patterns, the sets of expectations, tend to be changed ... by the acts of individuals in response to other influences." Firth has suggested the term *social organization* to indicate "the systematic ordering of social relations by acts of choice and decision." Even the most apparently rigid social structure requires that people who use it as a guide to action make numerous choices. Thus structure and organization are two aspects of every social system: "In the aspect of social structure is to be found the continuity principle of society; in the aspect of organization is to be found the variation or change principle—by allowing evaluation of situations and entry of individual choice" (1951:31,40).

Some scholars have reasoned that since we cannot predict the choices that an individual will make, a scientific understanding of culture change is impossible. Others feel that we can completely disregard the individual and study cultural phenomena to establish universal laws of cultural development that will be true of all societies (White 1949:121–145).

The position of this book on the issue of free will versus cultural determinism is an intermediate one. Culture change and, for that matter, cultural stability are the results of many thousands of individual choices. In making choices, members of a society take into account the expectations of others and the probable consequences of conformity or deviance. Some choices are automatic and unconscious, while others require extensive consultation, soul-searching, and emotional upheaval. Although we cannot predict exactly what a specific individual will do in a given situation, the behavioral sciences are rapidly improving their ability to predict the behavior of groups. In the long run, the changing pattern of individual choices within a group determines the direction of cultural change.

People use culture for their own ends, but it is important to remember that the ends they desire are largely dictated by their culture. Individuals vary, but the *kinds* of wealth, prestige, security, or pleasure that they seek and the *ways* in which they pursue these valued ends depend on what the society deems valuable and legitimate (see Chapter 10). Thus a careful study of social structure and social organization reveals a good deal about the contexts that influence individual behavior.

Every language and social structure offers many alternatives, and the more alternatives people are aware of, the more choices are open to them. For example, the greater our command of language, the more varied and precise our speech can be. The availability of many alternatives, however, calls for many decisions, and decisions require evaluation of alternatives. Constant attention to alternatives can be exhausting. Thus, one important function of social structure is to *limit* one's choices on the basis of prior decisions. (Cf. Bettelheim 1971:79–83.)

Standardized patterns and restrictions on choice make communication possible and relieve individuals of the need for constantly making decisions. From the anthropologist's point of view, the categories and plans that produce these regularities of behavior constitute the culture. Carried to extremes, this limiting could result in people's always saying or doing the most obvious things: clichés in speech and conformity in action. But since human motives and experience vary greatly, such complete uniformity is most unlikely. Speech and social organization are the manifestations of language and social structure, under the direction of human purpose.

ANTICIPATION

A spider constructs its web and a bird builds its nest in anticipation of future needs. Such behaviors are considered instinctive because they are present in the animal's nervous system at birth and have only to be set off by a combination of internal and environmental factors. Animals can also be conditioned to perform various actions in anticipation of coming events. If a rat receives an electric shock on one side of its cage a few seconds after a buzzer is sounded, it soon learns to associate the sound with the coming shock; thereafter, whenever the buzzer is sounded, the rat seems to anticipate the shock and moves to the safe side of the cage. There are many ways to interpret this phenomenon; we need not attribute to the rat any conscious awareness of what is taking place.

Human beings can be conditioned in similar ways without consciously knowing what is controlling their behavior, but some kinds of human learning clearly do involve awareness of what a person should do under a given set of circumstances. Culture, particularly language, makes it possible for people to anticipate and to prepare for many kinds of future events, including some they have never before personally experienced. Human anticipations are primarily the results of enculturation.

The conditions that call for role performance are of two general types: scheduled and unscheduled. *Scheduled events* are those whose occurrence is fixed and known in advance: holidays, mealtimes, work periods, markets. The actual timing of such events may be set by clock and calendar, or in relation to any regular occurrence, such as the flowering of a bush or the winter solstice. An *unscheduled event* is one whose occurrence cannot be reliably predicted: a murder or sudden death, an earthquake, an unannounced visit. By providing a plan of expected behavior for various crises, culture attempts to convert the unscheduled into the scheduled, so that the unexpected event sets in motion a chain of other events in which each person concerned may anticipate his or her part. For example, although murder is usually unscheduled, its occurrence influences the subsequent behavior of many categories of persons. Among the Cherokee, when a person was killed, all the other members of that person's clan were responsible for avenging the murder; at such times the structure of Cherokee society was drastically reorganized until this purpose was accomplished (Gearing 1958).

Preparations for scheduled role performances are part of social organization— they anticipate the ways in which the social structure will be put into action in particular cases. Preparation for role performance may be subdivided according to what is being prepared: personnel, resources, or the setting of the performance. If any performance is to take place, each of these factors must receive some consideration.

Preparation

Learning the social roles that one will be expected to play is part of the process of enculturation (Chapter 2). In this sense, people begin to prepare for the future from the moment they are born.

Preparation for highly specialized roles (such as the Tapirapé shaman, Navajo singer, or American doctor) may be lengthy and exhausting. One reason for the widespread conformity to role expectations is the need to invest a great deal of time, effort, and self-esteem in learning a specialized role. After a long and often painful learning process and the giving up of many more immediate satisfactions, it is extremely difficult to abandon a hard-won role.

Learning to speak the language of one's group is an essential part of preparing for any social role, and the most specialized roles require the mastery of additional vocabulary, or even entire languages. Merchants who travel through areas of linguistic diversity must learn a trade language (or several languages); Hindu and Christian priests must master one or more archaic tongues. Nearly every occupational group has its own jargon, and part of loyalty to an ethnic group consists of the ability and willingness to speak its dialect.

The *practice* of individuals and the *rehearsals* of groups in anticipation of future performances also come under the heading of social organization. Here structural patterns are applied to concrete behavior. Anthropologists can learn a great deal more by watching a wedding rehearsal and listening to the comments, promptings, and advice given than they can by witnessing the actual polished performance of the ceremony.

At a rehearsal, the various roles called for by the social structure are assigned to particular persons. The assignment of roles corresponds to the division of labor within the society as a whole, with the processes of recruitment and social control brought into sharper focus on this smaller scale. *Modifications* are made as the structure is put into action: various details of a performance are altered to fit the requirements of a concrete situation—the skills of the performers, the number of persons involved, the setting in which they are to perform, and so forth. During the summer of 1959, the author witnessed three separate Sun Dance performances by members of the Southern Ute tribe. (The Southern Ute Sun Dance lasts for three or four days, during which time the dancers remain in the lodge and have nothing to eat or drink.) Although the basic structure of all three dances was the same, there was considerable variation in details, much of which was due to the experience and preparation of the participants. At the third of these dances, the ethnographer had to step out of his role as observer and become a participant because none of the regular singers who knew the Sunrise Song had appeared when it was time for the dancing to begin. On another occasion, the start of the Sun Dance was delayed because someone had neglected to bring the large drum that is beaten by the singers.

Performances must also be anticipated by the preparation of the resources that will be needed for the event. For example, throughout the world people celebrate important social events by consuming large quantities of food. If a feast is to be successful, the food resources to be consumed must be accumulated and prepared. The feast itself is an important part of the social structure, but the anticipation of the event affects people's behavior for days or even months beforehand, and all such anticipation is part of the social organization.

Accumulation of resources may be *direct* (as when the Polynesian mother gathers breadfruit and coconuts for a family meal), but more often it is quite *indirect*, involving many intermediate steps (as when the Bantu laborer works for months or years in the copper mines to accumulate enough money to buy cattle to use as bridewealth to acquire a wife). Similarly, the fabrication of resources into culturally approved forms may take time and effort. The elaborately carved wooden posts that decorate a Tiwi grave can be made only by those few older men who have sufficient experience and leisure. The fabrication requires many days of effort; this is one reason that Tiwi funerals are held several months after a death has taken place.

Preparation of the setting involves the *allocation* of time and space to a particular performance and the *distribution* of both personnel and resources within the setting. The setting for an event should be chosen to minimize distraction and interruption. Cultures vary, however, in the activities they prescribe for a given setting. Latin American businessmen prefer to conduct a variety of affairs at once, in contrast to the usual North American pattern of one thing at a time. Edward Hall reports the following revealing anecdote:

> An old friend of mine of Spanish cultural heritage used to run his business according to the "Latino" system. This meant that up to fifteen people were in his office at one time. Business which might have been finished in a quarter of an hour sometimes took a whole day. . . . However, if my friend had adhered to the American system he would have destroyed a vital part of his prosperity. People who came to do business with him also came to find out things and to visit each other. . . . To us it is somewhat immoral to have two things going on at the same time. In Latin America it is not uncommon for one man to have a number of simultaneous jobs which he either carries on from one desk or which he moves between, spending a small amount of time on each [1959:29–30].

The distribution of personnel and resources within the chosen setting leads from the phase of preparation into the performance itself. If preparations have been complete, the role performers speak and act appropriately, all necessary resources are readily available, and there are no interruptions or distractions. But how often is the social structure so perfectly translated into action? Unanticipated intrusions are always possible, and personnel or resources are seldom as well prepared as they might be. There are many discrepancies between the ideal structure and its concrete manifestation in behavior. How often does a famous speaker have a coughing fit, or an actor fail to appear for a performance? We know that often too little food is prepared for a feast and that the Sun Dance drum is occasionally forgotten.

To note these imperfections of social organization is not to deny that there is a social structure behind the variable manifestations. Lapses simply show that culture *influences* and does not determine behavior. People must anticipate many factors if a performance is to be a success. As George P. Murdock once wrote:

> Actual social behavior, as it is observed in real life, must be carefully distinguished from culture, which consists of habits or tendencies to act and not of actions themselves. Though largely determined by habits, actual behavior is also affected by the physiological and emotional state of the individual, the intensity of his drives, and the particular external circumstances. Since no two situations are ever exactly alike, actual behavior fluctuates considerably, even when springing from the same habit. A description of a culture is consequently never an account of actual social behavior but is rather a reconstruction of the collective habits which underlie it [1960:249].

CHOICE AND CHANGE

The preceding discussion of anticipation deliberately omitted the factor of choice. We assumed that for a given initiating event (scheduled or unscheduled) only one kind of behavior would be expected of the players of a given role. Within these limitations, anticipation involves the ways in which role players prepare for their performance. In reality, social structure generally provides *alternative* ways of behaving in a given situation, and people must constantly choose among the structural possibilities offered to them. Many of these choices are trivial, involving only personal preference and having little effect upon the social system, but in the long run, *patterns of individual choice change the social structure.* That is, the expectations that influence social behavior are themselves affected by that behavior. In general a rule that is continually violated will ultimately disappear from the structure (as did the prohibition amendment from the Constitution), whereas a pattern of behavior that is regularly repeated comes to be expected.

When you order lunch in a restaurant, it makes little difference whether you choose a hamburger or a tuna sandwich. If no one ever orders the hamburger it will eventually disappear from the menu, and if enough people request an item that is not on the menu, it may eventually be added. To take a more usual anthropological example, imagine a society in which the residence rule is *ambilocal:* a newly married couple may live with the kin of either the bride or the groom. Suppose that for some reason the patrilocal alternative is chosen more and more frequently until matrilocal residence becomes quite rare. At some point, the repeated choice will affect the expectations of the group as a whole, and patrilocal residence will become the rule. Thereafter, couples who for some reason wish to live with the bride's kin will be violating an expectation rather than just choosing an alternative. In the same way, new alternatives may become part of a social structure. As a result of repeated violations of shared expectations, the new patterns are eventually accepted as legitimate, sometimes replacing the original pattern. Murdock has stated this point most clearly:

> From the point of view of cultural change . . . actual or observed behavior is of primary importance. Whenever social behavior persistently deviates from established cultural habits in any direction, it results in modifications first in social expectations, and then in customs, beliefs, and rules. Gradually, in this way, collective habits are altered and the culture comes to accord better with the new norms of actual behavior [1960:249].

Decision-Making

We come now to the question of how people decide among the structural alternatives that are open to them. The following discussion of decision-making is based on two assumptions: (1) that more than one alternative is actually available to a person and (2) that given knowledge of available alternatives and their probable consequences, most people make reasonable choices. This is a *rational model of decision-making.* Though it may not be applicable to all choices, it can help us to understand social organization as a dynamic process.

An individual faced with the need to make a rational decision begins by consciously or unconsciously *scanning* the available alternatives and *eliminating* some. A person's range of scanning is limited by awareness of alternatives, and this awareness is primarily determined by past experiences. As noted above, the greater our command of a language, the more varied and precise our speech can be. Similarly, the more knowledge we have of the structure of our society, the more alternatives are available to us. People differ in their awareness of structural possibilities, so that a decision that is obvious to one person may not even be considered by another.

In addition to this differential *awareness* of alternatives, there remains the factor of differential *access* to alternatives. Persons must often eliminate alternatives of which they are aware because they lack certain ascribed qualities, elements of personal preparation, or resources. A young college student, looking for a summer job in the classified ads (scanning), may eliminate certain possibilities because the positions call for a person who speaks Spanish or owns a car. Spatial and temporal factors may also eliminate some possibilities, such as a job in a distant city or one for which the application period has already passed.

Assuming that our student has objective access to a number of opportunities (possesses all of the role attributes required for recruitment), still other alternatives will have to be eliminated because of *incompatibilities* between the job requirements and other commitments. She may have to turn down a perfectly good job because to take it, she would have to give up her role as student. The decision-maker tries to avoid or to minimize the probability of *role conflict*—a situation in which incompatible behaviors would be expected of her.

Many of us manage to perform roles that are apparently incompatible by keeping our performances separated in time and/or space. The army officer who moonlights as a jazz musician carefully selects the places where he plays, to avoid meeting his fellow officers or his subordinates. In a monogamous society, the role of husband is expected to be performed in relation to no more than one woman at a time, but the successful bigamist is able to schedule his role performances so that others are not aware of his double life. In a polygynous society such deceptions are not necessary. Role conflicts and incompatibilities are relative to the social structure of a given group.

Having scanned the possibilities of which they are aware and having eliminated some on the basis of potential access and incompatibility, decision-makers must *evaluate* the remaining alternatives: estimate the satisfactions that may be derived from each alternative and choose that which offers the greatest value and/or the least risk.

Value conflicts are probably unavoidable in human social life. Most decisions represent a compromise between two or more possible types of satisfaction, rather than the all-out pursuit of one type. Even if we could commit ourselves exclusively to the maximization of one type of satisfaction, we would eventually meet with conflicting demands from our own bodies and from the various groups of which we are members. Many such conflicts are the products of differing expectations held by the societal group on the one hand and subcultural units (such as the family or the peer group) on the other. Walter Miller's studies of the delinquent subculture show how young men seeking to maximize their prestige within the peer group inevitably come into conflict with representatives of the larger society (1958). Other studies have shown the conflict between the impersonal bureaucratic ideals of a society and the narrower personal or familial loyalties of its members (Fallers 1955).

Conformity and Alternatives to Conformity

Having decided to comply with a given set of cultural or subcultural expectations, the individuals concerned still have considerable freedom as to the *manner* in which they conform. People can control both the *timing* and the *intensity* of their performances for their own purposes. This may be true even when the social structure provides no alternatives. For example, among the Turu (a Bantu tribe of Tanzania), each man chooses the time and place of his own circumcision; initiation is a voluntary act, although all men must eventually submit to it (Schneider 1966).

The use of timing for personal ends is well illustrated by the Tiwi marriage system. Tiwi girls are betrothed early in life to much older men, but they continue to reside with their parents until after puberty. If a girl's father dies before she joins her husband-to-be, the stepfather gains a certain degree of control over her which he can use for his own purposes. Although he is not usually able to break the engagement, he can delay her change of residence. By postponing her departure (or by threatening to do so), the stepfather can generally gain some benefits from the aging husband-to-be, who is eager to acquire his promised bride (Hart and Pilling 1960).

By the intensity of a performance we mean the manner in which an expected but quantitatively variable action is carried out. In many cases, the structure prescribes an action but leaves the intensity of the act to be determined by the processes of social organization (anticipation and choice). In total institutions such as prisons and the army one often finds an elaborate vocabulary describing the intensity of a role performance. Such special vocabularies develop because many members of total institutions are not participating by their own choice. Terms such as "serving time," "goldbricking," and "gung ho" express the attitudes that may be taken toward a performance. As Erving Goffman has pointed out, total institutions are excellent settings for the study of social organization because their members often develop ways of simulating intense performances without expending much real effort: the most successful goldbrick is the person who can *appear* to be gung ho in the presence of superiors.

If one has chosen to conform with the expectations of a given role, one's freedom is pretty much limited to modifying the timing and the intensity of role performance. There are, however, at least three types of *alternatives to conformity* with the requirements of a role. The first possibility we shall call *deception.* That is, one can *appear* to comply with a set of expectations, even simulating a highly intense performance, while one's purposes are actually far from or even opposed to those of the role one is playing. An extreme case is the secret agent who masquerades as a gardener. It is essential that he give a creditable performance, even though his motives for adopting this role have nothing to do with love of flowers. His apparent conformity to the role will be maintained only so long as it furthers his true purpose of espionage. Deception in less extreme forms is found whenever individuals represent themselves as kinds of people that they are not; in this form, it is familiar to all of us.

A second possible alternative to conformity we may call *negation:* the refusal of a person to fulfill some or all of the expectations associated with a role. Negation can take many forms, from an outright refusal ("Hell, no, we won't go!") to an elaborately reasoned denial of obligation ("Well, I'm only sixteen, I've got a ruptured spleen . . .''). Most negations are eventually met with sanctions, but some are built into the social structure itself, and may be viewed as legitimate alternatives to conformity. In our society, the "sick role" is one such form: by claiming a certain type or intensity of ill health, a person may be able to negate many of the usual requirements of occupational, kinship, and other roles. Among the Plains Indians, adoption of the berdache role (see p. 87) allowed some men to escape the usual obligations of being a male. The Cheyenne called such individuals "half-men, half-women," implying a reduction and combination of expectations from two standard roles.

Philip L. Newman's " 'Wild Man' Behavior in a New Guinea Highlands Community" analyzes another structural alternative to conformity. Among the Gururumba, men between the ages of twenty-five and thirty-five occasionally indulge in public behavior of an extremely bizarre nature. The "wild man" rushes about, shouting and scattering things with an apparent loss of bodily control; he seems to be unable to hear and he speaks only in a kind of pidgin English; he also steals a variety of objects, which he destroys just before returning to a normal state. The consequences of such an episode are described as follows:

There are no recriminations against the wild man after he has gone wild, and no one in his clan or village will mention the episode to him. They do talk about it among themselves, however. It is evident from these conversations . . . [that] they do not think of him as the same kind of person he was formerly thought to be. . . . The Gururumba are aware of the kinds of pressures social life imposes on them. When a man goes wild they also become aware of the fact that this particular individual is not as capable as others of withstanding those pressures. Specifically, there is an observable reduction in the expectation others have of the degree he will participate in exchange transactions and a corresponding reduction in the intensity of demands made on him: He may still have debts, but repayment is not pressed aggressively. . . . The outcome of wild man behavior is thus a reduction of demands made without loss of social support [Newman 1964:16–17].

The similarity of the "wild man" to an American who has had a "nervous breakdown" is quite striking.

Innovation

The last type of alternative to conformity is called *innovation,* that is, any creative response to a situation in which an individual cannot or will not comply with expectations. In one sense, we are always innovating since our behavior never exactly repeats itself; even repetitions of the same word show some phonetic variation (see Chapter 3). In addition to this kind of unavoidable free variation, it is possible to place any item of behavior on a continuum from most to least conventional. This continuum can be divided into four major parts, as shown in Figure 6.1.

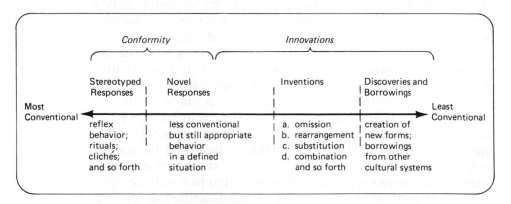

FIGURE 6.1 Continuum of Action Probabilities

Stereotyped responses, such as shaking hands or saying "How are you?" when meeting someone, are the most conventional actions an individual can perform in a given situation. Religious rituals, such as the Roman Catholic mass, are also highly stereotyped. There is always a certain amount of free variation, but close conformity to social expectations is itself highly valued in these situations, and general forms of speech and behavior tend to be highly predictable.

Novel responses, as noted in Figure 6.1, are usually appropriate to the social situation but less predictable than stereotyped behavior. In such instances the individual exercises some degree of choice while remaining within the alternatives offered by the shared structure. Most of our daily behavior falls within this range of actions that are acceptable but more or less novel. For example, our choice of clothing for a given occasion frequently combines standard items in a novel manner.

Inventions often involve the accidental or deliberate *violation* of cultural rules (see Introduction to Part Two). The four types listed in Figure 6.1 do not exhaust the possible kinds of inventions, but are intended to suggest the major ways in which people break social rules. According to Homer Barnett's book *Innovation,* most things that we think of as inventions can be analyzed as rearrangements, substitutions of one cultural element for another, or combinations of cultural elements already known to the innovator: *different plans applied to traditional categories* (Barnett 1953). Clothing made of paper and the electric toothbrush are clear examples of substitution and combination inventions.

Innovations in social structure often involve combination or rearrangement of the attributes of old roles rather than the creation of entirely new roles. The reorganization of a business or a governmental agency usually means the multiplication of vice-presidents or the consolidation of several functions under one supervisor. Within a kinship system, changes from polygamy to monogamy or from endogamy to exogamy involve alterations of plans without the creation of any really new categories. In a complex society, each advance in knowledge seems to call forth a new category of persons to master and transmit it. The astronaut and the anesthesiologist are relatively new occupational roles that have developed in response to scientific and technological advances, but though the *content* of these roles is new, their attributes are modeled after familiar military, scientific, and medical roles.

The least probable type of innovative behavior is the *discovery.* A discovery need not involve the violation of a cultural rule because many discoveries are so improbable that cultures have no rules concerning them. For example, the discovery of radium or of the planet Neptune, though surprising and unexpected, did not violate any cultural prescriptions such as "You shall not discover radium." Discoveries often require extensive rearrangements of our expectations. Inventions alter the plans associated with known categories, but discoveries involve the creation of new categories or new plans or both.

The *borrowing* of new cultural elements from another system is essentially the same as a discovery. Like discovery, it introduces unconventional categories and plans into a culture, often with far-reaching consequences. The borrowing or discovery of a new food plant, weapon, or form of political organization may set in motion a chain of events that will affect every aspect of a culture.

Borrowed elements will usually undergo changes of form and of significance as they fit into the new cultural system. This is called the *process of reinterpretation.* As Melville J. Herskovits has pointed out, reinterpretation goes on between generations as well as among societies: new meanings are assigned to old forms, and borrowed elements are fitted into different categories and associated with different plans. The American-made alarm clock becomes a striking chest ornament in New Guinea; the sacred maize plant of the Maya becomes pig fodder in Nebraska; and the stylish clothes of our parents' youth become, for us, funny costumes or nostalgic "camp." Reinterpretation is a constant and universal process; it accounts for much of the variability of behavior in the realm of social organization (Herskovits 1964:190–194).

Innovation can be the first step toward structural change, but the innovative behavior of a single person must be distinguished from the *acceptance* of that innovation by others who perform similar or complementary roles. It is only with the spread of a pattern of behavior that we may speak of a structural change: that which was highly unconventional must become increasingly conventional and finally expectable. When the cartoonist Robert Osborn invents a new type of caricature by omitting the noses on the faces of his subjects, he is clearly an innovator; unless other cartoonists adopt this innovation, it will remain an attribute of Osborn's personal role—part of his unique style— and it will not affect the code shared by cartoonists and their public. On the other hand, the rearrangements of parts of the human face and body employed by Pablo Picasso and other European artists early in this century became expected attri-

COLLECTION, THE MUSEUM OF MODERN ART, NEW YORK, THE LILLIE P. BLISS BEQUEST

Influenced by African sculpture, Pablo Picasso's innovative paintings established a new style in European art.

butes of the Cubist school of painting and, as such, part of the structure of Western culture.

Acceptance of an innovation, then, requires that many people choose to act in the new way. The innovation may persist as an alternative mode of action, or it may replace the former pattern. On the other hand, it may rapidly disappear (this is what we mean by a fad) or lose its novelty and pass into the realm of stereotyped responses and clichés (as with the phrase "Sock it to me").

No cultural system is entirely static. In a primitive society, stereotyped responses are likely to be highly valued for their own sake and to be closely related to other conventional actions; it is unlikely that they will be quickly replaced by new patterns. Still, *innovations are constantly taking place.* People in every society enjoy some degree of novelty, and most people can alter their expectations very quickly if it is clearly to their advantage to do so. Structural change is the inevitable result of the process of social organization (anticipation and choice), with innovations providing the new materials from which major structural changes may develop.

ADAPTATION

There are several intentional parallels between the ideas put forward in the last section and the modern synthetic theory of biological evolution. In contemporary evolutionary theory, *mutations* provide the new materials from which major structural changes may develop. Mutations are alterations in DNA molecules (genes) due to omissions, substitutions, rearrangements, and combinations that take place in the course of reproduction. Like social inventions, mutations introduce variations that may or may not be "chosen" (selected for) in a given environment.

The synthetic theory explains biological evolution as the result of *natural selection* acting on the variability produced by mutation. Natural selection is the process that, in the long run, fits a population to its environment by eliminating poorly adapted organisms and favoring the better adapted individuals. A genetic mutation that decreases the adaptation of an organism to its environment will be eliminated by selection, while a mutation that increases adaptation will be favored because individuals inheriting this trait have a better chance to reproduce than other members of the group.

Natural selection applies as much to cultural development as it does to biological development. A new tool, technique, or social innovation cannot persist if it leads to the extinction of any population that accepts it. On the other hand, an innovation that significantly improves the adaptation of a group to its environment will give that group an advantage over other groups. An innovation that leads to the expansion and dominance of one society may mean the decline and even extinction of another. Cultural evolution can be directly studied, because a human population can vastly change its way of life in less than a generation, whereas only the slow, opportunistic process of biological evolution alters the structure and behavior of other species.

Not all parts of a culture have equally direct connections with a group's adaptation to its physical/biological environment. Human adaptation is much more complex than that of other ani-

Level	Environment To Be Adapted To	Goals	Basic Processes	Units Involved
I.	Physical/ biological (nature)	Maximum energy utilization; control of population size; adaptability	Evolution (capture and transformation of *energy*), both biological and cultural	Genetically inherited structures and behavior; culturally transmitted tools and techniques
II.	Social (others)	Social integration; continuity of group	Enculturation (exchange of values: *reciprocity*); social change (acculturation)	Roles, groups; plans for social interaction; conceptions of space and time; situations
III.	Internal (self)	Cultural coherence; personal satisfactions; individual identity	Culture growth (elaboration of *symbolic forms*: art, religion, law)	Ideology; world view; personal construct system; mazeway

FIGURE 6.2 Three Levels of Human Adaptation

mals; it proceeds simultaneously on at least three levels, with different goals, processes, and units on each level. Figure 6.2 summarizes these three levels of adaptation (based on Meighan 1966).

Adaptation on any of the three levels may produce either stability or change. When adaptation ceases, the result is not stability but death. The rest of this chapter will deal with adaptation of the *social environment* (Level II), in terms of the processes of acculturation, revitalization, exchange, and reciprocity.

Acculturation

When societies that have been relatively isolated come into contact with larger, more powerful, more technologically advanced societies, both groups undergo a process of adaptation that is called *acculturation.* Adaptive changes are more noticeable in the smaller group: they range from minor borrowings and modifications to virtual replacement of whole cultural subsystems.

The Micmac Indians first came into contact with Europeans around 1500. Their initial contacts were with sailors who had come to exploit the rich fishing banks off the coast of what is now Nova Scotia. Occasional trade began, the Indians exchanging fresh food and furs for brandy, metal tools, and trinkets. By 1600 the French had established a flourishing fur trade in their colony of New France (eastern Canada); they built forts and enlisted the Micmac on their side against the British. French missionaries were also successful in converting the Micmac to Roman Catholicism.

The fur trade, military innovations (especially guns), and the new religion altered Micmac culture in many ways. Nevertheless, these changes in the social, technological, and ideological systems helped to maintain the total culture. Some tribes tried to ignore the powerful outsiders and were soon extinct. The Micmac had to modify their way of life if they were to survive as a people under changing social and ecological conditions. Despite (or perhaps because of) adaptive changes in technology and social structure, they clung to their native language and managed to *reinterpret* (see p. 154) the European religious and political doctrines in terms of their aboriginal beliefs and values.

More than four hundred years of acculturation have not destroyed the Micmac sense of identity or their desire to live as Indians. Today, despite disease, warfare, and restriction to tiny, unproductive "reserves," the Micmac number more than 6,000 persons—probably more than at the time of first European contact. The men work when they can as fishing guides, in lumbering, and in construction; recently many young Micmac have gone into "high steel," building bridges and tall buildings in the cities of eastern Canada and New England. The adoption of these occupations is an adaptive change in one part of the social structure which permits other parts (family and community organization) to maintain themselves (Guillemin 1975). The Micmac have strongly resisted attempts by missionaries and government agents to make them take up agriculture. Choices made in the past have produced structural changes, often far beyond what was anticipated, but these adaptations have given continuity and stability to Micmac society and culture (Bock 1978).

Revitalization

Revitalization movements arise when societies are under intense stress (possibly as a result of acculturation). They are social movements that attempt to relieve a crisis by means that may appear bizarre to outsiders. Radical or reactionary, and despite apparently irrational elements, these movements, when successful, often bring about vast changes in a whole series of societies in a surprisingly short time.

The cargo cults of Melanesia are probably the best known of modern revitalization movements. In the wake of World War II, many native peoples who had been briefly exposed to the military and economic might of the United States attempted to lure precious cargo to their own societies by constructing piers or landing strips and performing magical rituals under the leadership of a prophet who promised great wealth to all who followed his teachings. Followers often had visions and engaged in frenzied dancing and destruction of property. Although the anticipated cargo did not arrive, these cults generally resulted in major alterations in leadership patterns, division of labor, and ritual practices. In many places, the fantastic programs were followed by more practical attempts at social reform and economic development.

Paula Brown (1968:484) has suggested that the distinctive features of cargo cults are "the dream or vision of the prophet, the belief in access to supernatural beings, miracles, the swoons, and seizures of individuals and massed dancers." She also makes the following, more general point:

> In order for people to join any movement for social change, their wish for a different life must be very strongly held. Their wishes can vary greatly in content. They can wish to return to the golden age of the past (as in the American Indian Ghost Dance); they can wish for a somewhat better standard of living in the present (a labour movement); or they can have millennial dreams of a perfect age and salvation. In its common Melanesian form the wish is for the achievement of European wealth and power. These feelings are often linked with resentment at the native's position. "The white man shall go" is a common, though not universal, element; nationalism is often involved as well [1968:474].

The American Indian Ghost Dance was a much more conservative movement than the Melanesian cargo cults. Nonetheless, it comes within the classic definition of a revitalization movement as "a deliberate, organized, conscious effort to construct a more satisfying culture" (Wallace 1956:265).

In 1870 and again twenty years later, prophets appeared in various Great Basin and Plains Indian tribes, preaching the return of the dead. They organized elaborate ceremonials designed to ensure the magical defeat of the whites and the return of the buffalo, which had become nearly extinct.

The Ghost Dance was clearly a response to the crisis of white military pressure, colonization, and the whites' deliberate slaughter of the buffalo, which had been the Indians' principal source of subsistence. Dozens of Indian cultures virtually collapsed after the failure of the 1890 Ghost Dance. Elsewhere, similar movements have had notable success, winning thousands (or millions) of converts to their messages of reform and salvation. The similarities and differences among these movements are explored in a fascinating book by Weston La Barre, *The Ghost Dance: The Origins of Religion* (1970).

EXCHANGE AND RECIPROCITY

Social integration is achieved primarily through an exchange of values among the various parts of a system. Values are exchanged partly through the division of labor, but even in the absence of specialization and objective interdependence, integration stems from a universal rule of behavior: *the principle of reciprocity.* According to Alvin Gouldner, "There are certain duties that people owe one another, not . . . as fellow members of a group or even as occupants of social statuses within the group but, rather, because of their prior actions" (1960:170–171). For example, the social structure of a village in India rests not only on caste solidarity and interdependence but also on the specific ties between high-caste patrons and the individual workers who provide them with specialized goods and services (the *jajmani* system):

> In return for their services, the traditional workers are given biannual payments in grain and are sometimes given the use of a piece of land. The patron–worker tie is a hereditary one: a patron cannot arbitrarily change a traditional worker, and no one other than the hereditary worker will perform the traditional work of a patron under threat of outcasting. Similarly, a traditional worker cannot change a patron without the permission of his caste [Cohn 1955:56].

In this system, as in every society, people are guided by a general rule that "makes two interrelated, minimal demands: (1) people should help those who have helped them, and (2) people should not injure those who have helped them" (Gouldner 1960:171). This rule (norm of reciprocity), because it is so very general, can regulate behavior even if one does not know what kind of person one is dealing with:

> Being indeterminate, the norm can be applied to countless *ad hoc* transactions, thus providing a flexible moral sanction for transactions which might not otherwise be regulated by specific status ob-

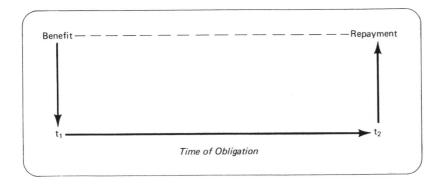

FIGURE 6.3 Temporal Consequences of Reciprocity

ligations. The norm, in this respect, is a kind of plastic filler, capable of being poured into the shifting crevices of social structures, and serving as a kind of all-purpose moral cement [Gouldner 1960:175].

A gift received or a service performed establishes a relationship where there was none, or reinforces existing social relationships. Gouldner also points out the *temporal consequences* of this norm (see Figure 6.3). The norm of reciprocity requires that debtors neither break off relations nor launch hostilities against their creditors; nor will creditors do so as long as they expect repayment. A gift or service initiates a social *time of obligation:*

> It is a period governed by the norm of reciprocity in a double sense. First, the actor is accumulating, mobilizing, liquidating, or earmarking resources so that he can make a suitable repayment. Second, it is a period governed by the rule that you should not do harm to those who have done you a benefit. This is a time, then, when men are morally constrained to manifest their gratitude toward, or at least to maintain peace with, their benefactors [1960:174].

According to George Foster, all citizens of the Mexican village of Tzintzuntzan cultivate exchange relationships (*dyadic contracts*) with equals and superiors in order to maximize their security in "the uncertain world" in which they live. Furthermore, this system requires that

> an exactly even balance between two partners never be struck. This would jeopardize the whole relationship, since if all credits and debits somehow could be balanced off at a point in time, the contract would cease to exist. . . . The dyadic contract is effective precisely because partners are never quite sure of their relative position at a given moment. As long as they know that goods and services

are flowing both ways in *roughly equal amounts over time,* they know their relationship is solidly based [Foster 1961:1185; italics added].

The dyadic contract is an aspect of social organization involving both choice and reciprocity, for "the formal social institutions of Tzintzuntzan kinship, neighborhood and godparenthood provide an individual with more potential associates than he can utilize. . . . By means of the dyadic contract, implemented through reciprocity, he patterns his real behavior" (1961:1188, 1189).

In societies that desire long periods of obligation, it is improper to repay a debt too eagerly. Among the Seneca Indians of New York State, for example, a person who wants to repay a gift too quickly is considered ungrateful. Similarly, many American retail businessmen feel that a person who buys on time is obligated to his creditor and thus likely to make more purchases at the same establishment; credit managers refer disparagingly to those who avoid time payments as "cash bums."

Like any other cultural rule, the universal norm of reciprocity *influences* behavior rather than determining it; that is, it can be violated or used by individuals for their own ends. What we call a bribe is only a gift that creates an obligation of which we do not approve; bribery could not work if the recipient did not feel obligated to reciprocate.

When reciprocity between two persons or two groups breaks down, it is often replaced by hostility. This can happen when one party fails or refuses to repay his or her obligations. The norm of reciprocity can also be used to humiliate an opponent by means of a gift that the recipient cannot hope to repay (or even to maintain, such as the proverbial white elephant).

The general principle may therefore be modified as follows: *the exchange of goods or services between parts of a system produces social integration only if* both *parties to the transaction feel that the values exchanged are roughly equivalent.* Exact equality of exchange tends to terminate a relationship, while extremely unequal exchanges tend to produce hostility. In an unequal exchange where *A* gives more to *B* than he receives from *B,* the hostility may be felt by *A* if he thinks he is being exploited; but it may also be felt by *B* if he thinks he is being humiliated (cf. Hyman 1966).

It should be emphasized that the exchange of equivalent goods or services produces integration among *groups* as well as among individuals. The incest taboo serves as a source of social integration, since people are considered valuable in all

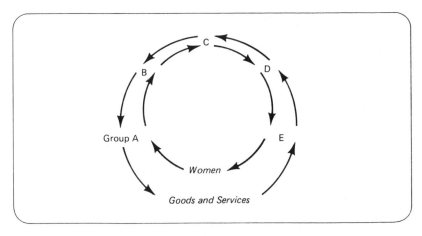

FIGURE 6.4 Integration by Exchange

societies (though not necessarily for the same reasons) and the incest taboo makes it necessary for men and women to seek their mates outside of their immediate families. The biological and social consequences of this taboo are so adaptive that it has become universal. Similarly, various rules of exogamy and preferential marriage found throughout the world promote social integration by ensuring the regular exchange of mates among lineages, clans, or districts.

Claude Lévi-Strauss (1963a) has pointed out that in a caste society such as India, where strict rules of endogamy prevent the exchange of mates among major social groups, the occupational specialization of the groups produces social integration by requiring a constant exchange of goods and services. There are many societies in which a number of social units are integrated by what amounts to the exchange of women for other types of valuables. Thus, when two men marry each other's sister, we have an exceedingly *direct* form of exchange; but a larger number of groups can be integrated by means of an *indirect exchange* in which women travel in one direction while valued objects go in the opposite direction (as shown in Figure 6.4).

At the level of the national state, exchange of goods via foreign trade is an important means of international integration. We must not underestimate the historical importance of the exchange of women even on this level: royal marriages ensure cooperation just as royal divorces lead to hostility (compare the cases of King Henry V and King Henry VIII of England). Also, in many African feudal states where the ruler takes a large number of wives, his wives generally come from noble families in different districts of the kingdom; they thus serve, in part, as hostages to guarantee the loyalty of their noble relatives.

Finally, as Lévi-Strauss has made clear, words and other significant symbols are still another type of value, so that the *exchange of messages* plays an essential part in the integration of all kinds of social systems (1953:524–525). When we say of two persons that they are not speaking or that they don't talk the same language, the implication is that cooperative activity is difficult or impossible. The free exchange of messages makes possible smooth interaction because it is only through the regular flow of information that we can develop reliable expectations about the behavior of others. When communication breaks down between the parts of a system—be it a family, a business, or the nations of the world—the degree of integration of the system is lowered, and hostility is the likely outcome. Dictators have long known what social psychologists have experimentally verified: the one who controls the flow of information within a social system controls the system.

Individuals put their culture to work for them in order to achieve their purposes and maximize their satisfactions. In all societies, people act within the framework of their social structure, *anticipating* its demands, *choosing* among structural alternatives, *modifying* the manner of their performances, *innovating* more or less novel responses, and *adapting* to their social environment by various means, including exchanges guided by the norm of *reciprocity*. These major principles of social organization produce a much more dynamic picture of the operation of social systems than does a static description of social structure in terms of roles, groups, situations, and the standard plans for action associated with each of these categories. Regular patterns of choice ultimately change the structure, but *it is the shared structure that makes choice possible and meaningful.*

RECOMMENDED READING

Ivan A. Brady and Barry L. Isaac, eds., *A Reader in Culture Change*, 2 vols. Cambridge: Schenkman Publishing Company, 1975. An anthology of theoretical articles and case studies dealing with cultural change in a wide variety of societies.

Clifford Geertz, *Agricultural Involution*. Berkeley: University of California Press, 1971. A classic study of ecological change in Indonesia and its consequences for social organization. The author compares the course of development in Indonesia with the pattern in Japan.

George M. Foster, *Tzintzuntzan*. Boston: Little, Brown, 1967. In this intensive case study of a Mexican peasant community the author identifies several general processes and "cognitive orientations" that, he argues, contribute to both stability and change in traditional societies.

Jeremy A. Sabloff and C. C. Lamberg-Karlovsky, eds. *The Rise and Fall of Civilizations*. Menlo Park: Cummings Publishing Company, 1974. A collection of readings illustrating the contribution of archaeology to the understanding of cultural processes.

Julian H. Steward, *Theory of Culture Change*. Urbana: University of Illinois Press, 1955. Although these essays were written more than twenty-five years ago, they are still essential reading for anyone interested in processes of change and their relationship to environmental adaptation.

PART THREE
TECHNOLOGICAL SYSTEMS

The part of a culture that enables people to produce objective changes in their physical and biological environment is called the *technological system.* It consists of learned categories and plans for action that are manifested in the tools, techniques, and skills employed by the members of a society. The technological system is intimately related to the social system of a group. Because technology does not operate all by itself, changes in technology and in social structure go hand in hand. The techniques and skills that make possible the survival of a human society must be shared and applied by specific categories of persons. Techniques are attributes of social roles and, as such, are expected to be performed in culturally defined situations. The technological ability of a population also limits its size and social structure.

Americans and others who live in modern industrial societies that possess complex machine technologies and scientific medicine tend to take these advantages for granted, not realizing how recent such developments are in the history of human culture. The study of primitive technological systems provides a valuable perspective from which we can better appreciate our advantages as well as our debt to the past. The technological systems of primitive peoples are truly remarkable in the way they make possible adaptation to difficult and hazardous environmental conditions, with the use of only the materials immediately at hand. Furthermore, our own complex civilization is largely built upon the achievements of our unknown primitive ancestors. Ina C. Brown has put this point very well:

> We who are citizens of the United States are apt to think of our country not only as self-made but as generous to a fault in giving to the rest of the world. Actually, we are deeply in debt to other peoples. The plants and animals we use for food, our form of writing, the paper and printing presses that bring us the news of the world, the basic inventions that underly our technological civilization, even our ethical values and religious concepts were discovered, invented, developed, or thought out by peoples in other times and places [1963:136].

The following chapters deal with the principal tools, techniques, and skills that have been developed by primitive peoples to help them to survive in various environments, the kinds of environmental adaptation that specific technologies make possible, and the forms of thought and social structure that accompany these adaptations.

CHAPTER SEVEN
TOOLS AND HUMAN NEEDS

A n *artifact* is any portion of the material environment that has been deliberately used, or modified for use, by humans. Tools are thus a subclass of artifacts. A *tool* is any artifact that is used to augment our ability to act upon the physical world. This is a very broad definition, but such a definition is necessary if it is to encompass everything from hand axes to lasers and from clay pots to space capsules, for these are all parts of human technology.

Tools are useful because the human body is not equal to all the tasks it must perform. To understand the adaptive functions of tools, we must bring them into relation with the human needs they help satisfy. The *adaptive function* of a tool is the contribution it makes to the survival of populations that use it.

Many artifacts have no direct connection with the physical survival of human groups. Works of art, sports equipment, flags, jewelry, and other similar objects promote social integration or cultural coherence rather than environmental adaptation (see Figure 6.3). Such objects naturally conform to the laws governing the physical world, but they are not tools because their action upon that world is incidental to their primary functions.

TOOLS THAT REGULATE TEMPERATURE

The human body, like that of other animals, can function only within a fairly narrow temperature range, and this fact leads to our most immediate need for tools. Like all mammals, we are warm-blooded. We have physiological mechanisms for regulating our own temperature, but they are not sufficient for survival in many of the environments in which humans are found. *Homo sapien* was originally a tropical animal—a primate—and is able to inhabit temperate and arctic zones only with the assistance of certain tools.

The development of temperature controls is older than our species, for we know that *Homo erectus* (Pekin man) controlled fire. More than 50,000 years ago, early members of our own species (the Neanderthals) lived near the edges of Pleistocene glaciers, surviving under conditions of severe cold (see pp. 11–13). All animals use naturally occurring shelters, so it is hardly surprising that early humans lived in caves—and that thousands of people still do today. A cave without fire is uncomfortable, however, and it may present more hazards (for example, dampness and intruding carnivores) than advantages. In the tropics fire is important for the insect-repelling qualities of its smoke. The mastery of fire, then, was one of the earliest and most important steps in learning to control the environment.

Shelters

Shelters are also tools for controlling environmental conditions, and thus regulating body temperature. In tropical regions, shelters function primarily as protection from solar radiation and rain. They are built quite ingeniously, from materials available in the immediate vicinity. C. Daryll Forde describes the shelters built by the Semang, a nomadic hunting and gathering people of the Malay Peninsula:

> Three or four stout sticks are driven into the ground in a line, sloping over toward the central clearing, and supported by forked struts or held in position by fibre strings pegged in the ground. The outer side of the sloping stakes is then closely thatched horizontally, working from the bottom to the top. Rattan leaves are used, and each is folded on its midrib to give a double thickness of fronds. This sloping thatch-like wall is adjustable, and its angle is raised or lowered according to the weather. In stormy weather more foliage is heaped

MARC & EVELYNE BERNHEIM/WOODFIN CAMP & ASSOC.

Grass thatching and woven mats can produce a shelter that is both beautiful and practical, as in this Baganda royal tomb.

on outside and held in position by branches. Beneath it, their heads to the back, raised couches are built to lift their occupants from the damp earth and vegetation [1963:13–14].

This simple lean-to dwelling fits the needs of the Semang perfectly. It is no more than a roof that deflects the sun's rays and sheds water. It performs these functions while offering minimal interference to cooling breezes. The leaves used in this single wall have a very low heat capacity; they reflect solar radiation rather than absorb it. Finally, the shelters may be quickly constructed from materials that are readily available in all parts of Semang territory—an important feature for these nomadic bands.

Throughout the tropics, where heat, humidity, and heavy intermittent rains are the major climatic problems, the dominant element of human shelter is a water-repellent roof. The roof is often combined with a raised floor and walls of low heat capacity, all made of local materials. Woven mats are commonly used, for in wet weather the fibers expand to repel water and in dry periods they contract to admit air. One particularly ingenious arrangement has been reported from the plateau area of Nigeria: a dome-shaped mud roof is topped with wooden pegs and a second roof of thatch is set on the pegs. The water-repelling action of the thatch is combined with the heat absorption of the mud roof and the insulating property of the air trapped between the two roofs.

In hot, arid areas such as the American Southwest, where temperatures fall very low at night, the adaptive problem is to level out the extreme temperature differences between day and night. For this purpose, high-heat-capacity materials such as mud and stone serve very well. These materials absorb solar radiation during the day, and at night they radiate the heat energy to the interior of the shelter. Houses built of stone, mud, or mud bricks, finished in light colors, with small openings for light, help keep the inside temperature fairly stable. Such shelters are extremely functional provided the group using them is sedentary, for they take considerable time and effort to construct.

Nomadic groups in temperate and subarctic environments often use some kind of tent since they cannot count on finding building materials. The tent is what engineers call a tension structure; its design gives a maximum of enclosed space with a minimum of materials—an important advantage for nomads who must carry both frame and covering materials with them. The Indians of the Northeast usually used birch bark to cover their conical or hemispherical *wigwams,* whereas the conical *tipi* of the Plains Indians was, understandably, covered with buffalo skin. Some pastoral nomads of central Asia use felted animal hair (an excellent insulator) as a tent cover. For example, the *yurt* of the Kalmuk and the Kazak consists of a collapsible willow-rod frame, something like a trellis, which is set up in a circle, topped with an umbrella-like frame over which large sheets of felt are stretched and lashed down with horsehair rope. The floor is covered with felt and a curtain of felt hangs across the doorframe. Such easily transported shelters are obviously well adapted to the needs of their nomadic inhabitants.

Probably the most striking example of primitive architecture is the Eskimo snow house, or *igloo*. Wood, which is the usual building material and fuel of primitive tribes, is not available to the Eskimo. The igloo is made from

> large blocks of snow, cut from a drift of fine-grained, compacted snow with a bone or ivory knife . . . laid spirally and sloping inwards to build up a dome without any scaffolding. Each block is rapidly and skillfully cut out by eye to fit in its place with the right slope and to afford a firm foundation for later courses. The final key block is lowered into position from outside. Any crevices are tightly packed with snow and the main structure is complete. With use during the winter cold its solidity increases, for the meltings on the inner walls are soon frozen again to solid ice. . . .
>
> In some areas the main chamber is lined with skins held in position by sinew cords passing through the walls of the dome and held by toggles. A considerable air space is left between the skin ceiling and the snow roof. With such a lining and an air exit hole in the roof a temperature of ten to twenty degrees above freezing can be maintained without serious melting of the igloo, since there is always cool air between it and the interior [Forde 1963:117–120].

The excellent performance of the igloo is a result of both its form and its material. The streamlined hemispherical shape offers minimum obstruction to winter gales while exposing the least possible surface to chilling. The dome, as you may recall from solid geometry, encloses the largest possible volume within a given surface; at the same time, it is effectively warmed by a single source of radiant heat. Dry snow may seem an unlikely material, but it is one of the best imaginable materials for the arctic environment, because of its low heat capacity. This means that the walls have excellent insulating properties, and when glazed with ice the interior acts as a radiant heat reflector. In short, the igloo is a first-rate shield against icy winds and a nearly ideal container for people and heat energy (Fitch and Branch 1960).

In addition to these design factors, the igloo requires a dependable source of radiant heat, and wood for fuel not available in the Arctic. Thus the Eskimo's adaptation to their environment rests in part upon a simple but essential device: the oil lamp. This is a shallow stone dish with a moss wick which enables the Eskimo to burn oil derived from seal blubber—the only readily available fuel. A single oil lamp, placed near the center of a small igloo, provides all the heat needed to warm the interior.

Clothing

Like fire and shelter, clothing helps people control their body temperature. The forms of clothing are influenced by considerations of style, but the materials used depend primarily on adaptive requirements. For example, the Indians of the Northwest Coast had clothing well suited to the high humidity of their area and to their seagoing way of life. They wore waterproof hats of finely woven basketry and garments of cedar bark. Red cedar bark was shredded and made into conical, water-repellent rain capes, and yellow cedar bark was woven into warm robes. Other garments were woven of goat or dog hair. Bark garments can be used only in areas of high humidity because elsewhere they quickly lose their flexibility and fall apart. In parts of South America and in the Pacific, bark cloth was made in long strips, which were wrapped around the body. In these regions, grass skirts were also made and worn by both sexes.

The hair of mammals is a natural insulating material, and can be used to replace the hairy covering that humans have lost in the course of evolution. The techniques of felting and of spinning and weaving are found mainly among groups with domesticated animals. Similarly, extensive use of vegetable fibers such as cotton, flax, and hemp tends to be limited to settled societies with agriculture.

The primary adaptive function of clothing in an arctic environment is to shield the body and to assist in the conservation of natural body heat. Eskimo clothing is admirably suited to its tasks. In some regions it is made from caribou hide and carefully shaped:

> Eskimo garments are no shapeless wraps. They are carefully cut out and tailored on established patterns for men and women. For protection against water and damp, waterproof suits of gut are made. Clothing is made by women. It is finely stitched with sinew thread and often beautifully finished with border strips of contrasting colour. To protect their eyes against the continual glare of snow and ice during the spring on the coast the Eskimo wear slit goggles of ivory [Forde 1963:121].

This passage brings out two important points. First, the temperature-regulating properties of clothing cannot be divorced

Traditional women's garments of Mauritanian nomads provide protection against sun and sand while satisfying local ideas of modesty.

from other functions, such as shielding from glare, dampness, or insects. Second, adaptive functions combine with (and sometimes contradict) notions of modesty and traditional esthetic values. Ornamentation seldom contributes to the effectiveness of a tool, and standards of propriety and attractiveness (which are both conventional and variable) often diminish the comfort of those who maintain them. Thus in analyzing the technological functions of a tool, we must examine all of its uses in relation to the physical world and as far as possible separate them from the implement's nontool aspects. Finally, various categories of clothing are associated with particular categories of persons (the doctor's white coat, the widow's veil) and thus are systematically connected with social structure.

Perhaps the most striking example of environmental adaptation comes from our own culture, for in the twentieth century we are moving into entirely new environments: outer space and the depths of the ocean. As astronauts and deep-sea divers enter these environments, they encounter extremes of heat, cold, pressure, and radiation never before faced by human beings. When they leave the controlled environment of their capsule containers, they must protect themselves against these hazards. The space suit, with its special materials and integral sources of heat and oxygen, represents the first major advance in human clothing since the bearskin robe.

THE NEED FOR FOOD AND WATER

Water must be consumed in some form, or life cannot go on. The main problems facing a group in connection with its water supply are finding a source, extracting the usable portion, and storing or transporting the water.

The only "tool" used to locate water is the widely distributed but totally ineffective divining rod. To find sources of moisture, members of hunting and gathering societies rely principally on their intimate knowledge of their territory and of the characteristics of local plants and animals. Even in extremely arid environments, finding drinking water is more a matter of techniques than of tools; it involves knowing the location of water holes or of moisture-containing plants, plus a keen sensitivity to signs of moisture. People who live in arid environments also develop the ability to persist in spite of thirst, and this ability gives them an advantage over others who tend to give up (and thus die) in the same situations.

Once a source of moisture is found, tools may be needed to extract the drinkable portion. The Eskimo melts some snow in a soapstone bowl; the Bushman inserts a drinking tube (a hollow reed that is carried everywhere) into a crack in a hollow tree. In both cases, the tools used are simple, but are nevertheless essential.

For nomadic peoples in arid environments, storage and transport of water are serious problems. Many hunting peoples use the paunches, bladders, or skins of animals as canteens, and these receptacles must be prepared with stone knives and scrapers or sewn with bone or ivory needles. Pottery jars are either unknown or impractical because of their weight and fragility, though they may be employed by nomads who possess beasts of burden. The Bushmen of the Kalahari desert use ostrich eggshells to carry water.

Many peoples who lack pottery or metal containers heat water by "stone-boiling." This method is used with containers that cannot be placed directly over a fire—made, for example, of basketry, leather, bark, or wood. Stones are heated in a fire and then dropped into the water, and the heat is transferred to the water without burning the container. In the days before European contact, the Micmac Indians used this method to heat water in the large, hollowed-out tree stumps that served them as kettles.

Large sedentary societies in any environment must bring drinking water to the population centers, often over great distances. Where rainfall is not sufficient for agriculture, large quantities of water must be stored and transported to the fields. Digging wells, building dams, and constructing irrigation systems or aqueducts require both an advanced technology and a social structure that can enforce large-scale cooperative efforts. It has been suggested that the earliest civilizations in China, the Middle East, and Central America all originated in connection with such irrigation projects (Wittfogel 1957).

Food-Gathering Tools

Though constantly on the move, hunting and gathering people do a remarkable job of exploiting the food resources in their environments. Once again, intimate knowledge of the territory and of its flora and fauna plays a major role: without it, these people could not survive.

Among food collectors, the gathering of plant food is almost invariably the task of women. The work is commonly carried out with the help of the digging stick, which is simply a strong stick that tapers to a point; the point is often hardened by being tempered in a fire to drive out the moisture. The digging stick is an all-purpose tool used as a prod to locate edible roots, as a pick to loosen the soil, and as a lever to extract plants from the ground. According to E. A. Hoebel, the Cheyenne Indians believe that this tool

> was given by the Great Medicine Spirit and it figures in the ritual paraphernalia of the Sun Dance, for it has its sacred aspects. Cheyenne [digging sticks] are of two types. The short kind has a knob at one end and is pushed under the desired root by pressure against the stomach when the digger is down on both knees. The other kind is long, and used as a crowbar. The sharp ends are fire hardened [1960:59].

The digging stick enables food gatherers to procure starchy roots, and various pulverizing or grinding tools such as the maul and the milling stone enable them to get at the nutritious kernels of seeds, which are usually encased in hard, inedible shells.

> The basic household item of the [Cheyenne] woman is her stone maul—an oval river stone with pecked-cut grooves on the short sides around which is fixed a supple willow withe firmly fastened with green rawhide. When dried out, the rawhide shrinks and holds the maul within the handle with the grip of a vise. With the maul she breaks up fuel, drives tipi pegs, and crushes large bones to be cooked in soup. With smaller handstones the housewife crushes her chokecherries and pulverizes her dried meat [1960:61–62].

From ethnographic accounts such as this archaeologists can get some idea of the many possible functions of prehistoric tools.

The milling stone is essential to an economy based on the gathering of seeds or the cultivation of grains—the most common types of subsistence economies found in the world. Milling stones appear in the archaelogical records of both the Old and the New World about 10,000 years ago. This fact does not necessarily indicate contact between, say, the eastern Mediterranean and central Mexico at this period, but it does show that following the end of the Ice Age, people in widely separated parts of the world were learning to exploit the food energy found in wild seeds. Such experimentation eventually led to the development of agriculture.

Another characteristic tool of plant collectors is the seed-beater, a paddle-shaped implement that is used to knock seeds off plants into a container. The Paiute used them in connection with conical baskets when harvesting grass seeds and pine nuts. In the Great Lakes area, many tribes have used similar seed-beaters in harvesting wild rice: one person would slowly guide a canoe through the swampy regions where the rice grew, while another bent the rice stalks over the canoe and knocked the grains into its bottom.

A final example of tools used in food processing comes from California, where the Indians developed a number of ingenious methods of preparing the acorn. Oak trees are abundant in central California and their annual crop of nuts is quite dependable. The only problem is that most varieties contain a high proportion of tannic acid, which makes them inedible. The devices used to remove this acid are simple, and they made possible the accumulation of a sizable food surplus. The acorns were cracked open between two stones and the nutmeats ground with a mortar and pestle.

> When the meal was ground sufficiently fine, it was taken to the bank of a stream where there was a handy water supply for the leaching process. Most frequently the meal was placed directly on the sand in a shallow depression or basin which had been prepared for the purpose. In southern California, however, the meal was placed in a porous basket. Then water was dipped from the stream and poured over and through the meal in the manner of making drip coffee. Sometimes the water was heated by placing hot stones in a closely woven basket filled with the liquid. Warm water dissolved the tannic acid more readily, but if too hot carried away some of the fat which was a desirable nutritive element. Cold water took longer, but washed away none of the food value. This leaching process was repeated until the bitter taste of the tannic acid was eliminated. The meal was then ready for cooking [Driver and Massey 1957:235].

Acorns were also used for food in the northeastern United States, but here a *chemical process* was used: to neutralize the tannic acid, the whole kernels were boiled in water to which lye (derived from wood ashes) had been added. The nuts were then dried or roasted and stored.

Since the human body is not provided with built-in pouches, the use of seeds, roots, and berries as sources of food also requires strong, lightweight containers for transport and storage. Such containers are less likely to last for 10,000 years than are milling stones, but the arid climate of the American Southwest has preserved a few examples, and ethnographic studies of modern seed gatherers can be used to fill out the prehistoric picture. Burden baskets, woven and used by women, were essential tools. Net bags were probably used to carry larger objects. The *tumpline,* a strap slung across the forehead, distributed the weight of a load carried on the bearer's back. Food was processed and stored in baskets, skin bags, covered pits, or, in some cases, pottery jars.

Hunting and Fishing Equipment

The adaptive problems involved in hunting are similar to those involved in obtaining water and plant food, except for the tendency of animals to avoid being located and killed. In itself the human body is too slow and clumsy for efficient hunting, but with tools and socially transmitted techniques people can become skillful and effective hunters.

Clubs and spears are probably the most ancient weapons; every known human group possesses some simple crushing and piercing tool. A fairly ancient improvement on the spear is the spear-thrower, often called by its Aztec name, *atl-atl.* The spear-thrower serves as an extension of the arm, providing additional leverage and thus multiplying the force that can be applied to the end of a spear. Using a spear-thrower, an average person can learn to hurl a weapon as far as a champion javelin thrower and to throw it with considerable force at close range. Other improvements on the simple spear include separate points (initially stone, later metal) and detachable heads (as with the Eskimo harpoon).

The simple bow is a mechanism consisting of a single curved piece of wood to which a strong fiber or sinew cord is fastened. The resiliency of the bow is sometimes improved when strips of sinew are fastened to its exterior surface; this is the sinew-backed bow. When wood is lacking or when a powerful small bow is desired, a compound bow can be fashioned from several pieces of bone, wood, or horn. The Eskimo bow is usually made of three sections of wood or caribou antler strips bound together and reinforced with strands of sinew lashed to the outer face. The earliest archaeological evidence for the use of the bow comes from rock paintings only 10,000 to 12,000 years old. The first arrows were doubtless simple shafts, and the first separate arrowheads may have been only crude chips of stone. They were rapidly developed into finely flaked piercing implements—much lighter and thinner than any spear point. The Bushmen use tiny arrows tipped with a deadly poison, which enable them to hunt large mammals, including giraffes.

Some jungle hunters use the blowgun, a long tube through which a dart is guided, propelled by the hunter's breath. The Sakai, neighbors of the Malayan Semang, use a bamboo blowgun together with poison-tipped darts to hunt all kinds of small game. The Jívaro Indians of the Amazon basin are expert blowgun hunters; their blowguns are ten to fifteen feet long and can propel a poisoned dart up to forty-five yards to kill monkeys and birds.

The simplest animal trap is the pitfall: a hole dug in the ground and covered with leaves or branches both to shield the hole from sight and to allow only fairly heavy animals to fall through. In some areas sharp stakes are driven into the bottom of the pit to impale the falling animal. Snares are also constructed by primitive hunters, sometimes combined with other devices to secure the trapped animal. For example, a noose may be attached to the tip of a bent sapling, so that when the animal is caught, the sapling is released and lifts it into the air. A *deadfall* is a trap that, when triggered, releases a suspended weight, which falls on the victim.

Cage traps are used in Africa and Southeast Asia, particularly where bamboo is readily available. A *weir* is a "fence or barrier sufficient to block a fish yet permit the passage of water." Weirs are usually built in streams, but some are built on tidelands to impound fish stranded by the outgoing tide. Wood is the usual material, but in the Arctic some weirs are constructed of stone (Driver and Massey 1957:203).

Spearfishing, angling, and the use of fish rakes were all known in native North America. The use of fish poison was most highly developed in South America, where substances from about one hundred species of plants were used to stupefy or to kill fish. Among the Jívaro, for example:

> If the Indians are located on a large stream, they employ several devices for catching fish. Sometimes, if the water is low, a dam is constructed and a poisonous sap from the barbasco shrub distributed above the dam. As the juice permeates the water, the fish rise to the surface in a stupefied condition and are gathered by the assembled villagers. Fish are caught sometimes with rude traps and nets, or speared [Service 1978:205].

Food collecting is often the concern of organized groups. There is archaeological evidence going back to the Upper Paleolithic of cooperative drives, in which herds of gregarious animals were surrounded and driven over cliffs or into the water to be speared by waiting hunters. On the American Plains, in the days before the horse, fire was used to drive herds of bison into ambushes. The Pygmies of central Africa carry out cooperative hunts in which women and children drive game from a large area into nets three hundred feet long while the men stand ready with spears.

People have used dogs to supplement their senses since the end of the Pleistocene. The dog was the first domesticated animal, and functioned as a tool in the struggle for survival. The sheep, goat, and pig were the next animals to be domesticated, but they were used as sources of food and raw materials rather than as tools. Several thousand years passed before camels, oxen, and horses were tamed and the tools and techniques developed which made them useful as sources of energy (see below).

TRANSPORTATION: THE TRANSMISSION OF OBJECTS

The oldest and still most common form of transportation is walking, and the oldest cultural improvements in this process are paths and footwear. Once in existence, a path influences the behavior of those who use it, providing a channel for their activity. Paths are not usually thought of as tools, but they do satisfy our definition as portions of the material environment that have been modified for use. The path is a smooth channel through which people and objects can move. It is obvious that the nature of this channel must change with the type of vehicle used. A footpath is not suitable for a ten-ton truck, but modern-day engineers have often found aboriginal paths useful in planning the routes of new roads, since the natives know the most direct and convenient routes.

Many people go barefoot in their daily work, but in some environments footwear is highly adaptive. The fur-lined boots of the Eskimo and the moccasins of the American Indians provided important protection. Perhaps the best example of adaptive footwear is the snowshoe. In many cold areas, people were confined to their winter settlements during periods of deep snow until the invention of the snowshoe, "which enabled man to escape from his seasonal bondage, [and] completely changed his winter mode of life" (Birket-Smith 1965:215). The simplest snowshoe is a slab of wood or bark tied to the bottom of the foot. In the New World, this device developed into the netted snowshoe: an oval frame with crosspieces of wood, skin, or rope. The ski was invented in the Old World by 2000 B.C., and for the most part took the place of snowshoes.

Snowshoes and skis distribute weight over a broad area and prevent a person from sinking into the snow. The *sled* does the same for material objects. Three types of sled have been developed by northern peoples: (1) the hollowed-out tree trunk, including the boat-shaped sled, in which the sides of the trunk are extended upward with planks; (2) the plank sled, including the North American toboggan; and (3) the runner sled, which in its simplest form is only a pair of skilike runners connected by crossbars. The first two types of sled are, like the snowshoe, adaptations to soft snow, while the third type is better adapted to ice.

The Blackfoot Indian travois or slide-car, drawn here by a horse, helped these nomads to transport heavy or bulky possessions.

The dry-land equivalent of the sled is the slide-car, known in America as the *travois*. This tool consists of two trailing poles dragged along the ground, with a load attached at the center of the device. The travois was used by the Plains Indians, with a frame made of tipi poles, pulled by dogs, and later by horses. Birket-Smith feels that slide-cars are ancestral to wheeled carts, since "many primitive wagons are simply slide-cars equipped with wheels." The wheeled cart is only about 6,000 years old. The wagon is seldom used by primitive peoples, since it requires domesticated draft animals and reasonably good roads.

We shall use the term *boat* here to refer to all vehicles involved in water travel. There are four basic types of boat: the raft, the canoe, the double boat, and the plank boat. Each type appears in many forms, made with various materials and for various purposes.

The oldest means of water transport is probably the trunk of a tree. As recently as the nineteenth century, natives of some parts of Australia had no other boats; they would lie on a tree trunk and paddle with their hands. A raft is basically a number of tree trunks lashed together. Rafts are found all over the world. In the absence of sails, which are less widely known, the usefulness of rafts is limited to relatively shallow, quiet waters where they can be propelled and controlled with long poles.

Canoes appear in three subtypes: dugouts, bark canoes, and skin boats. A dugout is a tree trunk that has been hollowed out—generally with the aid of fire. Like the raft, the dugout is sometimes improved by the addition of planks to raise the sides. Simple dugout canoes are extremely unstable and require great skill in handling, yet they are found all over the world and in all sizes, from single-passenger models to huge boats over sixty feet long accommodating dozens of paddlers and many pounds of cargo.

The bark canoe is especially useful for long portages, since it has a large volume relative to its weight. Bark canoes were known in North and South America as well as in Africa and Australia. In northeastern North America, the combination of birchbark canoes with extensive river systems made possible rapid long-range communication.

One type of skin boat is the Eskimo *kayak,* which is used for summer hunting on rivers and lakes. This boat is made of sealskin tightly bound over a frame of wood or whalebone. The top is covered except for an oval hole in which the hunter sits. The kayak is very fast and extremely seaworthy, propelled only by a double-bladed paddle. The Greenland Eskimo often lace their watertight skin coats to the kayak hole; if it capsizes, they are able to right themselves with ease, without getting wet. The Eskimo also have a skin-covered open boat, the *umiak,* which can carry several passengers; it is used for travel and for whaling.

All these light boats are propelled by paddles, though the umiak is sometimes powered by sails. Sails are essential for long-distance ocean travel without mechanical sources of power.

One way to increase both the stability and the capacity of a boat is to lash two craft together. The double boat is simply a pair of canoes joined together by crossbeams on which a platform is constructed. A variant is the outrigger canoe: a beam of light wood is connected to the canoe so that it rests on the surface of the water parallel to the body of the boat. The Polynesians and other inhabitants of the Pacific Islands made many long voyages with boats of this type.

There is almost no limit to the size of a plank boat. Built of shaped boards covering a semirigid frame, these boats combine stability with large cargo capacity. The plank boat, compound sails, and the rudder comprised most of the elements involved in shipbuilding through the eighteenth century. Then, in a few short years, the development of the steam engine brought about a revolution in water transportation.

COMMUNICATION: THE TRANSMISSION OF MESSAGES

All human beings have a biological need for social contact with others of their species (Ashley Montagu 1972). Infants who are deprived of tactile stimulation (the earliest form of communication, through the sense of touch) deteriorate and eventually die. Early in life, contact (stimulation) must be physical and emotional. A warm, loving mother (or mother substitute) engaged in frequent communication with her child is essential to healthy development. Adults, too, suffer mental and physical disturbances if they are deprived of sensory stimulation for long, as in solitary confinement. Such facts led Eric Berne to say that "a biological chain may be postulated leading from emotional and sensory deprivation through apathy to degenerative changes and death. In this sense, stimulus-hunger has the same relationship to the survival of the human organism as food-hunger" (1964:14).

Through the process of enculturation, individuals are persuaded to give up the kind of physical intimacy they experienced as infants, and to substitute "more subtle, even symbolic, forms of handling, until the merest nod of recognition may serve the purpose to some extent, although [*the*] *original craving for physical contact may remain unabated*" (1964:14; italics added). The tools humans have devised to augment their capacity for social communication are responses to this need.

There are, of course, forms of human communication other than speech. We *receive* information through at least five senses, but we transmit information primarily through visual or auditory stimuli. As the principal means of human communication, *speech is a tool.* It enables people to transmit information in order to produce objective changes in their environment. A species or group that can transmit and store complex messages has a selective advantage over one that cannot. Other forms of communication are tools for storing or transmitting information when direct speech is not possible. Sign languages, drum signals, semaphore codes, and writing are all substitutes for speech.

In Africa, Middle and South America, and the Pacific, drum, gong, and whistle languages replace direct speech in certain ritual and interpersonal settings and are also used to transmit messages over considerable distances. They are found particularly (though not exclusively) in groups that have tone languages—linguistic systems employing contrastive pitch phonemes. True drum or gong language reproduces selected characteristics of the spoken message. In theory (if not in practice) any message could be sent by these systems. Simple arbitrary codes can signal only a limited number of messages (for example, "One if by land and two if by sea"). Musical instruments used for signaling in various parts of the world include whistles, horns, flutes, musical bows, drums, gongs, and marimbas.

All of these means are used to *transmit messages through space.* To *store information over time,* different kinds of devices must be used. The simplest examples are standardized ways of blazing a trail or indicating which fork of a path has been followed. Simple picture symbols or signs can communicate a limited number of messages when scratched on rocks, bark, or hide. Tally sticks, used to keep track of the score in a competition or to mark the time until a scheduled event, also fall into this category. The *quipu*, or knot record, employed by the Indians of Peru, preserved information (mainly numerical) in the form of knots tied in a series of colored hanging cords.

Prior to the information revolution of the present century, *writing* was the most remarkable tool devised for the storage and transmission of information. Writing is the transformation of speech into permanent visual forms, and functions to store information. A. L. Kroeber distinguishes three stages in the development of writing:

> The first is the use of pictures of things and actions, and, derived from these, pictorial symbols for qualities and abstractions. This is the pictographic and then the picto-ideographic method. In the second stage the representation of sounds begins, but is made through pictures or abbreviations of pictures; and pictures or ideographs as such continue to be used alongside the pictures whose value is phonetic. This may be called the mixed or transitional or rebus stage. Third is the phonetic phase. In this, the symbols used, whatever their origin may have been, no longer denote objects or ideas but are merely signs for sounds—words, syllables, or the elemental letter sounds [1948:510].

An alphabet is a system of the third type, whose symbols correspond to the significant sounds of the spoken language (its phonemes). Alphabetical writing makes possible the visual representation of the essential elements of speech in a compact form. Its adaptive significance for complex societies is enormous, for such societies must store and transmit vast quantities of information.

According to Kroeber (1948:514), "all the alphabetic systems that now prevail in nearly every part of the earth—Roman, Greek, Hebrew, Arabic, Indian, as well as many that have become extinct—can be traced to a single source." This first alphabet was borrowed, reinterpreted, subjected to all the processes of invention (omission, substitution, combination, and so forth), and borrowed again. It can serve as a model of cultural diffusion and change.

Modern developments in the transmission of goods, persons, and information have made possible, for the first time in human history, a worldwide network of communication. Since social groups are in part defined by the existence of stable patterns of communication among their members, this development could ultimately shatter the conventional cultural boundaries that divide group from group and nation from nation. A world society is now possible. But this does not mean that such a society will necessarily come into being, for there are also strong social forces opposed to such unification. Not the least of these forces is the process of enculturation itself, for this process must take place within a relatively small group. Each child must learn a

Wooden slit drums are used to transmit messages in the Cameroons, West Africa.

particular set of cultural and linguistic rules in the context of a specific family and local community. This means that one's primary social and emotional allegiance is necessarily directed to a small group and its provincial traditions. These local allegiances can, to some extent, be weakened and superseded by wider loyalties later in life; but they are never completely dissolved, and consciously or unconsciously they continue to shape our behavior. (See Epilogue.)

The mass media and modern methods of rapid transportation are perhaps the most important forces now operating to bind together human groups. They increase both mutual awareness and interdependence. It is only by communicating that people can come to share the categories and plans that make possible smooth interaction and genuinely adaptive behavior. In an age when a single misunderstanding could lead to the destruction of humanity, it is not difficult to see the hot line between Washington and Moscow as a tool essential to human survival.

RECOMMENDED READING

Robert Spier, *From the Hand of Man: Primitive and Preindustrial Technologies*. Boston: Houghton Mifflin, 1970. A clear discussion of how "primitive" tools are made and how they work.

Elman R. Service, *Profiles in Ethnology*, 3d ed. New York: Harper & Row, 1978. Brief descriptions of the technologies, social structures, and ritual activities of twenty-two societies on all levels of complexity, from hunting bands to agrarian states.

Philip Slater, *Earthwalk*. New York: Bantam, 1975. A highly provocative analysis of modern technological society and the problems that arise from distorted communication. Goes beyond dismal description to suggestions for some positive programs to remedy our ills.

Lewis Mumford, *The City in History*. New York: Harcourt Brace & World, 1961. A masterful account of the origin, forms, and functions of the city, that "container for containers" which Mumford argues is humanity's most complex (and most dangerous) tool. Clearly written, with a new and challenging idea in virtually every paragraph.

John H. Bodley, *Victims of Progress*. Menlo Park: Cummings, 1975. Brief but authoritative account of the devastating impact that Euro-American technology and the "culture of consumption" have had on primitive peoples for the last three centuries. The many case studies document Bodley's position on the destructiveness of even the best-intentioned development schemes and interventionist policies. Should be read by all anthropologists.

CHAPTER EIGHT
TECHNIQUES AND SKILLS

A technique is *a set of plans believed to achieve a given end.* Some techniques require the use of tools external to the human body. Thus, if I wish to drive a nail, I must find a hammer, hold it in a certain way, and strike the head of the nail with the head of the hammer (taking care to remove my thumb), because the carpentry techniques that I have learned require these actions. The difference between my hammering and that of a professional carpenter is primarily a matter of skill. A *skill* is *the acquired ability to apply a given technique effectively and readily.* One either knows or does not know a technique, but persons who share the same technical knowledge may employ it with varying degrees of skill.

Techniques logically precede tools, since they include knowledge of how to make the tools. If all tools were to evaporate tomorrow there would be chaos, but civilization could eventually be rebuilt; if all techniques were suddenly forgotten, however, our species would probably become extinct before the essential techniques could be rediscovered.

The skill component, though often neglected in discussion of technological systems, is also of great importance. Skill can develop only on a foundation of technical knowledge. Consider the case of a linguist who has compiled a grammar and dictionary of some language in an attempt to converse with a native speaker of the language. Though both of them may possess equivalent knowledge of the language system, it will be a long time (if ever) before the linguist achieves the fluency in speech of the native—that is, before she can apply her knowledge effectively and readily. The same holds for any technique, be it woodworking, athletics, or even science.

By definition, a technique is directed toward some goal, such as keeping warm, getting food, healing a sick person, or building a canoe. People use a technique because they believe it will enable them to achieve the end they desire. Sometimes they are mistaken—the technique may be invalid or inappropriate to the end in view. For example, some people fire guns in the air to drive plagues away from their villages; so far as we know, this does not affect the course of epidemics. In other cases, the chosen technique may be valid, but the performers may lack the skill necessary to make it effective; it *is possible* to make a fire by rubbing two sticks together, but a person can freeze to death while developing the necessary skill.

Members of different societies evaluate *specific ends* differently: one group may think that corn is the ideal food, while another favors acorns or taro or bison meat. But there are some general *kinds of ends* (such as good health and sufficient food) that are sought in every society and for which techniques will always be provided by the culture. The four groupings of techniques that we shall discuss have to do, respectively, with harnessing energy, getting food, healing sickness, and making useful objects.

TECHNIQUES FOR HARNESSING ENERGY

Societies differ vastly in the amounts and kinds of energy that are available to them, and in their abilities to convert one form of energy into a more useful form. Human muscle power is the most ancient and still most widespread source of energy used for social ends. Muscular energy can be applied to pushing, pulling, lifting, carrying, and so forth. The effectiveness of these actions can be augmented by practice and by a variety of tools, but the actual output of energy is fairly consistent. According to Leslie A. White, the "basic law of cultural evolution" is that,

> [o]ther factors remaining constant, *culture evolves as the amount of energy harnessed per capita per year is increased, or as the efficiency of the instrumental means of putting the energy to work is*

increased. Both factors may increase simultaneously of course. . . . But this does not mean that the tool and energy factors are of equal weight and significance. The energy factor is the primary and basic one; it is the prime mover, the active agent. Tools are merely the means that serve this power. The energy factor may be increased indefinitely; the efficiency of the tool only within limits. . . . When these limits have been reached, no further increases in efficiency can make up for a lack of increase in amount of energy harnessed. . . . And, since increase of energy fosters improvement of tools, one may say that it is energy that, at bottom, carries the culture process onward and upward [1949:368–376].

Aside from fire, the earliest energy source used to supplement human muscles was the muscle power of other animals. The muscle power of domesticated animals may be applied to tools. This application requires the invention or discovery of still other tools: harnesses and traces, yokes, collars, and reins. Techniques for training and handling the animals must also be developed. Once the mediating technology is developed, animal power makes many other developments possible. The speed of transportation may be increased; monotonous and fatiguing tasks (such as pumping water) can be assigned to animals; the beasts may be used for pulling plows or wagons, trampling grain, or lifting weights. Each of these inventions opens up many possibilities for cultural development, but in each case, the *advantages* of a new technique must be balanced against its *cost.* For example, draft animals or beasts of burden cannot be eaten; rather, they must be fed. Only a group with a reliable food surplus can make effective use of animal power.

Plants capture solar energy and, through photosynthesis, convert it to a form that people can burn either within their bodies (as food) or externally (as fuel). Energy in the form of moving gas or fluid (wind or water) can be harnessed only with the assistance of tools. The windmill and the water wheel have long been used to capture and convert these forms of energy, as have boats with and without sails.

Electrical energy occurs in nature, primarily in the form of lightning, but it is only in the last hundred years or so that devices such as hydroelectric generators have been invented to convert other kinds of energy into electricity. Future developments will involve nuclear energy and tidal power as well as the direct conversion of solar radiation into electricity. For the present, as in the past, we are primarily dependent on the energy stored in wood and the fossil fuels.

Basic kindling techniques are simple, but they do require

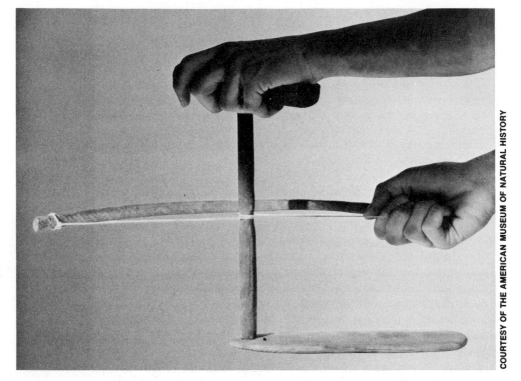

The bowdrill can be used to make holes or, as shown here, to kindle fire efficiently.

skill. Rubbing two sticks together will produce a fire if the sticks are dry enough and if they are rubbed in the proper way. A stick that is twirled rapidly between the palms with its end resting in a hole surrounded with tinder will also eventually produce a flame. This process is accelerated by the use of a bow-drill, a device that loops the string of a bow around the shaft of a drill to convert linear motion into rotary motion and to produce friction at the tip of the drill. The fire-plow consists of a grooved board and a stick, which is rubbed back and forth in the groove until the surrounding tinder catches fire. The modern match is really a chemical version of this device. The fire-piston, found in Indochina and parts of Indonesia, consists of a wooden cylinder enclosing a tight-fitting piston; when the piston is sharply struck, the air in the container is compressed and its temperature is thus raised high enough to ignite the tinder at the bottom. The strike-a-light is any device that yields by percussion a spark that can be nursed into a flame. Sparking stones were probably discovered accidentally by early toolmakers, since flint was one of the materials favored by Paleolithic peoples. In most areas, the combination of flint and steel has replaced earlier materials; it is used today in the cigarette lighter.

A few human groups do not possess any kindling techniques. For example, Allan Holmberg reports:

> Fire making is a lost art among the Siriono [of eastern Bolivia]. I was told by my older informants that fire (*tata*) used to be made by twirling a stick between the hands, but not once did I see it generated in this fashion. Fire is carried from camp to camp in a brand consisting of a spadix of a palm. This spongelike wood holds fire for long periods of time. When the band is traveling, at least one woman from every extended family carries fire along. I have even seen women swimming rivers with a firebrand, holding it above the water in one hand while paddling with the other [1960:11].

Knowledge of kindling techniques and skill in applying them are obviously of great importance to human survival. Only a few peoples are known who do not possess these skills (the Sirionó, the Andaman Islanders, and certain African Pygmy groups), but chances are they have only forgotten the techniques. This could happen because all peoples seem to prefer keeping a fire going to kindling it over and over.

Maintaining a fire requires the recognition and preparation of satisfactory fuel and the mastery of techniques for controlling and applying flames. Fire can be used directly for heat, light, and some kinds of cooking. Supplementary tools and techniques are necessary for other uses of fire. Stone-boiling (see page 177) is a widely used technique. Baking food in a pit or in an earth oven also seems to be a very ancient cooking technique. The techniques of drying and smoking are especially useful to hunting and fishing peoples who must preserve a part of their seasonal surplus for harder times. With the invention of fireproof ceramic and metal containers, fire became still more useful. Finally, the discovery and use of the fossil fuels made possible our modern industrial society. In the words of White:

> By tapping the vast deposits of coal, oil and natural gas, a tremendous increase in the amount of energy available for culture building was quickly effected. The consequences of the Fuel Revolution were in general much like those of the Agricultural Revolution: an increase in population, larger political units, bigger cities, an accumulation of wealth, a rapid development of the arts and sciences, in short, a rapid and extensive advance of culture as a whole [1949:373–374].

In this century, human societies have succeeded in tapping a new and immensely powerful form of energy in the nucleus of the atom. Whether this development will initiate a great new cultural advance or the end of humankind remains to be seen. It seems ominous, however, that the techniques for destructive use of atomic energy have thus far been developed far more quickly than techniques for its peaceful employment.

This section would not be complete without some discussion of spiritual energy: forms of energy other than those recognized by modern physics. Most human groups have beliefs in the supernatural, though they do not necessarily separate them from the rest of their beliefs (see Introduction to Part IV). Many technologies include techniques for harnessing spiritual energy. Such techniques include prayer, sacrifice, divination, ritual, and the use of amulets or fetishes. More direct attempts to control the supernatural are referred to as magic. In every known society, for example, we find the belief that certain verbal formulas can affect persons, objects, or future events.

Sir James Frazer (1953:12–52) distinguished two main types of spiritual technique. *Imitative magic* consists of procedures in which the desired end is depicted or acted out, as when hunters shoot arrows at an image of their prey before setting out on a hunt. *Contagious magic* involves some portion of a person (such as hair or nails) or a substance that has been associated with her (food or clothing). This material is subjected to a procedure believed to affect the person in a specified manner— killing her, curing her, or causing her to fall in love. Ingredients in a folk medicine may be used in the belief that their attributes (potency, speed, beauty, and so forth) will be transferred to the object of the procedure.

In most societies, spiritual and nonspiritual techniques are closely intertwined. Malinowski (1955) pointed out that people tend to employ spiritual techniques in addition to their physical efforts whenever the outcome of these efforts is *uncertain.* The Trobriand gardener does not simply perform his magic and then sit back, waiting for his crop to grow. He knows that he must plant, weed, cultivate, and harvest, but he also knows that the yield of his garden is affected by forces beyond his control. The Trobriand sailor, when he ventures out onto the open sea, recognizes the limitations of his boat and of his skills. It is here that fishing spells and canoe and trading magic become important to him.

Wherever uncertainty and anxiety enter into human life, spiritual techniques flourish. For the anthropologist, it is more important to understand the role that these techniques play in a society than to criticize their premises. Whether their functions are psychological (relieving anxiety or increasing individual confidence) or sociological (coordinating group efforts or promoting social integration), the fact remains that all human societies have developed some such beliefs and procedures. And careful investigation of the symbols used in these activities may reveal the complex social meanings that are, perhaps unconsciously, communicated.

TECHNIQUES FOR GETTING FOOD: SUBSISTENCE

Food Collecting

Only a minute proportion of the world's peoples lives today solely by food collecting. Until approximately 10,000 years ago *all* people engaged in this way of life and no other way was known (the total human population at that time was less than that of New York City today). The fact that the technique of food collecting is ancient does not mean that it is simple. The collection and use of wild foods require considerable knowledge and skill. For example, among the Tiwi, early each morning the women

> scattered in every direction from the camp with baskets and/or babies on their backs, to spend the day gathering food, chiefly vegetable foods, grubs, worms, and anything else edible. Since they had spent their lives doing it, the old women knew all about gathering and preparing vegetable foods, and they supervised the younger women. This was one important reason for men marrying widows, and even a man with many young wives was quite likely to remarry an elderly widow or two nonetheless. A husband with only young wives might have a satisfactory sex life, but he still needed a household manager if he wished to eat well [Hart and Pilling 1960:33].

Patterns of hunting (by men) and gathering of wild vegetable foods (by women) have been noted in hunting and gathering groups throughout the world. Recent studies of surviving groups such as the Bushmen of South Africa indicate that the contribution of the women to the diet of the group is often more important than that of the men, even though the techniques the women use are less dramatic. (See Lee and De Vore 1968.)

The *subsistence techniques* of a hunting and gathering group consist of their *categories of useful plants and animals* and the *plans for locating, capturing, preparing, and consuming each type.* Thus, wherever a group is largely dependent on the hunting skills of its men, it is essential that the hunters be familiar with their territory and with the characteristics of local animals. Tools are important to this process, but the knowledge and skill of the hunters are primary.

Food collectors are seldom content to take from nature only what they can find. All such groups make attempts to ensure or to augment their food supply by physical and/or spiritual techniques. For example, the Paiute Indians of Owens Valley had no domesticated plants, but they used irrigation to encourage the growth of wild plants. Other gathering groups sometimes fenced off areas where favorite wild foods were growing, to keep them safe from animals until they could be harvested.

Hunting peoples often believe that game is under the control of a supernatural protector who, if offended, will withhold it. This animal master is often pictured in folktales as an exceptionally large member of the species, who can also take on human form. He may be offended by a waste of food, by improper words or deeds, or by mistreatment of the blood or bones of "his" species. In most cases he can be placated by appropriate rituals. Hunters, whose success depends on unpredictable factors, seek to explain fluctuations in their success as the result of supernatural whim. The notion of an animal master is no more incredible than many of the tales told by modern weekend hunters and fishermen to explain their successes or failures. The animal master, totemism, and similar beliefs form part of an integrated world view in which humans and animals are much closer and more equal than most Americans consider them.

Many hunting peoples also participate in *increase rites*—ritual techniques intended to assure a continuing supply of game or other wild foods. Among the Australian aborigines, complicated increase rites are an important part of many tribal ceremonies. Each Arunta totemic group carries out great ceremonials to promote the increase of its totem species. These ceremonies are usually held

at the time of year at which the particular totem species produces fruit or seed or gives birth to its young. The ceremonies of each group differ greatly from one another in detail, but in all of them the following features are common:

1. The heart of the ceremony is the special and very detailed ritual performance which helps increase the numbers of the totem species.
2. The inkata [caretaker of the local group's totemic center] must eat a little of the species, as a sort of communion service.
3. Then the other members of the group ritually and sparingly eat a little of it.
4. After this, other people who are present (but who have not witnessed the secret ceremony) feast freely on the totem [Service 1978:27–28].

The requirement that certain groups avoid touching or consuming a species, item, or substance is known as a *taboo.* In some Australian societies, the totem animal of one's group is completely taboo; one may kill or capture it, but one must never eat it oneself lest the entire species perish. Here we find a special type of division of labor, since as a consequence of this rule, members of different totem groups are forced to exchange food with one another, just as the rule of exogamy forces them to exchange spouses.

Food Producing

Starting about 10,000 years ago, people in various parts of the world began to cultivate plants and to tame animals. The change from food collecting to food production was gradual; wild foods remained an important supplement to domesticated types until food production had become highly efficient. This transition was a matter less of new tools than of new knowledge: the crude sickles, axes, and grinding stones used by food gatherers were easily adapted to the new economy, but each new species brought under domestication was a triumph of practical knowledge and came as the result of hundreds of years of experimentation. It is a tribute to our prehistoric ancestors that though the ancient breeds have been much improved by modern technology, *no significant new food crops have been domesticated in the last 2,000 years.*

There appear to have been several independent centers of development of cultivation in both the Old and the New World. A seed-planting tradition based on wheat and barley spread from its Middle Eastern origin into Egypt, Europe, and Southwest Asia. Another seed-planting tradition, based on rice, spread in all directions from its probable area of origin in Southeast Asia. In the New World, the maize-planting techniques seem to have originated in Middle America. There was also an apparently independent center of cultivation of root crops in South America, where the techniques of vegetative reproduction were developed (that is, new plants were started from cuttings rather than from seeds).

The major techniques of hoe cultivation (or *horticulture*) include selection of seed or cuttings, preparation of the soil, planting, cultivation, and harvesting, and such supplementary techniques as fertilization, irrigation, and transplantation. Techniques used vary according to the crops planted, conditions of soil, topography, and rainfall, but there are several fairly widespread patterns.

The *slash-and-burn technique* of horticulture is found primarily in tropical areas. (See Russell 1968.) Overgrowth is cut, dried, and burned right on the field to be planted. In this way, the fields are cleared and fertilized at the same time, for the ash from the burned plants provides important minerals, making it possible to harvest sizable crops several years in a row. Robert Redfield has described the preparation of the *milpa* (cornfield) in the Maya village of Chan Kom as follows:

> The bush is felled with the small steel ax used throughout Yucatan. Everything is cut down except a few of the largest trees; these are left "because a little shade is good for the growing corn in a time of drought, and because too much ash would result if they should be burned." Small growth is cut at the roots; larger trees a foot or two above the ground. . . .
>
> Most of the felling of the bush for new milpas takes place in the autumn and early winter. At least three months is allowed to elapse before the milpa is burned. . . . The act of kindling the milpa is partly ceremonial and is accompanied by propitiatory offerings. The firing is usually done on a day when the wind is in the south or east. Two or more men set the dry bush on fire; some run along the east side and some along the south side, pausing at intervals to kindle the field with a torch, and whistling for the winds to come [Redfield and Villa Rojas 1962:43–44].

Once the rains begin, the cultivator places several grains of maize mixed with bean and squash seeds into three-inch-deep holes approximately one meter apart which are made with a digging stick. Little further care is taken of the field except to clear the second growth with a small hooked knife and to try to protect the ripening plants from marauding animals.

Similar patterns of cultivation are found throughout the world. There is always a mixture of physical and spiritual techniques. The Trobriand Islanders have "a whole system of garden magic consisting of a series of complex and elaborate rites, each accompanied by a spell. Every gardening activity must be preceded by a proper rite" (Malinowski 1955:192). The principal crop of the Trobrianders is the yam, several species of which are cultivated. They believe that at the call of a magician, yams can wander around beneath the surface of the ground. (What else explains the different yields of apparently similar gardens?) Therefore, they have numerous spells designed to encourage their yams to become deeply rooted and to stay in place. Since the burning of cut and dried scrub is a crucial stage of the gardening, here, as in Chan Kom, the burning is accompanied by spiritual techniques:

> Some herbs, previously chanted over, have to be wrapped, with a piece of banana leaf, round the tops of dried coconut leaflets . . . as torches to set fire to the field. In the forenoon . . . the torches were lit quite without ceremony (by means of wax matches, produced by the ethnographer, not without a pang), and then everyone went along the field on the windward side, and the whole was soon ablaze. Some children looked on at the burning, and there was no question of any taboo [although] in a neighboring village . . . the *towosi* [garden magician] got very angry because some girls looked on at the performance from a fair distance, and I was told that the ceremonies were taboo to women in that village [1955:194–195].

Many horticultural peoples are familiar with *techniques of intensive cultivation* such as fertilization, crop rotation, terracing, and irrigation. Wherever sufficient land is available, however, they seem to prefer *extensive* techniques, such as slash and burn, which involves constant shifting to land that has never been cultivated or to land where the brush has had time to grow back. New plots must be cleared and may be at some distance from the old settlement, but their high initial productivity and relative ease of preparation make them more attractive than the partly exhausted and weed-filled fields nearer home. Combinations of intensive and extensive techniques are also found. In parts of West Africa, for example, the staple grains (millet and maize) are planted on shifting plots, whereas bananas and plantains are harvested from permanent groves. In any case, given adequate land and the necessary techniques, horticultural systems can be brought to a high level of productivity with simple tools and with human muscles as the only source of energy.

The subsistence pattern known as *pastoralism* was found aboriginally only in the Old World, for the few domesticable animals native to the Americas could not support this specialized way of life. Pastoralists are nomadic, moving with their herds in search of water and pasture. There are many types of pastoralists, from the reindeer-herders of northern Siberia to the camel-breeders of Arabia. We shall limit our consideration to the important and well-studied cattle complex of East Africa, where the great interest attached to cattle provides "a dominating, integrating force" in the culture:

> Cattle determine a man's rank, as where, among the Bahima, chiefs were appointed to rule over a given number of cattle instead of a given region; or among the Zulu, where [rank] is established by the derivation of the cattle that passed on the occasion of one's mother's marriage. Among the Ba-Ila, a man has an ox that he treats like a pet, that sleeps in his hut and is called by his name. When this man dies, the skin of the ox is his shroud; its flesh supplies his funeral feast.
>
> The languages of the area yield significant illustrations of the importance of cattle. Evans-Pritchard, for example, cites forty different words, each of which applies to the color of a particular kind of cow or ox. The imagery in the poetry of the peoples living in this region is replete with references to their cattle [Herskovits 1964:104–105].

The Masai are a fairly typical group of this area. Although presently decimated by war and disease, they formerly roamed at will over large areas, raiding other pastoralists for cattle and trading hides or milk products for vegetable foods. The Masai keep some sheep and goats, but

> cattle are by far the most important live stock of the Masai, and nearly every family formerly had a considerable herd. . . . Most of the male calves are gelded soon after birth and kept to swell the size of the herd and to provide hides and meat for payments, gifts and feasts. . . . Cows are never slaughtered although they may be eaten when they die. They are indeed treated with the greatest care and much affection. Each has its personal name and the herdsman has his favourites among them [Forde 1963:295].

Nearly all pastoralists are aware of the techniques of cultivation; they cling to their nomadic pattern out of preference. In areas where pastoralists and cultivators are in contact, the pastoralists generally achieve political dominance because of their

superior military striking power. Waves of horseback-riding nomads conquered the Egyptian, Roman, and Chinese empires. In
stratified societies throughout Africa, cultivators are ruled by a
noble class with a pastoral background. In this area are also
found societies with mixed economies in which the men tend
herds while the women are solely responsible for cultivation.

For peoples who use animals only for their meat and hides,
domesticated animals are little more than tame game. Many pastoral peoples do not employ any dairying techniques, nor do
they use their animals for wool, as beasts of burden, or for rid-
ing. Such uses would be economical, however, since they do
not require that the animal be killed.

True *agriculture* (as opposed to horticulture) occurs when a
domesticated animal is put to the plow. Of all human subsistence patterns, agriculture has the greatest productive potential.
As Forde has observed:

> Plough cultivation is nearly everywhere associated with much
> knowledge and considerable equipment, in addition to the use of
> the plough itself. These include the use of water-lifting devices . . .
> the regular use of manures . . . crop rotation and an appreciation of
> the value of pulses as restorers of the nitrogen content of the soil
> which is depleted by cultivation of cereals. The ripe grain is trodden
> out by animals or threshed by driving over it wooden sleds. . . . All
> these and many other details of agricultural practice are unknown
> to the lower cultivators [1963:391].

Because intensive agricultural techniques can produce a
large and continuous yield from fixed fields, the farmer can afford to invest time and labor in constructing strong, permanent
facilities: fences, storage buildings, dwellings, and, above all,
irrigation systems. The plow and allied techniques allow a dependable crop surplus to be harvested in areas of moderate
fertility and rainfall. This surplus makes possible both a denser
population and a more extensive division of labor than do any
of the other food-getting patterns. With the development of metallurgy and its application to agricultural implements, food production becomes still more productive and a considerable
proportion of the population (though seldom over 20 percent)
can be freed from direct participation in food-getting activities.
Crafts can be practiced by full-time specialists, with a consequent improvement in both efficiency of technique and quality
of product. All complex societies have practiced intensive cultivation, and all the Old World civilizations had agricultural
bases.

TECHNIQUES FOR HEALING SICKNESS: MEDICINE

Medicine is an applied science: it consists of practical techniques that are part of a body of knowledge and belief about the human body and the causes of disease. When this knowledge is limited or the beliefs are inaccurate, the derived medical techniques *may or may not work.* For example, where blood-letting is a standard remedy for certain ills, people generally *do* feel better after such a treatment, because psychological and physiological processes are interrelated; therefore, it is unwise to dismiss the skills of native curers as mere superstition. Furthermore, the healers in primitive societies frequently make use of substances that Western medicine has found to be empirically effective and has therefore adopted. (Aspirin and quinine are probably the best known of these substances.) Large drug companies spend sizable amounts of money investigating the techniques of curers throughout the world.

The general formula for any healing technique may be stated as follows:

Illness X   calls for   Treatment Y
(category)   (plan)

This formula indicates the two major phases of medical action: (1) *diagnosis,* in which the category of illness is determined, and (2) *therapy,* in which a plan of action is carried out—a technique with the goal of restoring the sick person to health or at least relieving the symptoms. The treatment is based on the healer's understanding of the agent and cause of the diagnosed illness: a virus, a parasite, a poison, a psychological trauma, a sorcerer's spell. In general, healing activities try to avoid, remove, or nullify the influence of whatever or whoever is believed to be responsible for the illness.

Diagnosis of disease involves a folk taxonomy consisting of the categories of disease and the attributes by which they may be recognized. In American folk culture, for example, a cold is recognized by such symptoms as stuffiness, aches, slight fever, and so forth; but if the fever is high and accompanied by other discomforts, the disease may be categorized as the flu. (See D'Andrade 1976.) Charles Frake has given us an excellent analysis of the diagnostic process as carried out by the Subanun of the southern Philippines:

Subanun diagnosis is the procedure of judging similarities and differences among instances of "being sick," placing new instances into culturally defined and linguistically labelled categories. . . . There are 132 diagnostic categories which possess unique, single-word labels. The Subanun must consequently rote-learn unique and distinctive labels for the vast majority of his diseases [and] all Subanun do, in fact, learn to use such a copious vocabulary of disease . . . terms with great facility [1961:114–116].

The disease categories found in any culture are not independent of one another: they are grouped on several contrasting levels. For example, the general category used by the Subanun to indicate wounds is *samad*; this term contrasts with the general term for skin diseases, *nuka*. Within the latter category there are several more specific levels, including specific disease names such as *pugu,* 'rash,' and *bugais,* 'spreading itch,' and intermediate categories such as *beldut,* 'sore,' which itself includes a number of specific illnesses. Most types of disease recognized by the Subanun are diagnosed by observation and verbal description of their symptoms. If patients wish to know how and why they fell sick, however, they must consult a *belian,* 'medium,' who communicates with the gods to get this information and to request a cure.

The Navajo Indians have several types of diviners. One is the hand-trembler. To diagnose an illness, he prays to Gila Monster while sprinkling pollen on his arm and laying out four kinds of beads. Then he begins a song. "As soon as the hand-trembler begins to sing, and sometimes even before, his hand and arm begin to shake violently. The way in which the hand moves as it shakes provides the information sought" (Kluckhohn and Leighton 1946:148). Navajo divination reveals which curing chant should be performed for the patient.

Why is one type of treatment rather than another used in a given society? The answer to this question is related to the *belief system* of the society. (See Chapter 9.) For example, most American doctors have been trained in the germ theory of disease: since they believe that certain categories of infectious diseases are caused by bacteria that can be destroyed by penicillin, their plan of treatment is to inject the patient with a suitable amount of penicillin. *The technique is deduced from the belief system—* in this case, the beliefs in bacteria as agents of infection and in penicillin as an effective antibacterial drug. (This does not explain, of course, why thousands of doctors give penicillin injections for virus infections upon which the treatment can have no effect.)

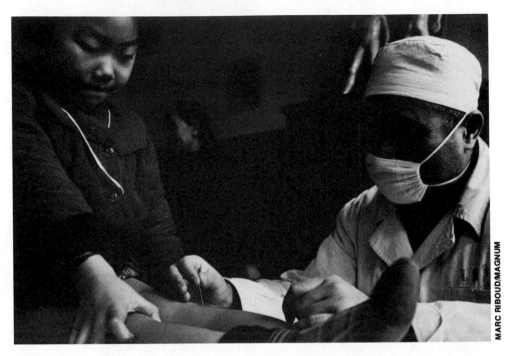

MARC RIBOUD/MAGNUM

Treatment through the technique of acupuncture, in the Children's Hospital in Peking.

If a culture includes beliefs in witchcraft, viruses, soul-loss, nuclear radiation, or possession by evil spirits, it will probably include techniques for dealing with these causes of illness, based on cultural expectations about the way these causes operate. For example, the Navajo Indians believe that violations of taboo or contact with bears, snakes, lightning, or enemy ghosts can bring on illness. The illness, however, is regarded as a *symptom of disharmony* between the sick person and the supernatural world. The Navajo distinguish between contagious disease (*naatniih*) and a more general category of body ache (*tah hooneesgai*), and they believe that

all ailments, mental or physical, are of supernatural origin. The notion of locating the cause of a disease in physiological processes is foreign to Navaho thought. The cause of disease, of injury to the body or to one's property, of continued misfortune of any kind, must be traced back to some accidental or deliberate violation of one of the [taboos], or to contact with a ghost, or to witch activity. It follows logically that treatment consists in dealing with these causative factors and not with the illness or injury as such. The supernaturals must be appeased. If a visible sign of attack is present, it must be removed, or the patient must be treated on the general principle that he has been attacked by supernaturals or by supernatural means and that his supernatural relationships need to be restored to normal condition again. The ultimate aim of every curing ceremonial is this restoration [Kluckhohn and Leighton 1946:132–133].

This does not explain why primitive cures are so often successful. How is it possible for unscientific practices to produce cures, or for black magic to cause illness and death? First of all we must recognize that when people are sick they want something done to make them well. It is nearly as important that *something* be done as that the medically correct thing be done. Even in our own society, physicians often produce apparent cures by giving anxious patients a *placebo.* Sugar pills and saltwater injections are common placebos. As Jerome D. Frank points out, however, until quite recently *most* prescribed medications were "pharmacologically inert," whether the doctors realized it or not. "Despite their inadvertent reliance on placebos, physicians maintained an honored reputation as successful healers, implying that these remedies were generally effective." In recent studies, placebos have been shown to be effective in curing such diverse illnesses as peptic ulcer, warts, and mental disturbances (Frank 1963:66).

How can a placebo produce a cure? When physicians in our society prescribe medication they are doing what patients expect of them—performing their role. This very action seems to raise patients' hopes and allay their anxiety. Placebos are most effective for patients who have favorable attitudes toward medicine and doctors. "It appears that the ability to respond favorably to a placebo is not so much a sign of excessive gullibility, as one of easy acceptance of others in their socially defined roles" [Frank 1963:70].

At least two factors are involved in such cures: suggestion and social support. The suggestion that "this [pill, prayer, amulet] will help you" is an important part of every healer's power— the more so if the patient really wants to believe. The successes of many faith healers can be attributed to this factor. (Suggestion can even cause some drugs to have the opposite of their usual effects.) In primitive societies, where shamans or curers have the confidence of their patients and where their powers are bolstered by sleight-of-hand and confident claims, suggestion probably plays a large part in the cures they achieve.

Social support also contributes a great deal to cures. In nearly every society sick people have a special place in the social struc-

ture—the sick role—which entitles them to special consideration. A severe illness generally results in the mobilization of a
social group to give aid and comfort. Among the Navajo, the
patient becomes the center of attention during a curing ceremony that may last as long as nine days and nights. During this
time, the patient's self-esteem grows, for relatives rally around
to pay for and assist in the ceremony while the singer—an older
man of high prestige and great experience—gives assurances
that the patient will recover.

Some techniques for curing illness involve considerable pain
or at least discomfort for the patient. Western psychologists
have come to the conclusion that many psychosomatic illnesses
are triggered by an individual's *need for punishment:* suffering
(which is genuine) represents an attempt to atone for unconscious feelings of guilt. A painful or humiliating treatment can
satisfy this need for punishment and indirectly relieve the patient of symptoms. Perhaps the effectiveness of some primitive
techniques rests on such a psychological mechanism. (It has
been suggested that the apparent therapeutic value of psychi-
atric shock treatments derives from this source.)

The superiority of scientific medicine is due to more valid
beliefs about human physiology and the nature of disease.
Western culture has accumulated an extensive body of such
knowledge and has developed elaborate means of recording,
evaluating, teaching, and applying this knowledge by means of
medical publications, schools, conferences, hospitals, and so
forth. But these techniques are expensive, and the costs are
not only monetary. There have been losses too. Part of primitive
curers' effectiveness comes from their intimate personal knowledge of their patients and what is likely to be troubling them—
for example, whether an illness is complicated by economic
problems or by family conflict. Scientific medicine tends to be
impersonal, with patients known to the doctors only as cases or
numbers. Hospitals, excellent as they often are, have become
total institutions that all too often deprive patients of the social
support they need.

The new subfield of *medical anthropology* studies both the
curing techniques of non-Western societies and the institutions
of Western society (hospitals, mental asylums, tuberculosis san-
itariums, and so forth) to understand how they do or do not help
those who need them. Anthropology has an important practical
role to play: the anthropologist can identify the positive and
negative aspects of medical treatment in all societies, including
our own, and may help in discovering more effective techniques
of healing. Medical anthropologists have studied such diverse

subjects as the training of medical students, nutrition, old people's homes, and resistance to scientific medicine in other societies. Such studies have important consequences for the populations studied and also for anthropological theory. (See Nader and Maretzki 1973.)

TECHNIQUES FOR MAKING OBJECTS: CRAFTS

Associated with most categories of objects made by human beings are plans (techniques) for making them. These *craft techniques* are often a mixture of practical knowledge and supernatural belief. Acquired skills are extremely important. Even within our own civilization, many skills and techniques—such as those involved in making fine violins or stained-glass windows—have been all but lost. A survey of the variety of techniques employed by primitive people in weaving, pottery-making, canoe-building, and metallurgy shows the ingenuity of many primitive cultures in meeting their needs without polluting or despoiling the environment.

Weaving Baskets and Fabrics

Weaving must be a very ancient technique, for woven objects are found in every society. Even the Siriono of Bolivia, who subsist with few tools, make two kinds of baskets from palm leaves, and spin both bark fibers and cotton for use in making hammocks, baby slings, bowstrings, and arrows (Holmberg 1969:11). Baskets are widely used as containers by hunting and gathering peoples. The Australian aborigines, for example, wove a few crude types of baskets. In general, basket-making is a female occupation, perhaps because it is closely associated with food-gathering, which is also usually women's work.

In southern California, baskets were made by *coiling*. This technique involves a spiral foundation (the warp), which is bound back upon itself with a more flexible material (the woof) and shaped upward as it grows in diameter. Farther north in California, coiling was combined with other techniques. Among northern California tribes such as the Pomo and the Maidu, basket-making reached great heights of perfection. The masters of this craft used dozens of materials and techniques for weaving and decoration. The very elaboration of the techniques showed an appreciation of the "aesthetic value of technical perfection." As Franz Boas wrote:

Virtuosity, complete control of technical processes ... means an automatic regularity of movement. The basketmaker who manufactures a coiled basket, handles the fibres composing the coil in such a way that the greatest evenness of coil diameter results. In making her stitches the automatic control of the left hand that lays down the coil, and of the right that pulls the binding stitches over the coil brings it about that the distances between the stitches and the strength of the pull are absolutely even so that the surface will be smooth and evenly rounded and that the stitches show a perfectly regular pattern. ... The same observation may be made in twined basketry. In the handiwork of an expert the pull of the woof string will be so even that there is no distortion of the warp strings and the twisted woof will lie in regularly arranged loops. Any lack of automatic control will bring about irregularities of surface pattern [1955:20].

The craftworker is seldom aware of exactly how her skill is applied. She may be able to state the criteria she uses in choosing and preparing materials for weaving, and the specific techniques of weaving can be communicated through verbal instruction and visual demonstration. Developing the skills is another matter.

In true weaving, two sets of threads are used, the warp and the woof, crossing each other at right angles. *Simple weaving* involves passing the woof under and over alternate warp threads. More complex forms of weaving (also found in basketry) include *twilling,* in which the woof passes over two or more warp threads, and *twining,* in which alternative woof strands either twist around one another or actually wrap around the warp threads (wrapped twining).

The loom—a device for holding warp threads and storing completed work—makes possible variations of weave and increased speed. Improvements in the loom include use of the *heddle rod,* with thread loops (heddles) attached to groups of warp threads to lift them together, and the *shuttle,* which carries the woof across the warp. In Europe, Africa, and parts of Asia warp threads were suspended vertically in an *upright loom,* a frame of posts driven into the ground. In South and Southeast Asia, the *horizontal loom* has long been the major form. The back-strap loom is one in which the horizontal warp threads are held taut by a strap passed around the weaver's back. (Horizontal looms were spread widely through the Pacific islands; the oc-

A Navajo woman weaves a rug on an upright loom. The complex designs are reproduced entirely from memory.

The pottery shown here is an example of the coiling technique used by the Pueblo Indians in New Mexico.

currence of the back-strap loom both in Indonesia and in pre-Columbian South and Central America has been used as evidence of trans-Pacific contacts.)

Making Pottery

Pottery-making is a much younger craft than weaving. The earliest known pottery appeared in the Near East somewhat less than 8,000 years ago. Pottery-making techniques spread rapidly in both the Old and the New World. This craft is found everywhere that cultivation is found and among some food-collecting peoples as well. Pottery is not really suitable for nomadic or highly mobile societies; but with settled villages and a food surplus it becomes most useful.

Coiling is the basic pottery-making technique throughout the New World and outside of true agricultural areas in the Old World. It is similar to the technique used in the coiling of a basket, as described by Boas:

Long round strips of clay are laid down spirally beginning at the bottom. By continued turning and gradual laying on of more and more strips in a continued spiral the pot is built up. Complete control of the technique will result in a perfectly round cross section and in smooth curvatures of the sides. Lack of skill will bring about lack of symmetry and of smoothness of curvature. Virtuosity and regularity of surface and form are here also intimately related [1955:21].

Coiled pottery may be finished in any number of ways. The exterior may be scraped smooth with a shell and polished with a stone or left plain. The potter may decorate it by pinching the coils together, by smoothing it with a paddle, by stamping or painting it with a design, by covering it with a slip of thin clay, and so forth.

Since pottery is one of the most varied and durable objects made, archaeologists can study its manufacture in great detail. They use their knowledge of materials, techniques, form, decoration, and firing to identify pottery and pottery fragments (potsherds) in order to discover chronologies, historical distributions, and past culture contacts.

The *potter's wheel* was developed in the agricultural areas of the Old World; it is derived from the true wheel. In its early forms it is turned by the hands or feet of the potter; in later forms it employs other sources of energy. The principal advantage of the wheel is that it makes possible the rapid manufacture of highly symmetrical and standardized pottery. In most places where the potter's wheel has been introduced, the making of pottery has changed from a skill practiced as part of the usual female role to a craft practiced primarily by male specialists.

Decoration and *firing* complete the vessel. Pots must be carefully dried, because an excess of moisture will cause them to break in the firing. The vessels must be heated to over 400° C. (about 750° F.) to transform the clay into pottery and to ensure that it will not revert to clay when wet. Too much heat, on the other hand, will melt the clay or make it too fragile for use. Baking is a delicate process, whether the pots are baked in open fires or enclosed chambers (kilns).

Building a Canoe

Canoe-building is another highly skilled craft. Since the consequences of a canoe's coming apart can be drastic, the entire process is often surrounded with ritual. Among the Trobriand Islanders, construction of the seagoing canoe (*masawa*) involves two stages of work and at least three systems of magic. In the first stage of the work

> the component parts are prepared. A big tree is cut, trimmed into a log, then hollowed out and made into the basic dug-out; the planks, poles, and sticks are prepared. . . . This stage generally takes a long time, some two to six months, and is done in fits and starts, as other occupations allow or as the mood comes. The spells and rites which accompany it belong to the *tokway* magic, and to that of the flying canoe cycle. To this first stage also belongs the carving of the decorative prow-boards. This is done sometimes by the builder, sometimes by another expert, if the builder cannot carve.
>   The second stage is done by means of intense communal labor. As a rule this stage is spread over a short time. . . . The actual labor in which the whole community is energetically engaged takes up only some three to five days. The work consists of the piecing together of the planks and prow-boards . . . and then of the lashing them together. Next comes the piecing and lashing of the outrigger, caulking and painting of the canoe. Sail-making is also done at this time. . . . The second stage of canoe-building is accompanied by Kula magic, and by a series of exorcisms on the canoe. . . . The lashing of the canoe with a specially strong creeper, called *wayugo,* is accompanied by perhaps the most important of the rites and spells belonging to the flying canoe magic [Malinowski 1961:125–126].

The *tokway* magic is addressed to the evil spirit who lives in the chosen tree; it is an attempt to expel him from the tree before it is cut down. The flying canoe magic is related to a mythological cycle and is intended to give the canoe great speed; it also gives protection from evil spirits, such as the dreaded "flying witches," believed to be the principal dangers to travelers. The *kula* magic is primarily concerned with ensuring a safe and successful trading voyage, and parts of it are performed in connection with building and decorating the canoe. Magic enters into every phase of the construction, and though some spells may be omitted, others must always be performed. The Trobriand natives do not separate the technical and the magical aspects of the construction. As Malinowski comments, "The magician does not produce the impression of an officiating high priest performing a solemn ceremony, but rather of a specialized workman doing a particularly important piece of work" (1961:142).

The uncertainty of most seagoing expeditions accounts for the association between canoe-building, sailing, and the supernatural. This association has persisted into modern societies:

in most contemporary fishing villages, there is an annual blessing of the boats, and all around the Mediterranean ships are
painted with large eyes to ward off evil. Nevertheless, most primitive sailors have remarkable skill and navigational knowledge
(Gladwin 1970).

Metallurgy

In the first attempts to use metals they were treated like malle-
able stones. Nuggets of gold and nodules of native copper
(metals that occur in relatively pure forms in nature) could be
cold-hammered into useful or decorative shapes, and these
techniques were known to many peoples who never found a way
to extract the metals from their ores. In some areas experience
with naturally occurring metals gave rise to true metallurgy. Like
pottery-making, metallurgy involves chemical transformation of
compounds by means of intense heat. It requires considerable
technical knowledge and precise control of fire.

Copper was the first metal to be extensively used, starting
perhaps 6,000 years ago in the Near East. Copper was known
there in its native form and some of its carbonate ores were
used as cosmetics. These ores can be reduced to metal at fairly
low temperatures, and it has been conjectured that the technique of reduction may have been discovered by accident—perhaps when some Egyptian matron left her makeup kit too near
the fire one windy night. In any case, the techniques of copper-
working were first developed in the Near East and spread from
there. By about 3000 B.C. two important new techniques had
been developed: *annealing* and *alloying.* When copper is hammered, it becomes quite brittle; but the technique of *annealing*
can soften it again. To be annealed, copper is heated white hot
and plunged into cold water. *Alloying* is the mixing of two or
more metals or of metal and a nonmetallic substance. Copper
mixed with tin produces bronze—an alloy that is much stronger
than either of its component metals alone.

The Bronze Age lasted for about 1,000 years in the Near East.
Techniques of working bronze were illustrated by the fine crafts-
manship of art objects, weapons, personal decorations, and agricultural tools. Among the refined techniques was *casting,*
which speeded and standardized the production of practical
objects: the molten metal was poured into open molds and then
finished by hammering and grinding. The Sumerians developed
a specialized casting technique, the *lost wax method:*

In casting an object by this technique, the craftsman first made a core of clay in the general shape of the object to be cast. When the core was thoroughly dried, he covered it with a layer of wax on which he modeled and incised the details which he wished reproduced in the casting. Lastly, the core and wax layer were enveloped in a clay shell, and the whole fired. The wax melted and ran out, leaving a cavity into which the molten metal could be poured. After the metal had set, the outer shell was broken off and the inner core dug out, leaving a hollow metal casting. This technique has never been improved upon for delicate metal work or for objects only one copy of which was required. It is still used by our own artists in casting small bronze figures [Linton 1955:106].

The Iron Age began about 1500 B.C. in the Near East and much later elsewhere. At first iron was so rare that it was used only for small decorative items. Actually, iron ores are much more plentiful than copper ores, but the techniques required for smelting iron from its ores are quite different from those that will work with copper. Attempts to transfer copper-working skills directly to iron-working can result in disaster. Annealing cast iron can produce a violent explosion; applying this technique to forged iron results not in softening the metal but in hardening it. (This process is technically known as *tempering*.)

The basic techniques of iron-working call for two things: patience and a source of intense heat. The heat, which can be provided by a forge with a forced draft, converts iron ore into "bloom"—a gray, spongy substance that must be patiently hammered to remove the encased iron droplets. Iron must be worked at a high temperature and repeatedly hammered (forged) to give it a toughness equivalent to bronze. Actually, iron remained inferior to bronze in most respects until techniques of smelting were improved and until metallurgists learned to produce a low-grade *steel*. Steel is iron containing a small amount of carbon, which toughens the metal so that it can be shaped and sharpened without becoming brittle. Steel-making techniques may have first been developed in southern India. Some groups in this area still use a simple technique in which "filings of relatively pure wrought iron obtained from the local ores are put in sealed clay vessels with grass and the whole heated in charcoal furnaces. The grass is charred to almost pure carbon, which combines with the molten iron to give steel" (Linton 1955:109).

The general use of metals in cutting tools and containers is quite new. Even in contemporary American culture, wood, basketry, and ceramics are much more important than we realize. A final point should be emphasized. We often read in the mass media about some Melanesian, South American, or African tribe "still living in the Stone Age" and about the difficulties such "backward" peoples experience in "moving overnight into the twentieth century," but how many of the "civilized" readers of this book know how to recognize or to smelt iron ore? Or how to mix copper with tin in the correct proportions to produce bronze? Or, for that matter, how to fashion a decent piece of pottery, basketry, or flint?

It is all very well to be proud of the accomplishments of one's culture, but let us recognize that it is our *culture*—socially shared and transmitted knowledge, beliefs, and expectations— that gives us such technological superiority as we may possess. Without the knowledge and skills of our society's metallurgists and engineers, every one of us would be more helpless than a Stone Age person. Luckily, the "primitive" is *not* thousands of years behind us, for the time required to acquire or to lose the most complex culture pattern is less than a generation. If this were not true, none of us could know all the things that we do know.

RECOMMENDED READING

Charles B. Heiser, Jr., *Seed to Civilization*. San Francisco: W. H. Freeman, 1973. A highly readable description of the domestication of plants and animals in various parts of the world in relation to human nutrition and social organization.

Horacio Fabrega, Jr., *Disease and Social Behavior*. Cambridge: M.I.T. Press, 1974. A contemporary account of disease and healing in various societies by a doctor with extensive anthropological experience.

Thomas Gladwin, *East Is a Big Bird*. Cambridge: Harvard University Press, 1970. A fascinating narrative of the navigational knowledge of Polynesian sailors based on fieldwork (and seawork) at Puluwat atoll. Includes material on the values that these people set on sailing and adventure.

Ralph Linton, *The Tree of Culture*. New York: Knopf, 1955. Still the best single source for a readable overview of human culture history, especially the origin and spread of tools and techniques that affect our lives today.

Leslie A. White, *The Science of Culture*. New York: Grove, 1958. A collection of provocative essays by an anthropologist who formulated an influential point of view on the relationship between energy and culture.

HERAKLION MUSEUM/JOSEPHINE POWELL

PART FOUR
IDEOLOGICAL SYSTEMS

The term *ideology* usually refers to a system of explicit beliefs concerning political and economic affairs. In addition, it has a rather negative connotation: one's enemies are said to have an ideology that distorts their view of reality, whereas one's own political or economic views are (of course) based on an unbiased and reasonable appraisal of "the facts."

In the following chapters, however, the term will be used in a broader and more emotionally neutral sense. *Ideology* denotes *any set of systematized beliefs* and *values shared by the members of a social group.* Every social group has an ideology, though the degree to which it is made explicit or systematic varies greatly from person to person and from group to group.

An ideology includes beliefs and values, that is, conceptions of both what *is* and what *should be.* Although these concepts can be separated for purposes of analysis, they are closely intertwined in human thought. Facts and values are not neatly separated into mutually exclusive compartments. Any real event or person is sufficiently complex that contradictory descriptions can be framed simply by the selection of different sets of equally factual points. Selection and emphasis can produce vast ideological differences, even when the same phenomena are regarded as facts.

These considerations have made many social scientists reluctant to study ideological systems, yet ideologies are no more abstract or subjective than are other parts of culture. Languages, social systems, and even technologies are all composed of shared ideas that must be *inferred from behavior.* No one has ever *seen* a morpheme, a social role, or a technique. These categories and their associated plans must be *discovered* by painstaking comparison of similar forms, aided by native judgments of rightness (grammaticality, appropriateness, and so forth). In the same way, an ideological system must be inferred from social behavior (including speech), supplemented by explicit native value judgments.

Probably the greatest advance in the systematization and explicit transmission of ideology came with the invention of *writing* and the rise of *literate elites* that examined their society's oral traditions, standardizing, elaborating, and codifying them in various ways. This is one of the characteristics of that relatively recent social development we call civilization. In the words of Robert Redfield:

> In a civilization there is a *great tradition* of the reflective few and there is a *little tradition* of the largely unreflective many. The great tradition is cultivated in schools or temples; the little tradition works itself out and keeps itself going in the lives of the unlettered in their village communities. The tradition of the philosopher, theologian, and literary man is a tradition consciously cultivated and handed down; that of the little people is for the most part taken for granted and not submitted to much scrutiny or considered refinement and improvement [1956:41–42].

Until the very recent development of tools and techniques for mass communication, the two traditions were usually separated by physical distance as well as by social class. (See Stover 1974.) The great tradition took form in urban centers, while the little tradition was rooted in the surrounding rural communities. The two traditions, however, depend on one another:

> Great epics have arisen out of elements of traditional tale-telling by many people, and epics have returned again and again to the peasantry for modification and incorporation into local cultures. The ethics of the Old Testament arose out of tribal peoples and

returned to peasant communities after they had been the subject
of thought by philosophers and theologians. . . . Great and little
tradition can be thought of as two currents of thought and action,
distinguishable, yet ever flowing into and out of each other
[Redfield 1956:42–43].

Even in the absence of a literate elite, a high degree of
systematization can take place within an oral tradition. Paul
Radin, in his book *Primitive Man as Philosopher,* has
suggested that in every society some individuals reflect on
their tradition and try to establish some coherence among its
parts; he has gathered many texts that demonstrate the
abstract concerns of such primitive philosophers. Remarkable
as these individual achievements may be, in all societies,
primitive and civilized, most people manage to get through life
with only the vaguest kind of ideology. This does not mean
that they are without beliefs or values—only that they have
little need to make their ideas explicit or logically consistent.

It is mainly in times of conflict that systematizations arise,
either to defend the status quo or to point out its
inconsistencies and call for its overthrow. This is even true of
highly intellectual ideologies such as the Western scientific
tradition. As Thomas S. Kuhn (1964:90) has pointed out,
"normal science" is a great deal like puzzle-solving; during
periods of normal science, scientists go about their work with
little theoretical discussion, guided by standardized concepts
and research procedures that Kuhn calls *paradigms.* It is only
when these paradigms begin to produce inconsistent or
inexplicable kinds of data that the traditional concepts,
procedures, and theories are genuinely questioned and
defended.

Each society considers its own ideology to be the only valid
view of the world. History can show us the *changes* that have
taken place in our own tradition, but it often leaves us
unaware of the continuities (because even the historian takes
them for granted). Anthropology, with its greater range in
space and time, can teach us what is universal and what is
particular, local, or conventional, while helping us to
understand how ideology, technology, language, and social
structure all interact to produce a living, changing culture.

CHAPTER NINE
BELIEF SYSTEMS

B elief systems include all kinds of historically developed and socially transmitted ideas. Some of these ideas are relatively obvious (for example, that the earth is flat and stationary, and that the sun travels across the sky from east to west every day). Other conceptions are based on more elaborate inferences from observations (that *Homo sapiens* evolved from lower forms of life, or that there exist various classes of spiritual beings that are interested in human affairs).

Within a given culture, however, the ideas held about the nature of the universe and our species' place in it tend to form a relatively coherent system. A homogeneous and well-integrated culture is one in which all such beliefs are consistent with one another and mutually reinforcing. Few if any cultures are actually so well integrated; indeed, a perfectly integrated ideological system would be highly unstable, since a change in any one part would have immediate repercussions throughout the culture. But cultures do exhibit a tendency toward internal coherence.

What is the world like? How did it get that way? What is our relationship to the world? Every culture provides implicit or explicit answers to such questions, and to questions that have no objective answers but must be answered if human society is to survive. An essential function of each society's ideology is to help its members answer the very personal questions: Who am I? and What must I do? An individual's *sense of identity* is largely constructed out of materials provided by his social tradition.

COSMOLOGY

Cosmology is that part of an ideological system which explains the origin, structure, and destiny of the universe. Every society has some such conceptions, and they are transmitted to each new generation through the process of enculturation. People tend to accept their society's cosmology as they do its language and technology, for it gives them a sense of identity along with an orientation in socially defined space and time (see Bock 1974:173–201). Even when one is aware of alternative cosmological systems, one's choice of beliefs is more often dictated by social position (group membership) than by objective evaluation of the alternatives.

The cosmologies of nonliterate societies are often articulated in the form of creation myths, which account for the present state of the world by relating past events. One extremely widespread notion is that the earth was once completely covered by water and that specific actions on the part of legendary individuals caused the dry land to appear. In Asia and North America, this idea is frequently encountered in the earth-diver myth, in which

> the culture hero has a succession of animals dive into the primeval waters, or flood of waters, to secure bits of mud or sand from which the earth is to be formed. . . . One after another animal fails; the last one succeeds, however, and floats to the surface half dead, with a little sand or dirt in his claws . . . which is then put on the surface of the water and magically expands to become the world of the present time [Wheeler-Voegelin 1949:334; cf. Dundes 1962].

Another widespread story describes the *emergence* of human ancestors who rose from an underworld by climbing a "world tree." One such myth is told by the Keresan-speaking Pueblo Indians of New Mexico:

> The world of the Pueblo Indians was not created in the beginning; it was always there—or here. But it was somewhat different in the beginning than it is now. The earth was square and flat; it had four

corners and a middle. Below the surface of the earth there were four horizontal layers; each one was a world. The lowest world was a white one. Above that lay the red world and then the blue one. Above the blue world, and just beneath this world that we are living in today, was the yellow world.

In the beginning the people were living deep down inside the earth, in the white world, with their mother, Iyatiku. Finally it was time for them to come out, to ascend to this world. Iyatiku caused a great evergreen tree . . . to grow so that the people could climb up its trunk and boughs to the next world. . . . The people climbed up into the red world and lived there for four years. Then it was time to climb up into the blue world. Again Iyatiku had a tree reach up to the world above, and . . . she had someone make a hole through the hard layer so the tree and the people could pass through.

At last the people were ready to ascend into this world. Iyatiku had Badger make a hole through the hard crust. . . . Badger looked out. "It is very beautiful up there," he told Iyatiku. "There are rain clouds everywhere." So Iyatiku decided it was all right for the people to complete their ascent and emerge into this world. Iyatiku had created societies of medicine men in the lower worlds and had given them their altars and ceremonies. These societies—the Flint, Fire, Giant, and Kapina medicine men—came•out with the people. There were some evil spirits, too, who also came out . . . but no one knew this at that time.

They came out at a place in the north called Shipap. Everything was new and "raw." The earth was too soft for people to walk upon so Iyatiku had the mountain lion use his magic power to harden it. . . . Iyatiku told them they were to migrate toward the south. She said: "I shall not go with you. I am going to return to my home in the white world, but I will be with you always in spirit. You can pray to me and I will always help you." Before she left she appointed a man to take her place. . . . She gave him an ear of corn. "Take this," she told him. "This corn is my heart. This is what you will live on; its milk shall be to you as milk from my breasts."

Iyatiku returned to the lower world and the people began their journey to the south. They stopped at a place and established a pueblo. They called it Kashikatchrutiya or White House. They lived here a long time [White 1960:54–55].

This emergence myth has many interesting features, such as the use of the magical number four and the color symbolism, both of which appear in many Pueblo myths and rituals. The origins of various cultural features are explained by the story— for example, the various medicine societies, the evil spirits, and the corn plant. Cosmologies often have the dual function of describing the world and explaining the origins of important social institutions.

Not all cosmologies include an emergence or even a creation tale. Among the Ojibwa Indians of the Great Lakes region, for instance, the characters in sacred stories "are regarded as living entities who have existed from time immemorial. While there is genesis through birth and temporary or permanent form-shifting through transformation, there is no outright creation" (Hallowell 1960:27).

Every cosmology includes ideas about the constitution of the world and about the various *categories of beings* that are believed to inhabit it, and their relationship to humankind. In nonliterate societies, such beliefs are codified in and transmitted through the myths and legends of the oral tradition. For example, in the following myth from Dahomey, in West Africa, the creator, Mawu-Lisa, gives birth to the major gods and assigns a function to each:

Since Mawu is both man and woman, she became pregnant. The first to be born were a pair of twins [a man and a woman]. The second birth was So [=Sogbo], who had the form of his parent, man and woman in one. The third birth was also twins, a male, Agbé, and a female, Naété. The fourth to be born was Agé, a male; the fifth, Gu, also male. Gu [the god of iron] is all body. He has no head. Instead of a head, a great sword is found coming out of his neck. His trunk is of stone. The sixth birth was not to a being, but to Djo, air, atmosphere. Air was what was needed to create men. The seventh to be born was Legba. Mawu said Legba [the trickster] was to be her spoiled child, because he was the youngest.

One day Mawu-Lisa assembled all the children in order to divide the kingdoms. To the first twins, she gave all the riches and told them to go and inhabit the earth. She said the earth was for them.

Mawu said to Sogbo he was to remain in the sky, because he was both man and woman like his parent. She told Agbé and Naété to go and inhabit the sea, and command the waters. To Agé she gave command of all the animals and birds, and she told him to live in the bush as a hunter.

To Gu, Mawu said he was her strength, and that was why he was not given a head like the others. Thanks to him, the earth would not always remain wild bush. It was he who would teach men to live happily.

Mawu told Djo to live in space between earth and sky. To him was being entrusted the life-span of man. Thanks to him also, his brothers would be invisible, for he will clothe them. . . .

When Mawu said this to the children, she gave the [first] twins the language which was to be used on earth, and took away their memory of the language of the sky. She gave to [Sogbo] the language he would speak, and took from him the memory of the parent language. The same was done for Agbé and Naété, for Agé, and for Gu, but to Djo was given the language of men.

Now she said to Legba, "You are my youngest child. . . . I will keep you with me always. Your work shall be to visit all the kingdoms ruled over by your brothers, and to give me an account of what happens." So Legba knows all the languages known to his brothers, and he knows the language Mawu speaks, too. Legba is Mawu's linguist. If one of the brothers wishes to speak, he must give the message to Legba, for none knows any longer how to address himself to Mawu-Lisa. That is why Legba is everywhere.

You will find Legba even before the houses of the *vodun* [priests], because all beings, humans and gods, must address themselves to him before they can approach God [Herskovits and Herskovits 1958:125–126].

The oral tradition itself is frequently divided into *categories of tales,* some of which are more important than others. For example, in Dahomey the older men do not tell *heho,* 'mere stories.' They concern themselves only with the class of narratives called *hwenoho,* 'traditional history.' The *heho* are told only at night, but the *hwenoho* are told during daylight hours. Sacred myths (such as the creation story given above) are narrated primarily by diviners and priests.

Shared beliefs about the nature of the universe give important clues to the pervasive attitudes found in a society. Beliefs in protective and/or malignant spirits, in a limitless or a bounded cosmos, in inevitable progress or certain calamity—all these beliefs indicate attitudes toward the place of human beings in the universe. One cannot understand the origins of Christianity without realizing that the Apostles expected the imminent destruction of the world. Among the Yaruro Indians of southern Venezuela, Anthony Leeds discovered a homogeneous world view that clearly corresponds to Yaruro social structure.

The Yaruro are simple horticulturalists who also do a limited amount of hunting and collecting. They have a strong sexual division of labor and property, but little other social or economic differentiation. Each Yaruro village is composed of several related households; the village has a spokesman, but his authority is slight. Great individual freedom of choice exists in economic, social, and even religious affairs. Each village constitutes a separate and independent center of relationships with neighboring villages and consequently has its own unique assortment of outside relationships. There are no political units above the village level. This situation is reflected in the cosmology:

According to the Yaruro, the cosmos originally lacked not only humans, but even gods. There existed only three, concentric, rigid, blue, celestial domes; below them, a flat, undifferentiated, vast savanna all of sand; and a cold, dark, flat underworld. Beyond these there was, and is, nothing. Thunder, already then, was to be found between the upper celestial domes, while Sun, his wife, Moon, and their children, the stars, were already revolving between the lower two.

Into this cosmos were spontaneously born the primordial gods. The goddess Ku'man, the grandmother of us all, who lives in a land to the west, out of the savanna created the discrete lands of her fellow gods and of the Yaruro. She created the . . . peoples. . . . She instructed the men and the women in their crafts. She ordained the social order.

The Yaruro do not consider the parts of the cosmos to be rigidly separated; rather, there is continuous communication among the various worlds. The gods are believed to be tied to one another and to humans by kinship and by visiting, just as the Yaruro households and villages are interrelated:

The relations between men and gods, the communication between the hither- and other-worlds, the cosmography itself, all show quite clearly that there is no separation of "natural" and "supernatural" as discrete classes of events. The cosmos, society, and man are a single system in Yaruro thought.

The principal mode of communication between the two worlds is the night-long religious ceremony known as the *tonghé,* during which a village shaman visits the other world and the gods, in turn, visit the village through his body.

The directness of contact between man and gods again emphasizes the unity of cosmos, society and man. Within this unity, the sharp division of a male sphere from a female sphere is found. These quite coordinate spheres, in the other-worlds as in the hither-world, in religion as in socio-economic life, are linked through the household [Leeds 1960:1–10].

Every cosmology also contains beliefs about *death,* and most include some conception of an afterlife. For the Yaruro the dead are not far away—they continue to help and advise their living kinsmen. During the *tonghé,* they speak through the shaman's body, urging peace and equality. They do not coerce or punish, nor are they manipulated by the living.

Among the Navajo, on the other hand, the ghosts of the dead are greatly feared, and anything connected with death is carefully avoided. Traditionally, if a death took place inside a Navajo hogan, that dwelling was abandoned or destroyed; Navajo patients have been known to flee from a hospital upon learning that a death has taken place there. The Navajo have no desire to establish contact with the dead; indeed, many of their elaborate ceremonies are designed to drive away ghosts or to cure illnesses that are believed to have resulted from contact with a ghost.

Among the Trobriand Islanders, as Malinowski observed, the attitudes of the people toward the *baloma* (spirits of the dead) are highly ambivalent. It is believed that the *baloma* will someday be reborn in another body; they are honored by feasts at harvest time when they return to their villages from the island of the dead. It is also believed, however, that another aspect of a dead person's spirit, called the *kosi,* leads "a short and precarious existence after death near the village and about the usual haunts of the dead man, such as his garden, or the seabeach, or the waterhole. . . . People are distinctly afraid of meeting the *kosi,* and are always on the lookout for him, but they are not in really deep terror of him. Nobody has ever been hurt, still less killed by a *kosi*" (Malinowski 1955:150–151). These two sets of beliefs exist side by side, and the Trobrianders do not usually attempt to reconcile them.

Ancestor cults are found in many Oriental and African societies, usually in those with unilineal descent groups. Each major lineage honors its own set of founding ancestors, and it is often believed that sickness or disasters affecting the members of a lineage are due to neglect of ancestors. In the case of clans, the founding ancestor may be legendary, but belief in common descent and participation in the ancestor cult serve to integrate such dispersed groups.

Whatever the specific contents of the belief system, it provides the survivors with something to *do* in the face of death and thus channels their grief into socially acceptable actions. Ritualized mourning and funeral procedures are found in most societies. In many groups, almost every death is believed to have been caused by witchcraft, and so the response to a death is a search for and punishment of the guilty party. Death in war often calls for retaliation against the group (though not necessarily the individual) held responsible (cf. Ariès 1974).

Individual attitudes toward death are strongly influenced by

social ideology. The dying and their kin may be comforted by beliefs about reincarnation or a happy afterlife. Personal bravery and disdain for mere long life were basic ideals of Crow Indian society. There was a notable development of stoicism among the warriors, and death was not feared by most people. One class of warriors, known as "Crazy-Dogs-Wishing-to-Die," was pledged to such recklessness that its members usually got their wish within a year, although only after doing great damage to the enemy. One vision-song was translated as follows: "Eternal are the heavens and the earth; old people are poorly off; do not be afraid." Lowie describes this sentiment as "one of the most characteristic of the Crow: mortals cannot expect to live forever like the great phenomena of nature; let them console themselves with the thought that old age is a thing of evil and court death while still young" (Lowie 1956:330, 114).

In most societies, religion is not a separate category of experience and action. There is, rather, a *religious dimension* to every part of life. The Western contrast between natural and supernatural is simply not relevant to the understanding of such societies. In the words of Dorothy Lee (1959:170):

> The world view of a particular society includes that society's conception of man's own relation to the universe, human and non-human, organic and inorganic, secular and divine, to use our own dualisms. It expresses man's view of his own role in the maintenance of life, and of the forces of nature. His attitude toward responsibility and initiative is inextricable from his conception of nature as deity-controlled, man-controlled, regulated through a balanced cooperation between god and man, or perhaps maintained through some eternal homeostasis, independent of man and perhaps of any deity. The way a man acts, his feeling of guilt and achievement, and his very personality, are affected by the way he envisions his place within the universe.

People everywhere attempt to understand and bring order and value into the natural world. In our own cultural tradition, science has taken over much of this task, but we can understand that the social function of myth and ritual is to create a "coherent pattern of meanings, in terms of which the worshippers understand the order of the world and their relation to it" (Lienhardt 1966:133; cf. Turner 1969).

Funeral rites in East Toradja, Indonesia, involve an elaborately constructed bier and professional mourners (in black) who cry, sing dirges, and dance.

CONCEPTS OF AUTHORITY

The problem of social authority can be stated quite simply: Why do followers follow? Given that some individuals command the actions of others, what allows them to do so?

Most social systems provide positive and negative *sanctions* (rewards or punishments) which are applied to ensure obedience. A follower may obey a command out of expectation of benefits (such as land, money, and prestige) or fear of punishment. In a military social system, the penalties for failure to obey an order are clearly defined, and rewards for obedience are also well understood (promotions, passes, medals, and so forth).

Still, although sanctions (or the threat of sanctions) are important to social control, they are not sufficient to ensure obedience. Throughout history, people have rebelled against authority for *ideological* reasons, especially when they have ceased to believe in the legitimacy of a leader's claim to authority over them. All social relationships require that both parties live up to the rights and obligations of their respective roles, but the leader/follower relationship always involves some asymmetry of authority, contrary to the norm of reciprocity. If authority relationships are to exist without constant conflict, the followers must believe in the *right* of the leader to make decisions and command actions (cf. Milgram 1974).

Political philosophers have tried to imagine a society in which no person was believed to have legitimate authority over another. They disagree as to whether anarchy is desirable (or even possible). Ethnographic evidence is also conflicting. The Nuer have been described, for example, as living in a state of "ordered anarchy." Lacking chiefs, courts, or any kind of centralized government, they nevertheless maintain order and ensure cooperation through the balanced opposition of lineage segments. Disputes are often settled through the good offices of certain religious officials (leopard-skin chiefs). Even the Nuer have a greater differentiation of authority than some simpler hunting and gathering groups, such as the Yaruro and the Canadian Cree, among whom the ideal of complete equality was very nearly realized. Many of the Indian tribes of the Canadian subarctic are characterized by a pattern of "fierce egalitarianism" that makes large-scale cooperation virtually impossible, since they reject all but the most temporary kinds of authority (Bock 1966:65–71).

Peter M. Gardner has described a similar pattern of life among the Paliyans of South India. This society represents an extreme of egalitarianism and individualism. The main feature of Paliyan social structure is what Gardner calls *symmetric respect,* according to which "one should avoid both aggression (hence competition) and dependence (hence cooperation)." This pattern is manifested in the following areas of Paliyan culture:

1. Socialization
Paliyan children, after an initial period of indulgence, receive a minimum of parental supervision and soon become extremely independent and self-reliant.

2. Noncooperative Behavior
The largest cooperating groups are nuclear families, and even here sharing is minimal. Marriages are unstable and many people never marry. Village membership is constantly changing. "No corporate functions are associated with village life. . . . There are no formalized ways of uniting, either 'democratically' or under leaders, during times of crisis." *Self-sufficiency* is expected of all persons. "To fail in this regard is to interfere with the rights of others." Paliyans "are hesitant to become emotionally involved with others and equally reluctant to unite toward practical goals."

3. Avoidance of Competition
The Paliyan ideal is nonviolent. "Avoidance of overt aggression is considered to be their first rule." Even competition in games is forbidden. "Social or economic differences must be minimized or denied and Paliyans are self-conscious about receiving anything which sets them off from others." *Disrespect* in any form is strictly prohibited: nothing must be said or done which appears to lower or disparage the status of another.

4. Social Control
No individuals or groups are empowered to resolve disputes, but a number of informal techniques are available. To avoid the outbreak of hostility, drinking of alcohol is forbidden and tension is released in fantasy. "When friction does arise, mature individuals frequently step forward and talk to the parties in conflict, joking with them or soothing their feelings. . . . The efforts of the conciliators are acted out without imposition of authority from above, for [they] have no mandate to order, arbitrate, or even suggest more appropriate behavior."

Separation of parties whose conflict cannot be conciliated is a frequently used device, and married couples often separate after their first serious quarrel; "serial marriages" are thus common. In serious crises, when decisions must be made, certain individuals become "possessed" and the gods speak through them. Thus necessary authority can be exercised without disrupting the "purely human patterns of symmetric roles and self-reliance."

5. Ideology

Individualism is found even in the sphere of everyday knowledge and beliefs; for example, informants frequently disagreed on the folk taxonomy of common plants, and "lacked either the ability or desire to repeat songs, prayers or rituals." They placed no special value on set or traditional versions: "There were no formalized bodies of knowledge. . .formal teaching did not exist. . . . Paliyans communicate very little at all times and become almost silent by the age of 40. Verbal, communicative persons are regarded as abnormal and often as offensive. Gossip is practically non-existent" (Gardner 1966).

The high degree of variation within the Paliyan belief system is both a cause and a result of the lack of communication and cooperation in the Paliyan social system. Sharing of common categories and plans is essential to smooth social interaction, but sharing of culture is *produced* by a high level of interaction. When people communicate freely with one another, they come to share common or complementary expectations; when communication within or between groups breaks down, interests and beliefs tend to diverge and cooperation becomes increasingly difficult. This process may be seen in the relations among all kinds of groups, from families to nation states.

Most of the small societies studied by anthropologists show a relatively homogeneous *core* of shared beliefs plus a variable amount of *specialized* or esoteric knowledge that is carried and transmitted by the performers of specialized roles (see Figure 9.1). This kind of cultural structure promotes social integration (through sharing and interdependence) while permitting cultural growth (through the addition of new specialized roles). Societies differ, however, in the kinds of knowledge they allocate to specialists and the ways in which these specialists are recruited.

The Siuai, described by Douglas L. Oliver, are a "society of forest-dwelling gardeners and pig-breeders" in the Solomon Is-

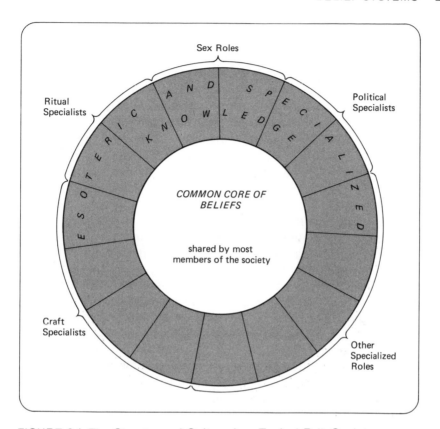

The circular diagram contains the following labels:

Sex Roles

Ritual Specialists

Political Specialists

ESOTERIC KNOWLEDGE AND SPECIALIZED

COMMON CORE OF BELIEFS

shared by most members of the society

Craft Specialists

Other Specialized Roles

FIGURE 9.1 The Structure of Culture in a Typical Folk Society

lands. They have a class of indigenous leaders known as *mumis.* The role of *mumi* is gained by achievement. He is not an official of a political system. The *mumi* gains renown (*poku*) and power through personal effort, primarily by acquiring wealth and distributing it generously in fulfillment of his kinship obligations and in competitive feast-giving.

Not all Siuai males aspire to become *mumis*: they recognize that the role takes a certain type of character as well as much hard work and sacrifice. As one native put it, " 'When he sits down he works and thinks about pigs and money; when we [non-leaders] sit down we sleep' " (1955:396). Wealth alone is not enough to make a man a *mumi*; it must be translated into symbols of prestige: a large and often frequented clubhouse, many slit-gongs, magical formulas, and feasts that are long remembered. Every powerful *mumi* in the course of his career builds a clubhouse and fills it with slit-gongs—or rather, has it built and filled for him. For it is by organizing the men of his community to do his bidding and then by compensating them with a generous feast that his renown grows. There are no great differences in the everyday living standards of the Siuai, but the miser who possesses wealth but does not give feasts or who skimps on his funeral contributions is held in contempt and could never become a leader.

The authority exercised by the *mumi* stimulates agricultural production and pig-raising for feasts, the building of structures and the manufacture of tradable articles, the procurement of shell money, the circulation, accumulation, and consumption of goods, and artistic activities, including music, drama, and various crafts. Thus the "political" leadership in this society has important implications for ritual and economic affairs. The leader does not possess any supernatural attributes himself, but the Siuai believe he controls a fierce demon (*horomorun*). This demon is thought to inhabit his clubhouse; it helps protect the *mumi's* property and person. While many Siuai have spirit-familiars, the *horomorun* is believed to be the most powerful in his area and must be appeased with many sacrifices and feasts. The more feasts a *mumi* gives, "the more nourishment is provided for his club-house demon, which waxes in size, in ferocity, and in loyal and protective adherence to the owner's person as well as property" (1955:379). The respect and fear that the Siuai display toward this demon is a reflection of their attitudes toward the leader; thus the *horomorun* provides supernatural sanctions for the authority of the *mumi.*

In most tribal societies, the political, economic, and religious functions of leadership are not separate. Whatever his title, the leader commands the actions of others for the benefit of the social group as a whole. He is a source of both continuity and change, a decision-maker, and a determiner of *social organization*. His choices are constrained by the social structure, but he introduces personal factors into his decisions, which affect the social structure. (See Chapter 6.)

The Soga peoples of Uganda offer a contrasting example of concepts of authority. Before the British colonial administration, the Soga were divided into fifteen small kingdom-states, each ruled by a king from the royal clan. Junior members of the royal clan were found throughout the kingdom in control of groups of villages. These princes constituted a threat to the king's authority. Civil war often broke out when the problem of succession arose, for there was no clear-cut rule of seniority within the royal group.

An important stabilizing influence in the kingdom, however, was the patron/client relationship. The king's administrative staff was made up of commoners bound to the ruler by personal loyalty. Since they did not share the inherited rank of the princes, these clients had no legitimate claim to the kingship, but they did act as "a check upon the ruler's power, since if he failed to govern within the limits set by custom they might combine in support of a rival prince and drive him from his position." The Soga royal hierarchy of Kings and Princes is *hierarchy* not unlike the feudal system of the late Middle Ages in Europe:

> At the top was the hereditary ruler—the paramount holder of authority and the central symbol of the kingdom's unity. At intermediate levels were the princes administering villages or clusters of villages and, counterbalancing them, the ruler's administrative staff of client-chiefs administering other villages or village clusters in the name of the ruler. Forming the broad base of the society were the communities of commoner agriculturalists organized into corporate patrilineal groups. Commoner and royal, kinsman and kinsman, patron and client, were bound together by highly personal rights and obligations. Subordinates owed superiors economic support through the payment of tribute, military support in war, the recognition of judicial and administrative authority, and personal loyalty. Subordinates in turn received paternalistic protection and aid [Fallers 1955:296–298].

Lloyd Fallers describes how this leadership system, based on kinship and personal loyalty, conflicted with the British colonial administration. After their conquest of Uganda in 1892, the British gradually established a *bureaucratic* civil service (the African Local Government) in which advancement was based on *objective competence.* During the 1930s, payment of tribute to chiefs was forbidden; literacy, education, and ability were increasingly made the basis of recruitment to positions of authority. At first, the rulers' and chiefs' sons, who monopolized the mission schools, had an advantage in gaining positions in the civil service, but with more widespread education, eligibility was extended to others.

The transition from hereditary to bureaucratic leadership was quite smooth. The traditional ideology, however, did not disappear: it continues to exist alongside the new beliefs and values, causing recurrent conflict. The principal incompatibility is between the traditional norms of kinship obligations and personal loyalty on the one hand and the bureaucratic norm of disinterested service on the other. Since both the traditional and the bureaucratic ideologies are accepted by most Soga, and since the same individuals are subjected to their conflicting demands, it is not surprising that there is a high casualty rate among chiefs. Whichever norm they follow, they deviate from the other. Fallers feels that this conflict is preferable to having Soga society split into opposing factions, but the contradictory demands do create a serious predicament for individuals in positions of authority. "There are indications that for chiefs who do contrive to avoid falling afoul of sanctions, and who remain in office, this success is achieved at considerable psychic cost" (1955:303).

CONCEPTS OF PROPERTY

Property is a cultural universal, but specific concepts of property vary widely among and even within human societies. There is variation in both the *categories* of property recognized by different peoples and the *plans* for action associated with each category. A personal possession in one society may be public property in another. The meaning of "personal possession" varies as well. In some societies, even highly valuable items may be taken or used without permission by specific categories of kin. For example, in both Polynesia and South Africa, a boy or man is "permitted to take many liberties with his mother's brother and to take any of his uncle's possessions that he may desire" (Radcliffe-Brown 1952:16).

There is an important distinction between rights of *use* and rights of *disposal*. A society may recognize the exclusive rights of a group or of specific individuals to use some category of property and yet may place limitations on their right to dispose of the property. In many nonliterate societies, what looks like ownership of tribal lands by a ruler is actually more like a public trust. In much of Africa, the usual pattern was symbolic ownership by the ruler, with constant redistribution and free use of land by members of the group. The idea that rights over land could be sold to an outsider was simply not present in the traditional ideology.

Hunting and gathering groups tend to range freely within their tribal territories, though particular fishing sites, berry bushes, or trees may be controlled by specific bands or families. Individual ownership of tracts is usually found only where the trapping of fur-bearing animals or the gathering of a cash crop (such as rubber) supplements or replaces subsistence activities.

It is the yield rather than the land itself that is important. Similarly, the herding peoples of Africa and Asia placed few limitations on land use within the tribal territory, though watering places (especially wells) were often controlled by specific families. As Herskovits has noted:

> Grazing land as such is rarely if ever owned by individuals, and . . . a presumption of group ownership is strong. It also seems probable that the vagueness of the boundary lines where restriction of tenure exists is a result of the seasonal nature of grazing and the large resources of land available to most herding peoples. This in turn must lower any scarcity value it may possess, making it a matter approaching indifference where a given herd grazes, since all herds can be adequately cared for [1952:349].

Horticultural peoples have a great variety of land tenure beliefs and practices. Where land is plentiful, anyone who can clear and plant a tract is entitled to its yield. Where land is scarce, or where considerable investment of labor in irrigation or terracing is necessary, notions of tenure are more complex. Individuals must assert their claims to rights over land on the basis of criteria recognized as legitimate by the society.

Corporate groups such as clans, lineages, and communities often control all of the productive land in a tribal territory, and individuals can acquire rights of use only through membership in or relationship to some such group. For example, in a society with corporate matrilineages, a man can claim certain rights in the land of his own (that is, his mother's) lineage. He may also have some claim to the land controlled by his father's matrilineage even though he himself is not a member. Among the Hopi, a married man usually works the fields allocated to his wife's household by her clan. A unilineal group that has more land than it needs may adopt members.

It is not unusual to find several types of land tenure within a single society. Malinowski described three different *categories of land* in the Trobriand Islands, each of which is associated with a different *plan for use.* The three categories are (1) village sites, (2) uncleared forest, and (3) garden plots. Restrictions are placed on the first and third land categories, while every member of the community has access to the second. The garden land is divided into plots, and an individual or a gardening team works each one (Herskovits 1952:351). There are at least nine distinct categories of persons who have an interest in each plot of garden land and its yield; they include the district chief and village headman (who receive some of the produce as tribute), the garden magician, the head of the local subclan, the village community as a whole (which retains certain rights over all surrounding land), the gardener, and the sister of the gardener (who receives much of the produce in the form of gifts made at the harvest).

In the landlord/tenant relationship the tenant's security of tenure and the amount of return owed to the landlord vary widely. In most tribal societies, the individual's right to use land is fairly secure, and rent paid to a landlord is difficult to distinguish from tribute offered to a ruler as symbolic owner of the land. The exploitation of tenants by a leisure class of absentee landlords is a development of "civilization" (Feder 1971; Stover 1974).

Disputes over ownership probably arise in every human society. Even in societies where intragroup theft is virtually unknown, overlapping or competing claims to property make conflict inevitable. One of the functions of a legal system is the resolution of such conflicts. A *legal system* consists of shared beliefs and expectations about the way conflicts should be resolved; it includes *categories of disputes* and *plans for dealing with them*—plans that range from self-help and the informal sanctions of public opinion to formal legal institutions such as courts and prisons.

Most primitive societies have plans for punishment of serious or repeat offenders, but conciliation is stressed. When there are competing claims, a compromise is sought, and when one party has clearly wronged another, the offender is encouraged to make restitution. Working against the common urge to retaliate, tribal legal systems seek to prevent widening of the conflict and to restore the social equilibrium through *compensation* of the victims and *rehabilitation* of the offenders.

John Beattie has described the "neighborhood courts" of the Nyoro of Uganda. The basic pattern, he says, is always the same:

> After the parties to the dispute have stated their cases and the witnesses, if there are any, have been heard, the assembled neighbors discuss the issues raised and usually reach a unanimous decision. They then direct the person who has been found to be at fault to bring beer and meat to the injured party's house on a specified day and time. If the person charged accepts the tribunal's decision, he does this . . . and there follows a feast, in which both the parties, and the neighbors who adjudicated on the case, take part. After this the dispute is supposed to be finished, and it should not be referred to again. . . . It is plain that the primary aim of these village tribunals is the restoration of good relations, not the punishment of an offender. . . . The beer and meat are not a "fine," for their purpose is to rehabilitate rather than to punish [1960:68–69].

Among the Cheyenne Indians, the greatest possible offense (other than homicide) was to hunt buffalo before the annual communal hunt. A single hunter "can stampede thousands of bison and spoil the hunt for the whole tribe. To prevent this, the rules are clear, activity is rigidly policed, and violations are summarily and vigorously punished." Yet the ultimate goal of the tribe members in dealing with offenders was rehabilitation. E. A. Hoebel has reported a typical case:

> All the hunters were in a line with the Shield Soldiers to restrain them until the signal was given. . . . Just as the line came over a protecting ridge down wind from the buffalo, two men were seen riding in among the herd. At an order from their chief, the Shield Soldiers charged down on them. . . . The first to reach the spot killed the two hunters' horses. As each soldier reached the criminals, he slashed them with his whip. Their guns were smashed.
>
> The offenders were sons of a Dakota who had been living with the Cheyennes for some time. He said to his sons, "Now you have done wrong. You failed to obey the law of this tribe. You went out alone and you did not give the other people a chance."
>
> The Shield Soldier chiefs took up the lecturing. The boys did not try to defend themselves, so the chiefs relented. They called on their men to consider the plight of the two delinquents, without horses or weapons. "What do you men want to do about it?" Two offered to give horses. A third gave them two guns. All the others said, "Good!" [1960:53–54].

Needless to say, in many cases arguments for restraint and attempts at conciliation are of no avail. Still, every human society has shared conceptions of legitimate property rights on the basis of which settlements may be reached and social equilibrium restored.

Societies differ in the extent to which they consider or treat various kinds of *persons* as property. In all societies individuals have certain exclusive rights over their own bodies and over the "personal space" immediately surrounding them. Thus, murder and forcible rape are everywhere considered to be crimes, but many societies consider them primarily as violations of property rights. All corporate groups have a common interest in their members. Clan vengeance is an instance of this principle (see page 122). It is also common for groups to accept *compensation* for the murder or injury of a member. In many parts of Africa the lineage of a murderer may avoid retaliation by paying a certain number of cattle to the victim's lineage, the size of the payment being proportional to the social importance of the murdered person. Compensation for damages to an individual's body or self-esteem is also found in many primitive societies. Among the Yurok Indians of northern California, an insult, a blow, and especially an injury that drew blood all called for the payment of compensation in shell money or other valuables; similar payments were common among the ancient Vikings.

In intergroup relations, men employ women as "valuables" in alliance-producing exchanges (see Chapter 5). Women are the highest type of valuable that men can exchange, so wife-givers are generally considered superior to wife-receivers. This is particularly true in patrilineal societies, where each exogamous descent group can perpetuate itself only by acquiring rights to the offspring of women from other descent groups. The payment of bridewealth is really the purchase of a woman's reproductive powers (not the woman herself) from her corporate group; this is certainly the case in societies where bridewealth is not returned upon divorce if the woman's children remain with her husband's group.

Elsewhere, the bridewealth payment serves as a stabilizer of marriage, for once it has been distributed among the members of the bride's corporate group, all acquire an interest in the marriage (that is, in avoiding repayment). In most societies where bridewealth is given, the legitimacy and the social status of a woman's offspring depend on the size and type of payment made at her marriage; women will brag about the circumstances of their "purchase." Women are a very special kind of property: part of the "prestige economy," as Herskovits calls it, rather than the subsistence economy. They are exchanged only for other "prestige items," such as cattle or ritual valuables. What is purchased is not the person as such, but rather certain limited rights in her reproductive, sexual, and domestic powers. In our own society it is still possible for a husband to sue another man (and receive monetary compensation) for "alienating the affections" of his wife and thus depriving him of the woman's "domestic services."

Slavery is rarely found in the primitive world, and where it does occur, the master acquires (whether through purchase, indebtedness, or capture) only *limited* rights over the person of the slave. In many areas, the children of a female slave are born free. Among the Lango of East Africa,

> the ownership of slaves is . . . so limited that the lot of the slave is almost indistinguishable from that of a freeman. On the payment of the usual dowry an enslaved girl is given in marriage by her captor, who stands in the place of a parent to her, and her only disability is that in the event of continued conflict with her husband she has no

family to summon to her aid. Male slaves are usually adopted by their owners; they marry Lango wives and are in no way discriminated against [Herskovits 1952:385].

In societies that lack means of producing an economic surplus, slavery cannot be very profitable; in such groups slaves produce little more than they consume. Except when an outside market for slaves has existed (in "civilized" nations), their main use is in the households of their masters. Slaves may have had some prestige value, but according to Herskovits:

whatever the manner of acquisition of slaves, and whatever the work required of them, their status as human beings invaded to a considerable extent their status as property. As a result, some limitations on free use and on unrestricted right of disposal were always present, and in many communities this operated eventually to take slaves out of the category of property, or at least to mark them off from other forms of property [1952:387].

In primitive economic systems, property rights, craft specialization, exchange within and among groups, and the ultimate consumption of resources are closely linked with other aspects of social life—kinship, leadership, religion, and so forth. Many of the characteristic features of what we think of as an economy—markets, money, banks—appear only sporadically in the primitive world. Specialization is limited, production is for personal use, accumulation for redistribution, and exchange for prestige or alliance. Among small-scale agriculturalists, capital goods are usually the common property of corporate groups. Accumulation of wealth is difficult because of the perishability of resources and the absence of any portable, durable "repository of value," that is, money.

Furthermore, built into many cultures are *leveling mechanisms* that ensure that "accumulated resources are used for social ends." As Manning Nash has written:

Leveling mechanisms are ways of forcing the expenditure of accumulated resources or capital into channels that are not necessarily economic or productive. Every society has some form of leveling mechanism, but in primitive and peasant economies leveling mechanisms play a crucial role in inhibiting aggrandizement by individuals or by special social groups. Leveling mechanisms may take various forms: forced loans to relatives or co-residents; a large feast following economic success; a rivalry of expenditure like the potlach of the Northwest Coast Indians in which large amounts of valuable goods were destroyed; the ritual levies consequent on holding office in civil and religious hierarchies in Meso-America; or the giveaways of horses and goods of the Plains Indians. Most small-scale economies have a way of scrambling wealth to inhibit reinvestment in technical advance, and this prevents crystallization of class lines on an economic base [1966:35–36].

Such practices can impede economic development in the Third World, but they cannot be eliminated without significant disruption of indigenous social systems.

EIDOS: INTEGRATING PRINCIPLES OF BELIEF

The term *eidos* was used by Gregory Bateson (1958) to designate the general principles that give *coherence* to a system of beliefs. The beliefs that make up an ideology are not a random selection: they fit together into an integrated pattern that makes sense, even if there are loose ends and unresolved contradictions. Explicit or implicit *premises* underlie every belief system. For example, in our own culture, hundreds of specific beliefs about legitimate legal procedures stem from the premise that "a person is considered innocent until proven guilty." Similar statements act as premises in other areas of American life. Cora DuBois (1955:1233) has suggested that four basic premises underlie much of American middle-class culture: "(1) the universe is mechanistically conceived, (2) man is its master, (3) men are equal, and (4) men are perfectible." (Cf. Hsu 1961:209–230; Slater 1970.)

Often the premises of a belief system are not explicitly stated by those who hold the beliefs, and it is up to the anthropologist to discover them. As Clyde Kluckhohn phrased it, the implicit philosophy of a people is in large part "an inferential construct based on consistencies in observed thought and action patterns" (1959:427). After many years of ethnographic and linguistic study, Kluckhohn attempted to present the implicit philosophy of the Navajo Indians in terms of its underlying premises, and the "laws of thought" that characterize Navajo reasoning. Here are a few of the basic premises that Kluckhohn has described:

1. The universe is orderly: all events are caused and interrelated.
   a. Knowledge is power.
   b. The basic quest is for harmony.

    c. Harmony can be restored by orderly procedures.
    d. One price of disorder, in human terms, is illness.
  2. The universe tends to be personalized.
    a. Causation is identifiable in personalized terms.
  3. The universe is full of dangers.

. . .

  7. Human relations are premised upon familistic individualism.
  8. Events, not actors or qualities, are primary.

Kluckhohn elaborates each of these points to show its consequences for social action. For example, number 7, the premise of *familistic individualism,* is explained as follows:

> The Navaho, particularly as contrasted with the Pueblo and some other communally oriented groups, is surely an individualist. Ceremonial knowledge is acquired—and paid for—by the individual. Certain animals in the family herd belong to definite persons. Some rites give considerable scope to individual self-expression. Yet this is equally certainly not the romantic individualism of American culture. No unacculturated Navaho feels his independence sufficiently to break from his relatives. . . . In his cognitive picture of his world the Navaho insists that family life is the hub of interpersonal relations. He does not consider himself primarily as a member of a local community, nor of his tribe. . . . One's first loyalty is neither to oneself nor to society in the abstract but rather, in attenuating degrees as one moves outward in the circle of kin, to one's biological and clan relatives.

In addition to these basic premises, Kluckhohn states four general *laws of thought* that he feels the Navajo follow in drawing conclusions from their premises:

  (a) Like produces like (e.g., the eagle flies swiftly so that the runner can well carry a bit of eagle down).
  (b) A part can stand for a whole (e.g., witches can work upon hair or nail parings as effectively as upon the victim himself).
  (c) *Post hoc ergo propter hoc* (e.g., the grass no longer grows as high as in the old days when taboos were strictly kept; therefore, the decrease in vegetation is caused by carelessness in observing the rules).
  (d) Every subjective experience must have its demonstrable correlate in the sense world. (It is not enough for a Na-

vaho to say "I *know* a witch is after me." Witch tracks must be found or dirt must fall mysteriously from the roof of the hut at night. All interpretations must be documented in terms of actual sensory events. . . .) [1968:678–686].

Statements of this type (describing integrative principles of thought or belief) are useful in that they summarize a wide range of observations. They may also be *compared* with statements about integrating principles in other societies.

Kluckhohn's description of Navajo familistic individualism may be fruitfully contrasted with a premise suggested by Edward Banfield to account for the economic and political behavior of a peasant community in southern Italy. Banfield defines *amoral familism* as the *belief* that one should "MAXIMIZE THE MATERIAL, SHORT-RUN ADVANTAGE OF THE NUCLEAR FAMILY; ASSUME THAT ALL OTHERS WILL DO LIKEWISE." He contends that the people of the village called Montegrano behave as *if* they were following this rule; it is a generalization that makes a large range of behavior intelligible to an outsider, and even predictable.

From this premise Banfield derives a number of logical implications that do indeed correspond to important features of social life in the village. For example, Banfield argues that in a society where people accept the premise of amoral familism, behavior outside of the nuclear family will lack any moral constraints; therefore, no one will further the interest of the group or community except as it is to his private advantage to do so. Since the hope of short-run material gain is the only recognized motive for participation in public affairs, only bureaucratic officials will concern themselves with public matters, for only they are paid to do so. It is assumed that they will take bribes and otherwise use their positions for private advantage. (This attitude extends also to teachers and other professionals.)

In a society of amoral familists, organized activity will be very difficult to achieve and maintain since it requires trust and loyalty, and these sentiments do not extend beyond the nuclear family. There are no leaders and no followers, for no one will take initiative, and if someone did, the group would refuse to cooperate out of distrust. Furthermore, there is no connection between political ideology and actual behavior. Claims of "public spirit" are regarded as fraud, and long-run interest, class interest, or public interest do not affect voting behavior *if* the family's short-run material interest is in any way involved

(1958:85–93). Not all of these attitudes and behaviors can be directly deduced from the premise of amoral familism, but they are certainly consistent with it. To this extent, the general principle is useful in understanding the ideology of these people.

A few principles of conceptual integration appear again and again, in various parts of the world. The cultures organized by these principles differ, but the structural patterns are clearly similar. One of these widespread principles is *dualism:* the division of conceptual and social realms into two opposed or complementary parts. In South and Southeast Asia, dualism often permeates every part of a belief system in the form of an elaborate symbolism opposing right to left, good to evil, male to female, purity to pollution, and so forth, and uniting these pairs into an overall duality. This pattern is frequently found in societies with dual organization of social groups into moieties.

One of the African societies with such a pervasive dualistic pattern is Dahomey (see Dahomey origin myth, page 226). As Paul Mercier noted:

> At the head of the Dahomean pantheon we have seen the dual divinity, creator or rather demiurge, *Mawu-Lisa,* a pair of twins or according to some, described as twins simply in order to express both their unity and their dual nature. The ideal type of every group in the divine world is a pair of twins of opposite sex or, more rarely, of the same sex . . . among men also the ideal birth is a twin birth. . . . This twin structure of the gods is the rule, even though, in the present stage of its elaboration, not everything has been integrated into this framework; it is typical that in many cases they speak of androgynous beings, to such an extent does the double nature seem entirely reasonable [1954:231].

The principle of dualism is even more apparent in the sphere of political organization:

> At the head is the king, and he is two in one. . . . There is only one royal personage, but there are two courts, two bodies of exactly similar officials, two series of rituals in honour of the royal ancestors. The reigning king bears two titles: 'king of the city' and 'king of the fields'. . . . Every title and every administrative office is conferred simultaneously on a woman within the palace and a man outside it. . . . Moreover, titles, already dual in themselves, are organized in pairs—one left and one right [1954:232].

Another widespread integrating principle is the notion of *hierarchy.* The officials controlling Dahomean society are arranged in a hierarchy under the king. Each of the principal chiefs who governs a large region of the kingdom has minor chiefs under his direction who are directly responsible to him. Likewise, each of the children of Mawu has under his control minor deities who are responsible to him. As Mercier comments, "There is a remarkable correspondence between the government of the universe and that of human society, between the structure of the world of gods and that of the world of men" (1954:233).

Finally, there is the important figure of Legba, the "spoiled child" of Mawu who transmits messages among the gods and from the gods to humans. Legba has no twin in the origin myth, but during the last two centuries he has become paired with an abstract principle, the conception of *impersonal fate.* This notion, introduced into the cosmology of Dahomey from other African societies, is known as Fa. Fa is believed to govern the destiny of groups and of individuals. Each individual is born under a double sign, and his destiny can be discovered through divination. Nevertheless, the Dahomeans do not believe in an absolute determinism, and this is where Legba enters the picture:

> He introduces into destiny the element of chance or accident. Man is not a slave. Though his fate binds him strictly to the structure of the world, it is no more than the guiding line of his life. He is not debarred from all freedom, and *Legba* ensures this in the world of the gods. *Legba* has stratagems and tricks to evade the rigid government of the world. It is clear that the mythology of *Legba* is connected with that of *Fa,* of which it is in some sort the reverse. He is not the power of evil, he may be the bearer of evil or of good, he may protect man but equally he may make his lot harder. *Legba* is universally venerated in all the cult groups and in every home. Each man has a *Legba* as he has a destiny, and he must propitiate him lest his destiny becomes worse [Mercier 1954:228–229].

The integrating principle of dualism has operated to bring two originally independent conceptions (Fa and Legba) into a paired relationship. In Dahomean culture, the dualistic and hierarchical *eidos* provides a general *plan for thinking* which, applied to all kinds of concepts, produces a coherent system of belief.

An alternative approach to the analysis of belief systems is found in the work of Claude Lévi-Strauss. In his book *The Savage Mind,* Lévi-Strauss rejects the notion that primitive thought is fundamentally different from that of contemporary civilized people. He cites the development of the "great arts of civilization—of pottery, weaving, agriculture and the domestication of animals"—as evidence of the mental capacity of early humans, for "these achievements required a genuinely scientific attitude, sustained and watchful interest, and a desire for knowledge for its own sake" (1966:14).

How, then, does primitive thought differ from "scientific" thinking? According to Lévi-Strauss, primitive people categorize their experiences on the basis of what they can see, hear, taste, smell, and feel; they then use this "repertoire" of categories to build *mythical* explanations of what they seek to understand. Unlike science, which develops analytic and mathematical methods to get behind the sensible qualities of experience, mythical thought uses these sensible qualities and the oppositions between them to explain the world. Oppositions such as male/female, light/dark, raw/cooked, living/dead, high/low, and plant/animal may, in a given culture, function to define categories and explain relationships. These oppositions (like the contrasts between vowel/consonant and voiced/voiceless in a phonological system) may be transferred from one part of a cultural system to another. For example, in a society with totemic clans, the oppositions recognized between natural species (e.g., bear vs. eagle) may be transferred to the realm of social structure (Bear clan vs. Eagle clan) or of mythology.

When Lévi-Strauss says that the cultural system has the same *structure* as the natural system he means that the oppositions between categories in each system are the same. Totemism does not claim that members of the Bear clan are like bears and the people of the Eagle clan are like eagles. Rather, it implies that the Bear clan *differs from* the Eagle clan in the same way that bears *differ from* eagles. It is thus essential to discover how a given society conceives of the differences. Bear and eagle can be differentiated in a variety of ways: low/high, slow/fast, friend/enemy, and so forth. Only the particular oppositions chosen by a culture are relevant to the social structure.

Animals and plants are important to mythical thought because they provide a natural model for the categories of culture. "The diversity of species furnishes man with the most intuitive picture at his disposal and constitutes the most direct manifestation he can perceive of the ultimate discontinuity of reality" (Lévi-Strauss 1966:137). It follows that by examining the detailed contents of myths and rituals we may be able to discover the unconscious principles integrating a primitive belief system.

Not all anthropologists accept the ideas of Lévi-Strauss, and few others can handle them with his elegance and productivity. Still, the search for ways to describe the general patterns of cultural systems is continuing under many names: symbolic analysis, cultural semiotics, world view, structuralism, and many more. The work of Lévi-Strauss will be an important stimulus to such studies for years to come, even if his particular analyses are found to be in error.

RECOMMENDED READING

Robert F. Murphy, *The Dialectics of Social Life*. New York: Basic Books, 1971. A difficult but rewarding consideration of the relationships between beliefs and actions in social life. Includes an excellent account of contemporary social anthropology and a sympathetic though critical account of structuralism.

Philip Pettit, *The Concept of Structuralism*. Berkeley: University of California Press, 1975. A brief, critical analysis of the concept of structuralism and its use in anthropology, linguistics, and literary analysis. Written by a philosopher, this book places Lévi-Strauss's work in a useful perspective, but it is not for beginners.

Gregory Bateson, *Steps to an Ecology of Mind*. New York: Ballantine, 1972. Stimulating essays by a Renaissance scholar whose work ranges from biology to psychiatry. Many of these essays are highly relevant to an understanding of human belief and value systems.

Elman R. Service, *Origins of the State and Civilization*. New York: W. W. Norton, 1975. An examination of authority relations in many types of societies and of the conditions under which a "state" level of organization may come into existence.

CHAPTER TEN
VALUE SYSTEMS

ultural *values* are shared conceptions of what is desirable: they are ideals that the members of a social group accept, explicitly or implicitly, and which therefore influence their behavior. As with other parts of culture, values may be violated, and individuals may use values for their own purposes. Such actions show an awareness of the very conceptions they violate. Revolutionaries are often the people most aware of their society's values, precisely because they wish to change them.

The *value system* of a society consists of explicit and implicit ideals together with their relative priorities and integrating patterns. Like beliefs, the values held by members of a social group tend to form a coherent system. Despite the presence of alternative or even conflicting conceptions of the desirable, it is usually possible to demonstrate some ranking of values and systematic connections among these values. The general conceptions that integrate a value system are usually referred to as *patterns* or *orientations* (rather than principles or premises).

THE PROCESS OF EVALUATION

Human behavior frequently involves judgment and choice. We are constantly called upon to respond to our environment by classifying our experiences and/or deciding among alternative courses of action. In daily life we must answer questions such as: Did he say *pin* or *pen*? Is that Mary Smith or her twin sister? Should I order steak or spaghetti? What kind of book is this? And on occasion we are faced with more crucial decisions: Which of these candidates should I vote for? Should I marry Lee? Which of these job offers should I accept?

In trying to answer such questions, the individual makes use of various *standards of judgment.* Some of them are highly personal, but most of the standards that we use are socially acquired: they are learned as part of the culture of the groups to which we belong or wish to belong. Culture provides *plans for making decisions;* it provides us with criteria for judging the kinds of evidence that are relevant and even how much evidence we need, although we may not be aware how frequently we rely upon socially acquired standards.

Even in so prosaic a matter as food preference, there are striking cultural differences. Most societies have a staple food that must be included in any meal if the meal is to be judged filling or satisfying, but whether this staple is rice, taro, milk, maize, potato, manioc, yams, or bread depends on local tradition. Even the judgment that some substance is or is not food involves a partly arbitrary evaluation: the insects that one group treats as a delicacy are thought disgusting by another group. The person making such a judgment must decide whether a given object or event meets the criteria for assignment to a given category. If ethnographers can discover the criteria that are used in making the judgments, they may be saved the trouble of listing all foods and nonfoods. They may be able to *predict* how the members of a society would classify some novel substance. Furthermore, it may be possible to discover relationships between food categories and other categories.

Edmund R. Leach has suggested that every culture divides the objectively edible part of the environment into three main categories:

1. Edible substances that are recognized as food and consumed as part of the normal diet.

2. Edible substances that are recognized as possible food, but that are prohibited or else allowed to be eaten only under special (ritual) conditions. These substances are *consciously tabooed.*

3. Edible substances that by culture and language are not recognized as food at all. These substances are *unconsciously tabooed.*

Leach argues that these categories and their associated plans for consumption are systematically related to cultural attitudes toward interpersonal relations. He notes that there is a "universal tendency to make ritual and verbal associations between eating and sexual intercourse," and he hypothesizes that "the way in which animals are categorized with regard to edibility will have some correspondence to the way in which human beings are categorized with regard to sex relations." He points out that "from the point of view of any male [ego], the young women of his social world will fall into four major classes," and "the English put most of their animals into four very comparable categories" (1966:31, 42–44). These classifications are reproduced below, side by side:

Categories of Women
(General)

1. Those who are very close—"true sisters," always a strongly incestuous category.

2. Those who are kin but not very close—"first cousins" in English society, "clan sisters" in many types of systems having unilineal descent. . . . As a rule, marriage with this category is either prohibited or strongly disapproved, but premarital sex relations may be tolerated or even expected.

3. Neighbors (friends) who are not kin, potential affines. This is the category from which [ego] will ordinarily expect to obtain a wife. This category contains also potential enemies.

4. Distant strangers—who are known to exist but with whom no social relations are possible.

Categories of Animals
(English)

1. Those who are very close—"pets," are always strongly inedible.

2. Those who are tame but not very close—"farm animals," mostly edible but only if immature or castrated. We seldom eat a sexually intact, mature farm beast.

3. Field animals, "game"—a category toward which we alternate friendship and hostility. . . . They are edible in sexually intact form, but are killed only at set seasons of the year in accordance with set hunting rituals.

4. Remote wild animals—not subject to human control, inedible.

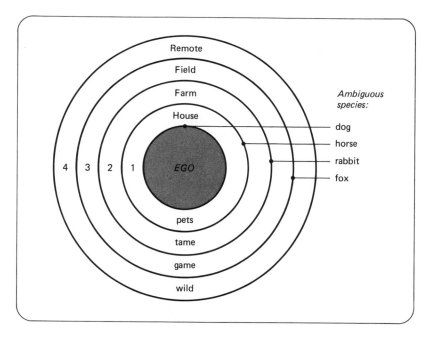

FIGURE 10.1 Animal Categories (after Leach)

Leach also suggests that the special importance of certain animals—shown by the elaborate taboos and rituals that surround hunting, racing, or eating them and the use of their names as terms of abuse when applied to human beings—derives from their *ambiguous* positions in the classification (see Figure 10.1). For example, the dog is "nearly human"; the horse is partly a pet, partly a farm animal; the rabbit is sometimes a farm animal and sometimes game; the fox is a wild animal treated like game in the ritualized British fox hunt.

Not all evaluations involve a simple classification. Many kinds of evaluation call for judgments of *equivalence* or *ranking*. Given a series of objects, events, or persons, we are sometimes required to judge which of them are in some sense the same or to rank them in a continuous series. These judgments may call for the use of a number of criteria, each of which must be weighed somewhat differently. Because of these complications, disagreement is common, and it is hard to discover how people make judgments.

The sensitive ethnographer can use the *disagreements in evaluation* as clues to the criteria that are actually being used. For example, in his study of prestige ranking in the Mexican village of Zinacantan, Frank Cancian attempted to judge the relative prestige of Zinacanteco men on the basis of their participation in the religious *cargo* system:

> The *cargos* are public offices, and Zinacanteco men fill them as community service. That is, the incumbents receive no pay and usually make very substantial cash outlays for saints' *fiestas* and ceremonies. The term of service is one year. . . . Almost all Zinacanteco males serve at least one cargo during their lifetime. . . . The cost of cargos varies tremendously, and only the rich can afford the most expensive ones.

Cancian found, however, that

> expense is not the only factor that determines the "prestige" (respect, deference) that accrues to a man for his participation in the cargo system. Other factors are important. The most crucial of these seems to be the authority that the incumbent of one cargo has over the incumbents of other cargoes in ritual situations. . . . In almost all cases it is difficult to decide how much expense is equivalent to how much authority in calculating the prestige a cargo brings to . . . the person who has completed it. Another difficulty is that the idiosyncratic features of some cargos, e.g., which fiestas they are featured in, seem to have influence on the prestige. In the end I had to construct a prestige ranking of cargos using the cost scale as a base line, changing the rank of some cargos according to my knowledge of the authority of the post and the idiosyncratic features involved [1963:1068–1069].

Since the people of Zinacantan were reluctant to discuss relative prestige, Cancian asked his informants which men had completed what *cargos* and then analyzed the *factual errors* that they made. He found that the errors were not random, but rather that his informants were guessing "in terms of some general impression of the cargo-holder's prestige in the community." That is, when an informant gave an objectively wrong answer, he usually indicated a *cargo* very close in prestige to the correct answer. Cancian concluded that "Zinacantecos, though they will not openly discuss it, actually do perceive cargos in terms of relative prestige; and are apt to remember the approximate prestige of an individual even when they have forgotten the particular cargo he passed in the process of achieving it" (1963:1073).

The institution just described is one type of leveling mechanism (as discussed in Chapter 9). That is, the *cargo* system of Zinacantan translates individual wealth into socially approved symbols of prestige and prevents excessive accumulation of resources by individuals. Persons who participate in such institutions are not being uneconomical or irrational. They are using their wealth as a *means* to achieve culturally valued *ends*.

The distinction between means and ends is extremely important. There is far more agreement among cultures about the ends that are valuable than about the appropriate means to achieve those ends. In addition, a valid end in one society may be viewed merely as a means to some further end in another group. As Robert L. Heilbroner has pointed out, the *profit motive* or the valuing of gain for gain's sake, which is common in our own cultural tradition, "is foreign to a large portion of the world's population, and it has been conspicuous by its absence over most of recorded history," while the positive "social sanction of gain is an even more modern and restricted development." Heilbroner states that until nearly the start of the sixteenth century in Europe, land, labor, and capital were simply not for sale:

> Economic life and social life were one and the same thing. Work was not yet a means to an end—the end being money and the things it buys. Work was an end in itself, encompassing, of course, money and commodities, but engaged in as a part of a tradition, as a natural way of life. In a word, the great social invention of "the market" had not been made [1961:12–14].

In trying to understand the value systems of other societies, we must beware of confusing means and ends. This is particularly true with respect to the high value that most Americans place on *efficiency*. All peoples have some notion of more and less efficient means to an end. If they did not, they probably could not survive. But in most societies, efficiency is only one of a number of criteria used in choosing a course of action. In American culture, this particular value often becomes an end in itself—or at least the sole standard of judgment. The pursuit of efficiency has contributed to our amazing economic development; but it has also led us to squander our social and natural resources, to upset the balance of nature, and to ruin the natural beauty of large portions of our continent.

A similar point can be made about American attitudes toward *education*. As Cora Du Bois has written, "To many Americans schooling has acquired the weight of a goal rather than a means. A college degree is a 'good thing' in itself, whether or not the education itself is prized" (1955:1237). It has also been observed that most Americans value *change* as an end, rather than as a means for reaching another goal. Objective analysis of means-ends relations can sometimes help to resolve conflicts. Some conflicts, however, are due to the inherent incompatibility of values, for example, the American middle-class desire for both privacy and community (Slater 1970).

JUDGMENTS OF GOOD ACTIONS: MORALITY

Every culture provides a set of categories and standards to be used in evaluating human behavior. Some of these standards ideally apply to all persons: the Golden Rule, the goal of self-determination, and the ideal of a single law "for you and for the stranger who sojourns with you" (Exodus 15:16); they are *universalistic* standards, intended for all human beings. *Particularistic* standards apply only to certain persons within specific social groups—not to outsiders.

Every society has numerous particularistic standards. The most important are role expectations—for example, conceptions of the way a good father or a good employer should behave. Even when moral standards are stated in universalistic terms, certain particularistic standards generally take precedence over them. Theodore Stern has analyzed the folklore of the Klamath Indians of Oregon to determine whether their mythology presents a consistent morality. On the basis of selected myths, Stern concluded that in Klamath society *loyalty to kin* takes precedence over "an all-embracing ethical code." Within the immediate family, warm personal ties may override moral expectations and even the norm of reciprocity. "It is only among neighbors and . . . strangers that a person is judged solely on his performance" (1963:27–28).

Among the Navajo, the ideal moral pattern was to treat all people as if they were relatives. This universalistic standard implies that a moral code must be *extended* from the in-group, where it is relatively easy to observe, to an out-group, where it is more difficult to follow. In complex civilizations, kinship relations frequently *symbolize* the ideal relationship among strangers: for example, the emperor is called "father of his people," and members of the women's liberation movement call each other "sister."

Another useful distinction is between *absolute* and *situational* morality. An absolute standard is one that should apply in all times and places, for example, "Thou shalt not kill." A

	Particularistic values	Universalistic values
Absolute values	Apply to certain people under all circumstances: "Honor thy father"	Apply to all people under all possible circumstances: "Thou shalt not kill"
Situational values	Apply to certain people under only specific conditions: "Feed the poor at Christmastime"	Apply to all people but only under specific conditions: "Tell the whole truth" (under oath)

FIGURE 10.2 Kinds of Moral Values

situational rule, on the other hand, is limited to specific social settings. There is considerable overlap between the concepts of absolute morality and universalistic standards. They differ in that the latter is an ideal for all kinds of persons, whereas an absolute value may be restricted to particular kinds of persons but applied regardless of the situation. For example, in Western society doctors are expected to save the lives of their patients regardless of the circumstances. The saving of life is thus an absolute value for doctors, but not for the average person, and certainly not for soldiers. (See Figure 10.2).

A situational morality can be just as demanding as an absolute one. Ruth Benedict observed that:

> in Japan the constant goal is honor. It is necessary to command respect. The means one uses to that end are tools one takes up and then lays aside as circumstances dictate. When situations change, the Japanese can change their bearings and set themselves on a new course [1946:171].

In *The Chrysanthemum and the Sword,* Benedict discussed the moral categories and standards found in traditional Japanese culture. She claimed that Japanese morality is organized around the concept of 'on,' which is translated as 'indebtedness,' and around two categories of repayment known as *gimu* and *giri. Gimu* repayments are limitless both in amount and in duration: they are obligations to one's parents and to the emperor, and Japanese say that "one never repays one ten-thousandth" of these obligations. *Giri* repayments, on the other hand, must be made "with mathematical equivalence to the favor received" and, to avoid losing face, one must pay them within clear time limits.

The category of *giri* is difficult for non-Japanese to understand. It has two subtypes: *giri*-to-the-world includes obligations to affines, distant relatives, and nonrelated persons who have done favors or loaned money; *giri*-to-one's-name is the duty to clear one's reputation of insult, to admit no professional failure or ignorance, and to fulfill the Japanese proprieties. Despite these subtypes, *giri* is considered a single virtue, whether one is reacting to benevolence or to scorn: "A good man feels as strongly about insults as he does about the benefits he has received. Either way it is virtuous to repay" (Benedict 1946:146).

The Japanese have developed many ways of avoiding situations in which loss of face may occur. They include the minimization of competition, the use of go-betweens, and above all, an elaborate code of *etiquette*. Extreme politeness was characteristic of traditional Japanese culture. It was an expression of care for one's honor and that of others. If one was insulted or shamed despite all precautions, vengeance or self-destruction became necessary to clear one's reputation. Revenge is an honorable act, and for a Japanese, as a last resort,

> suicide, properly done, will ... clear his name and reinstate his memory. American condemnation of suicide makes self-destruction only a desperate submission to despair, but the Japanese respect for it allows it to be an honorable and purposeful act. *In certain situations* it is the most honorable course to take in giri to one's name [1946:166; italics added].

Note again the situational standard: suicide is neither good nor evil in itself, but in certain situations it may be the most honorable action possible. It is a means to the culturally valued end of *giri*-to-one's-name.

Cultural attitudes toward suicide vary greatly, and the reasons for these attitudes are even more varied. In some societies, the act of suicide is simply unthinkable—if it takes place, a sorcerer (or mental illness) is blamed. In other groups, suicide is the expected response to specific circumstances. In Tikopia, if a man's family refused to accept his choice of a wife, the couple might drown themselves. In the Trobriand Islands, a young man hurled himself to his death from the top of a coconut palm when his incestuous relations with a clan sister were made public; this was regarded as the only action open to him. The Navajo regard suicide as undesirable in any circumstances. They are primarily concerned with *this* life, and there is no generally accepted doctrine of rewards and punishments in a future life.

Navajo morality is mainly situational. Certain actions, such as witchcraft and incest, are always condemned, while hospitality, courtesy, and deference to age are always approved. According to Clyde Kluckhohn, however, "the Navajo conceives of nothing as good or bad in and of itself. Correct knowledge and following the rules emanating therefrom are good because they lead to long life and happiness. Morals are relative to situation and to consequences rather than absolute. Everything is judged in terms of its consequences." Also, the emphasis in Navajo culture is on deeds rather than words: "Acts rather than beliefs count. Behavior is judged—not verbal adherence to a theological or ethical code" [1962:175].

When they hear the word "morality," most Americans think immediately and exclusively of sexual morality. Patterns of sexual behavior found throughout the world have been surveyed by C. S. Ford and F. A. Beach (1951). It is probably safe to say that in few other areas of culture do we find such a variety of beliefs and values combined with such frequent discrepancies between ideal and real behavior. Yet behind the mass of mating and marriage patterns, a few basic principles do emerge: the universal prohibition on incest, a general concern for legitimacy of birth, and a few recurrent patterns of social control over marital choices (cf. Schneider 1976).

Sexual behavior is restricted, to some degree, in every human society, but not all groups condemn the same actions, nor do all societies regard violations of their conventions as bad or evil. Homosexuality, masturbation, or adultery may be ignored or viewed as foolish. In the Navajo view, such acts may be condemned as likely to interfere with normal social relations, but not as immoral in themselves. On the other hand, many primitive societies are even more puritanical than our own in regard to sexual deviations, and any variation from the norm may be severely punished.

We are all aware that American *sex norms* are gradually changing. Although the *behavioral* changes that have taken place in recent decades have been far greater, there has been a general shift from relatively puritanical absolute standards to a set of more flexible situational standards. This trend has been related by anthropologists to the development in American culture of a "fun morality," the *obligation* to have fun. Some psychologists associate the change with a growing emphasis on the value of self-realization. As we observed in the discussion of Japanese moral concepts, however, a situational morality can be just as demanding as an absolute code. One popular author has suggested that Americans and Europeans, having finally freed themselves from guilt feelings over their violations of absolute moral standards, now torment themselves about the sincerity of their erotic attachments. In other words, although our sexual behavior is more liberated than formerly, we now question our motives much more closely, so that the net gain of "freedom" may be small (Vizinczey 1965). One of the benefits of the women's liberation and gay liberation movements has been a general raising of consciousness about the arbitrariness of conventional sexual morality. Only time will tell the ultimate consequences of these changes.

The study of moral values is an integral part of anthropological investigation. Moral evaluation of one's behavior and that of one's fellows is one of the characteristics that distinguishes humans from other animals. *Man is a maker of tools, rules, and moral judgments.* Universal moral principles are those that are necessary to the continuity of human society; no society in which indiscriminate murder, theft, and lying were considered desirable could continue. Beyond these universals, each culture has elaborated distinctive patterns of valuing—distinctive both in their categories of good and bad actions and in their plans for applying these categories. Suicide, blood vengeance, and even the accumulation of personal wealth are among the actions that, as shown above, may be highly valued in one group and strongly disapproved in another. Even within a given culture, categories may be applied in varying ways. We all value "humane" behavior, but on the humaneness of certain kinds of behavior (abortion, imprisonment, euthanasia, and so forth) it is difficult to arrive at a consensus.

Is it possible to evaluate value systems? A few anthropologists have suggested criteria for evaluating moral systems, but none of these is entirely satisfactory. The criteria proposed are often vague and difficult to apply. Some writers have suggested that the degree of *conformity* found in a society between behavior and ideals (whatever the ideals may be) is a suitable index of morality. But this solution simply redefines morality as conformity, and there may be occasions when an individual's violation of the society's moral code seems to involve an appeal to a "higher" moral standard. Ruth Benedict suggested that total cultures differ in the degree to which they promote self-realization of the people who live by them. But this emphasis on the full development of each individual is itself a value characteristic of a certain social class at a particular time in history.

Most anthropologists have adopted some version of the position known as *ethical relativism*. This is the view that we *cannot* evaluate value systems; indeed, we cannot even judge behavior outside the context of the individual's own social group and its morality. Ethical relativists must accept and try to understand actions that are personally distasteful or abhorrent, without passing any moral judgment on them. Such people need not approve of, say, torture or fascism, infanticide or cannibalism, but must try to prevent culturally determined emotional response from getting in the way of analysis and understanding.

Although ethical relativism presents difficulties as a philosophy, as a methodological assumption it is essential to anthropology. Even as a working principle, ethical relativism can be phrased in several ways. The emphasis here has been on the difficulty of comparing actions or value systems in the absence of any culture-free, absolute standard. Others have stressed the equal validity or arbitrariness of *all* cultural systems. On the other hand, Clyde Kluckhohn has suggested that the observed variation in ethical codes may be comparatively superficial, so that the anthropologist should examine questions such as:

> Is ethical *intent* very similar if not identical the world over? Are variations largely related to means rather than ends? Are means and some of the more proximate ends determined by historical accident and local circumstance? Is the whole picture needlessly confused by the local symbolisms for expressing ultimate goals and enforcing standards that are universal or near-universal? [1962:273].

In *The Primitive World and Its Transformations,* Robert Redfield (1953) suggests that a *moral evolution* may have taken place through human history, in the development of more humane standards and the extension of moral constraint beyond the immediate social group. He recognizes that there have been frequent and severe lapses from this trend and that a case can also be made for the moral inferiority of civilized peoples, but Redfield's basic view is optimistic and quite persuasive. Whether the behavior of civilized people will ever catch up with their highest ideals is another question.

An alternative viewpoint that has recently become quite influential in anthropology is that of *sociobiology* (e.g., Wilson 1975). These studies, usually based on analogies between humans and other animals, suggest that moral behavior and standards are best understood as the results of biological evolution, which has developed in each species characteristic "strategies" (from altruism to cannibalism) to ensure survival and genetic continuity. Many sociobiological theories are still highly controversial, but they are sure to stimulate reexamination of accepted ideas about morality. (See van den Berghe and Barash 1977).

JUDGMENTS OF BEAUTY: ESTHETICS

Esthetic judgments involve the appraisal of persons, objects, and events in terms of their pleasing qualities or beauty, though, as we shall see, moral and practical criteria sometimes enter into these appraisals as well. The categories and criteria used in making esthetic judgments are mainly implicit, at least in primitive societies, and their application calls for skills that can be developed only through a long acquaintance with a culture. For these reasons, esthetic judgments are often difficult for the ethnographer to understand or describe; by careful study of native evaluations and through systematic analysis of style and language, however, it is sometimes possible to discover the more obvious esthetic standards embodied in a culture.

Esthetic judgments typify the nature of a culture better than almost any other kind of human behavior. The art, music, and literature of a society—its "culture" in the narrower sense—embody ideals of form and content that give a tradition its distinctive flavor. These art styles result from the judgments and choices of many people acting in accordance with shared conceptions of beauty.

All the arts are characterized by a *striving for formal perfection* that goes beyond and is sometimes opposed to the mere usefulness of an artifact for some practical purpose.

> When the technical treatment has attained a certain standard of excellence, when the control of the processes involved is such that certain typical forms are produced, we call the process an art, and however simple the forms may be, they may be judged from the point of view of formal perfection; industrial pursuits such as cutting, carving, moulding, weaving, as well as singing, dancing and cooking are capable of attaining technical excellence and fixed forms [Boas 1955:101].

The craftworker not only produces useful objects; she also forms and decorates her baskets or pots to make them beautiful. The musician or storyteller does not just repeat traditional forms; he also embellishes them and creates new works pleasing to himself and his audience. All such creations and re-creations rest on a basis of traditional techniques and skills.

This jade figurine shows the characteristic style of the Olmec culture of ancient Mexico.

The artist uses these skills to produce improved or novel forms—forms that express cultural ideals and which must be judged by *esthetic standards.*

Every human society has some standards of excellence that may be called esthetic. The earliest material evidence of esthetic impulses goes back several hundred thousand years, to the Acheulean period. Artifacts from this period include beautifully formed axes—stone tools shaped with an eye for symmetry and balance that went far beyond the utilitarian purposes for which they were employed. During the Aurignacian and Magdalenian periods of the Upper Paleolithic, some 35,000 years ago, distinctive and technically accomplished art styles were developed at a time when humans were still hunters of big game. Much has been lost from earlier periods; but the impulse to decorate and to represent forms in various media is surely an ancient one. Folktales are probably as old as language itself, and music may be still more ancient. It is known from archaeological discoveries that the Neanderthals (and even *Homo erectus*) selected bright-red pigments from their environment and transported them to their living places (probably to decorate their bodies).

All artistic activities involve a selection of "some specific method, technique, manner, or plan of operations" from among several possibilities, and a development of this chosen style in the direction of formal perfection. According to A. L. Kroeber:

> A style is a way of achieving definiteness and effectiveness . . . by choosing or evolving one line of procedure out of several possible ones, and sticking to it. That means, psychologically, that habits become channeled, facility and skill are acquired, and that this skill can then be extended to larger situations or to somewhat altered ones. [Thus] every style is necessarily prelimited: it is an essential commitment to one manner, to the exclusion of others. . . .
>
> It is a commonplace that all esthetic styles rise and fall and perish. All art has constantly to get itself reborn with a new set of impulses, and then run a new course. . . . [But] the arts are by no means something wholly set apart from the rest of civilization. The same principles of style or method, and therefore of pulsation, tend to hold for most or all cultural activities [1948:329].

Graphic design, folklore, and music involve very different kinds of behavior, but each expresses the ideology of the society where it is found. Anthropologists insist that esthetic ideas can be understood only in relation to the total value system of the culture.

Esthetic Categories

One way to approach the esthetic values of a culture is by analyzing the linguistic terms used to describe or evaluate esthetic objects. Harold K. Schneider (1966) has made such an analysis of the key esthetic concepts of the Turu, a Bantu-speaking people of central Tanzania. He discusses four Turu terms: *-ja, luhida, nsaasia,* and *majighana.* The translation of these terms presents special difficulties. As Schneider notes, one Turu grammar defines the suffix *-ja* as 'good, beautiful,' but a Turu informant translated it as "useful":

> *-ja* encompasses all things of value to Turu, including those which are esthetic. The concept does not differentiate things which are manmade and natural objects, though according to one informant, *-ja* occurring in nature are "as if someone had made them," i.e., as if they had been fashioned for man's use. . . . Examples of *-ja* are cattle, cloths, songs, and even the useful actions of people. . . .
>
> *Luhida* may be contrasted to *-ja* as esthetically pleasing ornamentation, i.e., a design *added to* something else. *Luhida* is visible

... and has spatial continuity and isolation. It is designs which are geometrical or otherwise patterned, having rhythm, symmetry and balance but no precise symbolic meaning.

Several types of designs come under the heading of *luhida.* They include *madone,* a series of disconnected round units that are esthetically patterned (OOOOO), and *nsale,* a series of unconnected parallel lines occurring within a spatial field (|||||||). According to Schneider:

> The Turu would not see the parallel lines in a notebook as *nsale* because they run off the edges of the sheet, but if all the lines stopped short of the edge and the same distance from the edge of the page, they would be *nsale.* This design often occurs in the form of scarification of the body and as ornamentation on flour gourds.

The concept of *nsaasia* is more difficult to explain. It is sometimes thought of as a quality of action and sometimes as a quality of things, but in either case it must have a pleasing effect. Furthermore, *nsaasia* is always produced by human skill, whereas *-ja* and *luhida* may occur naturally. "A cow cannot be *nsaasia* no matter how pleasing to the eye, 'because it was born that way,' but a herd can be thought of as *nsaasia* because it is assembled by man." A person cannot look *nsaasia,* nor can an object that is flawless retain this quality:

> The essential qualities of *nsaasia* are regularity, smoothness, symmetry, cleanliness and color. Unlike *luhida, nsaasia* is also wholeness and completeness.... A stool which has no ornamentation may still be *nsaasia* because it is skillfully made with integral flourishes and fine lines. It loses this quality if disfigured, even if it is still useful. A clean, pressed shirt is *nsaasia* until it becomes dirty and rumpled or torn. A house may be *nsaasia* if the builder transcends utility by the use of matched and aligned poles.

The last of the four concepts, *majighana,* is closely related to the notion of *nsaasia* but is primarily "a voluntary action which makes people happy." Actions that are done under duress are outside of this concept; but a "man of *majighana* is one who customarily exercises freedom of choice to do things which make others happy." They may be simple acts such as sharing cigarettes, speaking pleasant words, or visiting with people to establish friendship, but the concept also includes sponsorship of "freely given" feasts and ceremonies such as ancestral sacrifices and fertility rituals:

Among the activities considered to be *majighana* is the circumcision rite, particularly the initial part in which the initiates are operated on and the feasting and dancing occur.... The pain in the act is discounted and the happiness it brings to others is emphasized. The dancing, drinking and eating make those attending the feast happy, and the achievement of social maturity by their child pleases the parents.

The Turu say that *"nsaasia is majighana."* This statement is the key to one of the most distinctive features of Turu esthetics, for it discloses their attitude toward the social function of art and the artist. As Schneider explains:

Nature can produce valuable and even esthetically pleasing things, but when they are created by men they are something special— *nsaasia. Nsaasia* is an act of *majighana* or altruism.... Art is an esthetically pleasing form that is produced by men. An artist is one who is able to perform acts of *majighana* by exercising his *nsaasia* to bring pleasure to others. Artists are one of the class of magnanimous people including any others whose actions bring joy to people. [See Figure 10.3]

A strong element of the practical runs through all of these concepts. Thus, the sky is not *-ja* because, as one Turu said, "When the sky can be seen there are no clouds so there will be no rain." A certain spotted beetle was said not to be *luhida* because it is destructive of crops, while "a well designed cigarette package is not *nsaasia* because when it is empty it is crumpled and discarded" (Schneider 1966:156–160).

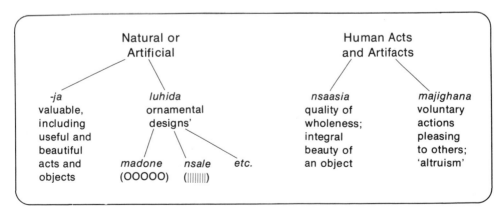

FIGURE 10.3 Turu esthetic categories with approximate translations

Esthetic concepts are firmly embedded in a social context and cannot be understood outside of this context. This is also true of the stylistic values embodied in traditional folklore. Samuel H. Elbert (1951) examined some nine hundred Hawaiian tales to establish their major stylistic features so that they could be compared with the principal emphases of the traditional culture. The "old culture" of the islands is clearly expressed in one or more of the following features of folklore style:

1. Exaggerations used in the tales are indices of cultural values. The heroes of Hawaiian tales are always described in extreme terms. "These heroes have great powers: they drink the sea dry, leap from island to island, or transform themselves into fish or animals. Their flawless bodies are so beautiful that strangers hasten to wait on them."

2. "The richly elaborated figurative language of the tales shows the cultural interest in nature. A bride is a flower, a child a lei, ignorance 'intestines of night' and wisdom 'intestines of day.' "

3. Word play and scatological jokes are the most frequent forms of humor found in the tales, with sarcasm and aggressive punning occurring less frequently. Joking shows a fascination with the human body, including its deformations. "Adultery and lechery are not sources of humor in the tales because of the lack of taboos on this kind of behavior."

4. Hawaiian mythology shows a great fondness for names. All the characters in a tale are listed at the beginning, and full personal names are frequently repeated where we might substitute pronouns. Genealogies are memorized and recited on many occasions. (According to some early missionaries, the Hawaiians thought that the "begats" in the Bible were the "best parts.")

5. The heroic tales illustrate the aristocratic emphasis of Hawaiian culture. Most of the tales deal primarily with persons of high rank; commoners appear only "to illustrate a virtue, such as hospitality, or to wait on or applaud a chief. The slave class is completely unrepresented." Animal characters are scarce. But the characters of heroes are treated realistically, and this can have a strong esthetic effect: "The sudden weaknesses of the hero, the fact that his mana occasionally fails, his fears and temporary setbacks, are realistic touches that serve as devices for heightening suspense and enhancing dramatic appeal."

Elbert also describes a number of stylistic devices used less for their meaning than for their esthetic appeal. These devices include antithesis, repetition, and catalogs, all of which serve as esthetic embellishments as well as ways of prolonging rituals and prayers in order to please the gods. According to Elbert:

Antithesis is a feature of nearly every myth. In a chant about the winds, the contrasting pairs little and big, long and short, successively qualify waves, a canoe paddle, and a canoe bailer.... Long catalogues or lists provide esthetic satisfaction and afford desired length, as in the case of a triumphant recital of sixty-one victories, or a list of one hundred eleven winds and where they live.

Repetition of key words in successive verses is much admired, and may be combined with antithesis:

One rain from the uplands,
One rain from the lowlands,
One rain from the east,
One rain from the west.

Long lists of personal names and place names are characteristic of many folklore traditions (for instance, the catalog of ships in the *Iliad*). These lists and genealogies often have very practical purposes: they may be used to validate the claim of a descent group to territory or to certain privileges. The recitation of such lists can also acquire an independent value and come to be enjoyed for its own sake.

A folklore tradition can be related to its cultural context more easily than other arts. Music is particularly difficult to work with. Nevertheless, in his study of the Enemy Way chant, David P. McAllester has made a significant contribution to our understanding of Navajo social and esthetic values. The Enemy Way is a three- or five-day chant, held for the explicit purpose of bringing relief to a person who is being troubled by the ghost of a non-Navajo. The ceremonial involves an alternation of sacred and secular songs. Each night, after the curing rituals performed by the singer, all the men present join in singing "sway songs" and "dance songs," usually until the dawn of the next day.

An important function of the social part of the ceremony is the "bringing out" of young girls who have reached marriageable age. The interest of the young men is clearly centered in the social singing and drinking and in looking over the available girls. The Enemy Way is felt to be a particularly enjoyable ceremony for the spectators. Any man may join in a good deal of the singing, and women have been known to do so, too. This is one of the rare occasions in Navaho life on which young men may dance with girls, and it is one of the few ceremonies to which a composer may bring his songs for a public hearing [1954:78].

The difficulties of investigating musical values are illustrated by one of McAllester's experiences. He asked several Indians, "How do you feel when you hear a drum?" The question was intended to evoke an esthetic response; but drumming is rarely heard in contexts other than Enemy Way singing. Feeling dizzy or otherwise peculiar at this ceremony is considered an indication that the spectator needs to have the chant performed. What the ethnographer thought of as an esthetic question "was interpreted by the average informant as an inquiry into his state of health." McAllester also found it impossible to separate esthetics and religion in any neat way because, for the Navajo, "what is desired in music is an *effect,* primarily magical, whether the song is for dancing, gambling, corn grinding, or healing. When a traditional Navajo is asked how he likes a song, he does not consider the question, 'How does it sound?' but 'What is it for?' " (1954:5).

Although some of McAllester's informants expressed their preference for songs that "make you happy" or that "aren't too rough," the traditional view of what constitutes beauty in music had to be inferred by a detailed musicological analysis of many Enemy Way songs. Only in this way was McAllester able to formulate the *implicit esthetic standards* that appear to govern Navajo music:

1. "Tonality should be consistent. A particular song should not change key while it is being sung, and a group of songs should be in the same key."

2. "A good voice is somewhat nasal, the vibrato is rather wide; the voice should be as high as possible, it should be capable of sharp emphases, and there should be an easy and powerful falsetto." These qualities are more common in younger than older singers; but endurance is also valued, and here the older singers seem to have the advantage.

3. Navajo group singing is characterized by a kind of wild freedom. There is little emphasis on careful rehearsal and uniformity: "Not all the singers seem to know the song equally well, nor do they all seem to be singing exactly the same version of the song. . . . The impression is of a group of individualists who tune their differences to each other at the moment of singing in a dynamically creative way which is very hard to describe." The singers do not appear to be distressed by this variation within the group.

4. Navajo rhythms "are characteristically fluid. The syncopations, the interrupted double beat, and the intricate variations in beat from one measure to the next evoke a gratified rhythmic

motor response from native listeners. It seems that the rhythm is not a steady background for the melody, as in the case of most Western European music, but is as keenly perceived as melody for its combinations and permutations."

5. Most if not all Navajo music is performed at a fast tempo, with a very limited range of note values: "If the most frequent value is indicated as a quarter note, one finds that quarters and eighths predominate overwhelmingly."

6. "Except in chant singing, the melodic line in Navajo music tends to start high and move down, often over the course of an octave" (1954:74–75).

It is unlikely that these standards would be explicitly formulated by a Navajo; nevertheless, since they influence the performance of songs and the creation of new songs, they may be accepted as valid statements of Navajo musical esthetics. In the last part of his monograph, McAllester shows how certain *nonmusical* values of the Navajo are expressed in the performance of the Enemy Way. These values include self-expression, humor, formalism, and individualism.

Alan Lomax and his co-workers at Columbia have attempted to formulate objective descriptions of musical styles and to relate these styles to other aspects of culture. They call their approach *cantometrics.* It includes both musicological analysis of the esthetic standards embodied in a corpus of folk songs and study of the social structure of performing groups. Lomax (1968) has been able to show correlations between the *organization of musical performances* in a society (for example, as individualistic or cooperative, democratic or authoritarian) and the more general *beliefs and values* of that society. The work of McAllester and of Lomax illustrates the way in which ethnomusicology is moving beyond the simple description of exotic musical traditions to the study of their relationship to the cultural contexts in which they occur.

ETHOS: INTEGRATING PATTERNS OF VALUE

The term *ethos* refers to general patterns or orientations formulated by the anthropologist to describe the integration of a value system. Ethos stands in the same relation to a value system as does eidos to a belief system. It reduces the complexities of a value system to a few *basic patterns* that influence all parts of the system and accounts for the *coherence* among, for example, economic, moral, and esthetic values. Some of the basic premises described in the section on eidos could be treated equally well under the heading of ethos (for example, Banfield's statement of amoral familism and its consequences for social and political behavior). As A. L. Kroeber has written, "Ethos deals with qualities that pervade the whole culture—like a flavor—as contrasted with the aggregate of separable constituents that make up its formal appearance. . . . The ethos includes the direction in which a culture is oriented, the things it aims at, prizes and endorses, and more or less achieves" (1948:294).

Ruth Benedict made one of the earliest attempts to characterize the ethos of cultural systems in her famous book *Patterns of Culture* (1934). Benedict felt that it was possible to describe whole cultures in terms of their general emotional approach to the world and to human relationships. Borrowing some of her terminology from philosophy and abnormal psychology, she described four very different societies as if each had a unique and consistent personality. The cultural ethos of the Zuñi Indians is described as seeking peace and order through self-control and cooperation, with a high degree of subordination of the individual to the group. The Plains Indians, on the other hand, are characterized as valuing violent emotions and stressing the individualistic quest for supernatural power. In a similar manner, she characterized the Kwakiutl Indian ethos as assertive and self-glorifying, while the Dobuans of Melanesia were termed hostile and suspicious. Benedict believed that such *configurations* (whole culture patterns) develop when the members of a society select a particular character type as their ideal and then elaborate their arts and institutions to be consistent with the chosen type. The outcome is a society in which a single "style" dominates the entire culture.

Although *Patterns of Culture* was and still is an important book, many of Benedict's statements have been criticized by later anthropologists as oversimplifications. It has been pointed out, for example, that the "peaceful" Pueblo Indians had a well-developed pattern of warfare, and that the "warlike" Plains Indians were quite capable of cooperative activities (as in their communal bison hunts, p. 241). Also, the Kwakiutl potlaches—which Benedict saw as expressions of the chiefs' craving for power and self-glorification—have been shown to have had important economic and integrative functions (Piddocke 1965). In presenting her four societies as unique configurations, Benedict failed to represent the *diversity* of values found in every human group.

To avoid oversimplification, Morris E. Opler suggested that

cultural value patterns should be described in terms of several *themes*—cultural ideals, "declared or implied," which control behavior or stimulate particular kinds of activity. According to Opler, cultural integration is the result of the dynamic interplay among a number of different themes, some of which reinforce one another while others contradict or limit each other (1945, 1968).

Anthony Leeds, whose discussion of Yaruro beliefs was cited in Chapter 9, summarized the Yaruro value system in a number of statements. The major themes of Yaruro culture are:

1. "The cosmos is static, limited, concrete, and internally continuous in that no barriers separate man and his society in the physical world from the nonphysical world."

2. "Goodness inheres generally in the cosmos as a system. The goodness manifests itself in understood causes and concretely and describably known parts of the cosmos which, whether places, persons, or things, are given exact locations."

3. "Evil, which is not polar to good, finds its locus in specific persons, things, or events inside or outside the cosmos, and is manifest in specific results. The underlying causes of evil, however, are inaccessible to the sense or to understanding. (Being neither known or localizable, they are not part of the unified kin and cosmic structure in which gods, the dead, and men and their respective lands are tied together.)"

4. "In the good cosmos, the good society consists of kin-related gods, the dead, communities and individuals living in tranquility and sharing all things."

5. "In the good society, action is guided by precept, suggestion, and by sensibility to the wants of others and of self; but compulsion and hostility are not permissible."

6. "The individual . . . is not compelled by the nature of the cosmos nor by the personnel in it to follow any particular path. He has free will with regard to the ordained order of things" (1960:1–10).

Philip L. Newman has also used the concept of theme in his description of Gururumba culture. One particularly important theme is the people's great "concern with growth and strength." As Newman comments:

> The Gururumba are horticulturalists and the growing of food is much on their minds. Casual conversation frequently turns around the state of one's garden or the health of one's pigs. Many of the songs they sing concern growth. . . . A concern with physical strength is also manifest in everyday life, since a strong body is

necessary for carrying out the tasks associated with gardening, hunting, and defending the group. It is a characteristic highly admired in both men and women, amounting to one of the major standards of beauty [1965:72].

Many Gururumba rituals are intended to promote growth and to ensure the strength of plants, pigs, and people. Beyond the practical basis of their concern, Newman demonstrates that the *means* of "achieving growth and showing strength have come to be values in their own right":

> The ability of an individual or group to be productive and assertive is among the most general values in Gururumba culture, and to produce food, to grow children and pigs, to protect the group, to seek out and discharge obligations vigorously, is to demonstrate the presence of that ability. The rituals of growth and strength, then, are not only of importance to the Gururumba because they add to their technical mastery of the physical world, but because they relate to the mastery of affairs in the social world as well [1965:75].

These general values are manifested in ideas and rituals surrounding sexuality and in the people's cosmology. The Gururumba are constantly striving for both productivity and assertiveness, while at the same time trying "to turn strength into nurturant channels":

> To a Westerner, daily life among the Gururumba appears to be carried on in a highly aggressive fashion: the constant banter about giving and taking, the frequency of fights and violent emotional eruptions, and the fact that many of the idioms in the language are built around "violent" verbs such as "hit," "strike," or "kill." "I hit him" can mean "I gave it to him," rather than the reverse as in our own language. In most contexts this kind of behavior is not aggression to the Gururumba; it is a display of the strength stemming from vital essence, the strength man draws upon to endure and flourish. Within that part of the social world defined by the sharing of food, assertiveness is not aggressiveness because it creates food and the social channels through which food flows. Furthermore, making a demand implies the obligation to be demanded of, and giving is not a means of overwhelming others because reciprocity will transform givers into takers [1965:89].

Once again the importance of reciprocity in maintaining social relationships is evident. The Gururumba express their relationships in a violent and unfamiliar idiom, but the social functions of their rituals and their elaborate gift exchanges are to bind local groups and kinship groups together by reciprocal obligations.

The Gururumba believe that their ancestors lived in a presocial era that lacked the institutions of marriage and of gift exchange (both of which are expressions of reciprocity). They did not live in villages and had no domesticated plants or animals. These ancestors were "strong," but they gave free reign to their impulses. "They raped, murdered and stole as whim directed them and ranged freely over the countryside without concern for boundaries." Significantly, the Gururumba sometimes liken themselves to these ancestors. At other times, they say that people are like their pigs: semidomesticated animals that frequently "tire of the rope and the fence" and break out of these constraints, doing great damage to houses and gardens. (See p. 152.)

Gururumba understandings about *human nature* contrast in a striking manner with the Yaruro ideology outlined above. Indeed, the positions of these two cultures almost define opposite ends of a dimension of values. According to Newman, the Gururumba position may be summed up in three general statements:

1. *"Man has selfish, destructive, and aggressive impulses in himself.* Witches are real people, ghosts and ancestors once were. Death releases harmful tendencies that have always been in man. Ghosts are not harmful because they are attempting to punish man or subvert his basically good nature; they are harmful in the same way men are."

2. *"These impulses are curbed by the forces of society.* This understanding is present in the statement that men would be like ancestors of the presocial era if they did not live in society, and in statements drawing a parallel between men and unwatched pigs. The Gururumba never indicated any particular longing to be like the voracious pig or the presocial ancestor, but their statements indicate an understanding that they would be that way more often than they are if it were not for social constraints. (They are this way toward . . . their enemies, with whom relationships are not modified by reciprocity and obligation.")

3. *"Society represses but does not eradicate impulses that cannot be allowed expression within its boundaries.* This is . . . apparent in the attitude toward men who exhibit a behavior pattern people refer to as 'being a wild pig.' These men run amok, attacking people and stealing objects. There is no attempt to restrain such behavior beyond keeping a watchful eye

on it to avoid serious injury and no recriminations are made when it is over. . . . The name given this behavior is instructive since there are no truly wild pigs in the upper Asaro valley, only pigs that have temporarily escaped their masters (1965:92–93)."

Some anthropologists hold that there are a number of universal issues on which every society must take a position. If so, it should be possible to characterize the value system of a given society in terms of its position on each of these issues, and to compare societies by noting their relative positions on each of these value dimensions. Florence Kluckhohn has suggested that each society must take a position on the issue of "human nature"—whether people are fundamentally good, evil, or both. The two ethnographic examples above illustrate the extreme positions: the Yaruro view people as inherently good, while the Gururumba think of people as evil (unless constrained by society). An intermediate position is represented by the Navajo, who regard good and evil as complementary and ever present, in both humans and nature.

On the issue of the relationship between humans and nature, both the Navajo and the Yaruro represent the intermediate position; they see humans and nature as existing in mutual *harmony.* The two extreme positions would be those in which humans are viewed as *dominant over* nature or as *subordinate to* nature; they are represented, respectively, by modern American culture and by the culture of the southern Italian peasants described by Edward Banfield (p. 246; cf. Kluckhohn and Strodtbeck 1961).

Other attempts to characterize the ethos of various cultures use such concepts as "ideal person," "dominant style," and "world view." In each case, the anthropologist attempts to discover and state a few basic patterns that will account for judgments, evaluations, and choices made in various aspects of social life. The approaches differ widely in their use of *materials,* which range from life histories and firsthand observations to questionnaires, projective tests, and "cultural products" (art objects, folklore, and so forth). They also differ in their *goals.* Some anthropologists, following Benedict, are content to formulate *unique characterizations* of a culture's ethos which can be compared with others only impressionistically, if at all. Others emphasize *comparability* and, like Kluckhohn and Strodtbeck, try to find universal categories of values in terms of which cultures can be systematically compared. Still others hope to *explain* the differences among value systems by examining patterns of child-training, features of social structure, subsistence, ecological relations, or various combinations of these factors.

It is the responsibility of anthropology to try to understand both the nature and the sources of human values, even if fundamental cultural differences cannot be explained. According to David Bidney (1953:698), "the most important and difficult task which confronts the cultural anthropologist is that of making a critical and comparative study of values."

Clearly, an ethnocentric approach that ranks other value systems as "primitive" or "advanced" to the extent that they approach our own views is unacceptable. The appreciation of the integrity of other cultures is an important and practical goal, one that anthropologists are pursuing today. In the interest of human survival, anthropology must go further, seeking a basis for intercultural understanding and cooperation. It is hoped that radically different means and cultural idioms can be reconciled so that men and women can work together toward a common end—the good of humankind.

RECOMMENDED READING

Clifford Geertz, *The Interpretation of Cultures*. New York: Basic Books, 1973. Elegant essays by the supreme intellectual among American anthropologists, dealing with values, religious and secular, and suggesting ways of understanding other cultural systems, including complex systems in which a variety of ideologies exist side by side.

Mary Douglas, *Natural Symbols*. New York: Vintage, 1973. Clear and exciting discussion of the relationships between social structure and values. Douglas is particularly interested in the way cosmologies are expressed in ritual action and symbol.

Clyde Kluckhohn, *Culture and Behavior*. New York: Free Press, 1962. Selected essays by an influential American anthropologist, many of which deal with moral and ethical issues, drawing on Kluckhohn's vast knowledge of Navajo culture.

Gary Witherspoon, *Language and Art in the Navajo Universe*. Ann Arbor: University of Michigan Press, 1977. A contemporary account of Navajo culture that emphasizes how the Navajo classify their world through language and beautify their world through art.

Dorothy Lee, *Freedom and Culture*. Englewood Cliffs, N.J.: Spectrum Books, 1959. Provocative essays on value systems and the relationship between individual and society by an anthropologist who possessed great sensitivity to language and to human needs.

PART FIVE
THE ANTHROPOLOGIST AT WORK

Observation and inference always go hand in hand when the anthropologist is at work. It is only by framing *provisional interpretations* of what they see that anthropologists know what questions to ask and where to look (or dig) next. Premature interpretations can lead any investigator astray, but without some guiding ideas one is completely lost. Science does not teach us to avoid inferences but rather to realize that they *are* provisional (hypotheses) and that we must search for data that may contradict as well as confirm our ideas.

The following chapter is not intended as a "how to do it" guide to anthropological field work; rather, it is hoped that this brief discussion will give the reader some idea of the *conditions* under which anthropological data are collected and the *problems* involved in drawing valid conclusions from such data. Anthropology differs from many of the sciences in that, as Robert Redfield once put it, "The anthropologist's own human nature is an instrument of work." This fact is both helpful and problematic. We are able to understand alien cultures partly because at one time we have all had to learn a culture (our own), but it is precisely because we have been enculturated that it is difficult to comprehend the patterns of a different way of life. Just as students of a second language must struggle to overcome a foreign accent, anthropologists must struggle to overcome ethnocentric biases, many of which they are not even aware of. It is part of our scientific faith that we can do so.

Ethnographic field work involves firsthand observation of social behavior from a relativistic viewpoint. It is an attempt to understand the historical basis and adaptive functioning of a cultural system without evaluating it in accordance with ethnocentric standards. Thus the first task of the ethnographer is to *learn the culture* of the group he is studying; in this respect, his task is similar to that of a child born into the group, for both must discover the categories and plans shared by other group members. But whereas a child must also develop the skills appropriate to his or her position in the society in order to function as a regular group member, the ethnographer is required to formulate, consciously and explicitly, the rules that appear to guide the various classes of group members in their daily interactions. The ethnographer's learning is *more explicit* and *less skillful* than the child's enculturation.

Of course, not all ethnographers (or archaeologists) set out to describe the total culture of a single group. Often the anthropologist is concerned with some particular aspect of culture. Nevertheless, most ethnographers try to get a general feel for the society they are studying so that they can judge the significance of their data in the total cultural context. In the following chapter, our model of field work will be the attempt to describe a total culture, even though most actual studies involve more limited ethnographic problems.

CHAPTER ELEVEN
OBSERVATIONS AND INFERENCES

FIELD METHODS

When ethnographers set out to observe a society or archaeologists to dig a site, they are faced with an enormous range of observable phenomena. From this nearly inexhaustible richness, these trained observers select the events and objects that are most relevant to their purposes.

The anthropologist who plans to observe and describe social behavior must have some criteria of relevance to guide her observations. Her professional training has taught her the kinds of facts that have proved significant in previous studies. Since her time in the field is limited, she cannot possibly see everything, so she starts with phenomena she has been trained to observe. In a primitive society she will usually begin with the kinship system, the subsistence technology, and the process of enculturation. These studies will lead her to all other areas of the culture. Ideally, the ethnographer has been trained to observe and report accurately all phenomena she may encounter, from techniques of fishing to religious ritual.

The extent to which she can prepare depends on how much is already known about the region in which she is to work. She will read the reports of explorers and of other field workers, familiarize herself with the history and geography of the region, and if possible prepare herself in the local language. Thus she can make the best use of her time and be aware of specific problems she will encounter.

In addition, there are practical problems to be resolved. Adequate funds, suitable clothing, medical supplies, inoculations, and special equipment (cameras, tape recorders) must be acquired; transportation must be arranged; lines of communication and supply must be established; in many cases, permission must be requested from a variety of government officials before research can begin. The field worker must also be prepared to adapt himself and his research techniques to the local situation, for one never finds exactly what he has anticipated, no matter how careful his preparation. *Flexibility* is probably the most essential characteristic of the good field worker if he is to keep his sanity, much less accomplish his planned research.

A classic description of the difficult conditions under which field work must sometimes proceed is given by E. E. Evans-Pritchard in his book *The Nuer* (1940:14–15):

> Besides physical discomfort at all times, suspicion and obstinate resistance encountered in the early stages of research, absence of interpreter, lack of adequate grammar and dictionary, and failure to procure the usual informants, there developed a further difficulty as the inquiry proceeded. As I became more friendly with the Nuer and more at home in their language they visited me from early morning till late at night, and hardly a moment of the day passed by without men, women, or boys in my tent. As soon as I began to discuss a custom with one man another would interrupt the conversation in pursuance of some affair of his own or by an exchange of pleasantries and jokes. . . . These endless visits entailed constant badinage and interruption and, although they offered opportunity for improving my knowledge of the Nuer language, imposed a severe strain. Nevertheless, if one chooses to reside in a Nuer camp one must submit to Nuer custom, and they are persistent and tireless visitors. The chief privation was the publicity to which all my actions were exposed, and it was long before I became hardened, though never entirely insensitive, to performing the most intimate operations before an audience or in full view of the camp.
>
> Since my tent was always in the midst of homesteads or windscreens and my inquiries had to be conducted in public, I was seldom able to hold confidential conversations and never succeeded in training informants capable of dictating texts and giving detailed descriptions and commentaries. This failure was compensated for by the intimacy I was compelled to establish with the Nuer. As I could not use the easier and shorter method of working through

regular informants I had to fall back on direct observation of, and participation in, the everyday life of the people. From the door of my tent I could see what was happening in camp or village and every moment was spent in Nuer company. Information was thus gathered in particles, each Nuer I met being used as a source of knowledge, and not, as it were, in chunks supplied by selected and trained informants. Because I had to live in such close contact with the Nuer I knew them much more intimately than the Azande [another large Sudanese tribe], about whom I am able to write a much more detailed account. Azande would not allow me to live as one of themselves; Nuer would not allow me to live otherwise. Among Azande I was compelled to live outside the community; among Nuer I was compelled to be a member of it. Azande treated me as a superior; Nuer as an equal.

The techniques of the field worker must adapt both to the problems being studied and to the exigencies of the field situation. This is why it is difficult to describe how field work should proceed. Following are some kinds of methods that often prove useful.

To begin with, the ethnographer must *enter* the community. Entry involves not only physical presence (which may itself be difficult) but also social acceptance. The anthropologist must find a *social position* within the group, in which he will be tolerated and allowed to carry on his work. He must deal with the tendency of the group to assimilate him to their earlier experiences with American or European officials, missionaries, or traders. In colonial or formerly colonial areas, one is likely to be taken for a government agent of some kind—a tax collector, policeman, or administrator. Such stereotypes can interfere with his access to many kinds of information; even in fairly open areas, the field worker (either ethnographer or archaeologist) is likely to be considered a spy and to be viewed with great suspicion.

The anthropologist must explain his purpose in terms that are understandable to group members and avoid being categorized as a kind of person from whom the community will withhold information. It is difficult to tell in advance what will work. Some explanations that sound quite plausible may backfire. For example, at the beginning of my field work with a band of Micmac Indians I stated that my intention was to do a "historical survey" of their community. The idea of having someone study their history was quite acceptable to most of the Micmac to whom I spoke; a few, however, interpreted the word *survey* too literally, and within two days rumors were flying that I was a government "surveyor" who had come "to divide up the lands." The Micmac, like most Native Americans, are extremely sensitive about their reservation lands, since they have been cheated so often. It took me several weeks to overcome this rumor, and many Indians remained suspicious throughout the period of field work.

The members of a society must somehow fit the anthropologist into their set of social categories (roles, groups, and so forth). Once they have managed to do so, the plans for interaction with him follow automatically. The anthropologist does not easily fit into the traditional categories. Nevertheless, he must be given a position in the social structure. In a kin-based society, he must be attached to one or more specific kin groups and perform the minimal expectations associated with his kin role; in a caste society (including military organizations), he must be given a temporary rank so that others will know whether to treat him as a superior, an inferior, or an equal; and so on. Any assigned status will open some sources of information to the field worker and exclude him from other sources. Such restrictions, however, are usually a lesser handicap than those experienced by the ethnographer who tries to establish a marginal position on the outside of a social system.

Once the field worker has entered the community and established herself in a social role that leaves her relatively free to gather information, there are two ways to gather data: (1) use of *selected informants* and/or (2) *participant observation.* Usually both will be employed in different proportions, depending on the field worker, the research problem, and the field situation. As Evans-Pritchard observed, some societies insist that the ethnographer take part in the social life, while in others such participation is difficult or impossible. In the latter case, the ethnographer has no choice but to work intensively with a few people who are willing to talk to her. This is also the preferred method when time is limited or when the field worker is trying to *reconstruct* an earlier cultural situation. It is usually possible and desirable to participate to some extent in the normal social life of the group, if only to verify the statements of informants and to resolve discrepancies.

A high degree of participant observation is possible only when the ethnographer has gained general acceptance in a nonrestrictive role and when his own temperament enables him to take part in the social life actively and without becoming too emotionally involved. One danger of participant observation is that by performing a specific social role the anthropologist may lose perspective on the total system. Another is the danger of "going native" to the extent of refusing to reveal information about the group; obviously, anthropological science could not progress if this always happened. Nevertheless, participant observation is essential for experiencing the interaction between the culture's structural rules and the organizational processes through which they are put into action. (See Chapter 6.)

The ethnographer does not simply collect facts in a random manner. Rather, as pointed out in the Introduction to Part Five, she organizes her observations and places provisional interpretations on them. These *hypotheses* come from the interaction of her observations with her theoretical training. They guide her continuing observations so that a line of questioning with an informant or a series of participant observations can contribute to her understanding of the cultural system (instead of just adding up to a collection of curious customs). For example, if questioning of two informants reveals a discrepancy between their accounts of some custom, the ethnographer will try to understand the discrepancy in accordance with what she knows about the society and her informants' statuses. She will question other informants and/or arrange for participant observation either to resolve the discrepancy or to show how it is related to other social factors (the sex, age, or group membership of the respective informants).

Whenever an ethnographic hypothesis is stated in a *quantitative* form, it is desirable to make enough observations to permit *statistical* treatment of the data. Take, for example, the study of marriage rules. Suppose that a number of elderly informants in a patrilineal tribe say that in the past a man *always* married a member of his mother's clan, but the younger informants say that while there is a preference for marriage with a member of the mother's clan, most men today do not consider this important in choosing a wife. A provisional interpretation of these statements would be that a former strict marriage rule has broken down. Before trying to explain the reasons for this cultural change, however, the ethnographer would be wise to examine a *sample* of marriage choices over the last few generations, noting each man's mother's clan and the clan of his wife. Analysis of actual marriage choices may show that marriage with a matrilateral relative was *not* so common in the past as the older people believe (say 70 percent rather than 100 percent), while a high proportion of recent marriages (say 65 percent) *do* follow this rule; that is, young men still tend to marry matrilateral kin, whether they realize it or not.

Cases of this sort are very common in ethnographic work. They form the basis for a distinction between *ideal culture* (what people say they should do) and *real culture* (how they actually behave in a given situation). Our example shows that there can be a discrepancy between ideal and real, and that the ideal culture may change while the real culture stays pretty much the same.

Ideal culture can also remain relatively constant while the actual behavior of persons increasingly deviates from the structural rule. An example is the contrast between American sex norms and the premarital sex behavior of college students. Such changes in behavior will *eventually* bring about a change in the structure. For instance, the coeducational dormitories that are now taken for granted on hundreds of campuses would have been unthinkable as recently as 1960.

COLLECTION OF TEXTS

The distortions that affect our memories in everyday life are multiplied many times in an unfamiliar or exotic situation. Most ethnographers therefore attempt to collect and record their data in permanent forms, called *texts.* Here are a few specific techniques used by ethnographers in gathering and recording data.

1. Field notes

Every ethnographer must keep a running record of his experiences in the field, from his first contact with the group he intends to study through his departure. The only general rule for taking field notes is this: the more detailed, explicit, and legible, the better. These notes should include all of his observations, the time and place they were made, and the names of others present. He should also write down his provisional interpretations of these observations, keeping facts and inferences as distinct as possible. Particularly at the start of field work, *everything must be recorded,* for observations that seem unimportant often turn out to be extremely significant. Part of the ethnographer's continuing education comes from rereading his notes and seeing how his perceptions of the society he is studying have changed with increasing familiarity. Still, first impressions have a special significance (in field work as in personal relations), and it is essential that they be fully recorded.

2. Informant interviews

Interviews range from informal conversations to all-day (and sometimes all-night) sessions for which informants may be paid. Notes or tape recordings made during interviews are useful, but in many situations they are impossible to take or would interfere with the free flow of information. In such cases, notes must be made as soon as possible after the interview to avoid loss of details or possible distortion in the ethnographer's memory.

Unless the ethnographer is able to establish some degree of rapport with an informant, she must be very cautious in using the information she gets. Rapport involves mutual confidence, understanding, and emotional affinity. There are no general rules for establishing rapport, but it helps if the ethnographer demonstrates genuine interest in and respect for the native culture; also, she must convince her informants that their personal remarks will be kept confidential. Field workers cannot be gossips; like all other professionals, they must protect their sources of information. Violation of confidence is poor ethical practice and bad ethnographic technique.

3. Genealogies

The collection of genealogies (family trees) has long been a standard part of the ethnographer's task. Extensive genealogies are collected from several reliable informants and supplemented by interviews with others. In a kin-based society, knowledge of the genealogical relationships among persons is essential to an understanding of the social system. Genealogies are used in analyzing kinship terminology, descent group recruitment, marriage rules, political organization, and so on.

This type of fact-gathering seldom meets with much resistance from community members.

Since genealogical information invariably proves to be valuable, it is a convenient place to start an ethnographic investigation. Not that genealogies are always easy to compile. Among the Tiwi, for example, whenever a woman remarries, her new husband *renames* all her children. Since most Tiwi men marry for the first time at a rather advanced age, an individual may have four or five different names given by his father and various stepfathers. Elsewhere, there are stringent taboos against even mentioning the name of a deceased person, while in some communities there are dozens of living individuals with the same name. In Bali, young people are usually addressed simply as "first-born," "second-born," and so forth, and members of a village community may not know of the other names an individual possesses. It is exactly this capacity for leading into other aspects of the culture that makes genealogies so useful.

4. Community mapping

Careful mapping of the community and region under study is useful in the study of residential groups, interaction patterns, land tenure, and conceptions of social space. Locating all members of the community is important for sampling and for determining the relationship of locality to other social phenomena. In Latin America, for example, it is common for the homes of influential citizens (as well as political and religious buildings) to be located around the central plaza of a town or village, while craftworkers and the poor are localized in other areas. Large communities are further divided into *barrios* ("quarters"), each of which tends to duplicate this structure on a smaller scale. Mapping of such a community reveals a great deal of information and should prevent hasty generalizations on the basis of data gathered from only one of the subdivisions.

5. Structured observations

A technique increasingly used by ethnographers is the control of their observations by deliberate sampling in space and time—the use of structured observations. For example, once the general structure of a community is determined by mapping, the ethnographer may make it a point to spend roughly equal periods of observation in each of its subdivisions. Another type of control involves brief, intensive periods of observation with an attempt to record many details of the interactions among particular classes of persons. Such observations may be recorded in terms of a predetermined set of categories. For example, in a comparative study of child-training in six societies, field workers were instructed as follows:

> The fieldworker should make 12 five-minute observations on each child. These observations should be scattered as widely as possible over time and setting. The fieldworker should describe all instances of the situations in which we are interested that occur in each of these five-minute observations [Whiting et al. 1966:94].

The writers were interested in instances in which the child hurt himself, had difficulty, broke a rule, or started an interaction, or in which another person assaulted, insulted, hurt, or reprimanded the child. Their goal was to obtain comparative material on childhood experience in a representative sample of the child's environment in each society. The main advantages of structured observations are that they keep the ethnographer from being overwhelmed with data, and at the same time prevent him from overemphasizing striking but unrepresentative occurrences that he happens to observe.

6. Trait lists

For some comparative and historical purposes, particularly when time is limited, it is useful for the ethnographer to employ a list of cultural elements (traits) which she can simply record as being present or absent in a given community or society. In a living culture, trait lists may serve as guides to observation, helping the ethnographer to take note of things she might otherwise neglect. Where aboriginal life exists only in the memories of a few elderly informants, trait lists derived from archaeological or ethnological studies of neighboring groups may serve as a stimulus to the informants' memories and thus aid in the reconstruction of a culture that can no longer be directly observed.

7. Questionnaires

In large-scale investigations employing a team approach, questionnaires may be used as part of an attempt to standardize interview procedures for greater comparability of data. Well-designed questionnaires can be quite useful, particularly for gathering quantitative data on topics that are already understood in a general way. Their greatest disadvantage is that a person often gives different interviewers differing responses to the same question. If the investigators have no contact with the respondent except while administering the questionnaire, linguistic and personal difficulties often prevent the establishment of rapport. In any case, it is essential that proposed questions be pretested on a small sample to determine both their *reliability* (the degree to which they elicit consistent responses) and their *validity* (the degree to which they elicit accurate information). Some sociologists have developed methods for deriving data from censuses and from large-sample surveys that were originally taken for other purposes; anthropologists could make good use of these methods, particularly in studying communities within modern nations.

8. Psychological tests

The use of psychological tests depends on both the training and the interests of the ethnographer. Some tests can be given with little preparation, while others, such as the Stanford-Binet intelligence test or the Rorschach personality test, require many months of intensive training to administer, let alone interpret. Relatively few ethnographers have these skills, though on large-scale projects it is possible to employ a psychiatrist or clinical psychologist to administer the tests. Their main problem is *cross-cultural validity*: that is, when a test has been designed for use with, say, American schoolchildren, it cannot be used in other societies without extensive modifications (after which, of course, it is no longer the same test and results are not really comparable). *There is no such thing as a culture-free test.* Even fairly straightforward tests of perception or of memory involve situations and stimuli that are likely to be unfamiliar to nonliterate persons. Although significant work has been done with psychological tests of various kinds, this is one of the most difficult types of ethnographic work, and it should be undertaken only with careful planning and safeguards. (See Price-Williams 1975.)

9. Elicited texts

In three major areas of study it is desirable to transcribe lengthy statements made by informants. Native language *linguistic texts,* on tape and/or in a detailed phonetic transcription, provide data for linguistic analysis. Linguistic texts are of many types. Often the ethnographer or field linguist will try to elicit sequences of utterances that will reveal the structure of the language—for example, minimal pairs or sentences that differ only in verb tense or person of the subject. Once phonology and grammar are fairly well understood, samples of normal speech or repeatable stories may also be elicited.

Linguistic texts often overlap with *folklore texts,* in which the field worker attempts to elicit one or more versions of a traditional tale, legend, or myth. Such texts are most valuable in a phonetic or phonemic transcription accompanied by a word-for-word translation plus a relatively free translation with remarks on specific cultural concepts necessary to an understanding of the material. Other texts, such as magical formulas, court records, and recipes, can be profitably treated in the same way.

The third type of extended text most often elicited by ethnographers is the *life history.* Such documents, particularly

CORNELL CAPA/MAGNUM

An ethnographer records the speech of an Amahuaca Indian in Peru.

when accompanied by explanatory notes, can be highly revealing of cultural patterns. A series of brief life histories may also be collected in connection with studies of personality or of culture change. The elicitation of a reliable life history requires considerable skill and a high degree of rapport between ethnographer and informant. In general, it should be attempted only after the anthropologist has been in the field for some time, and must be interpreted with great caution (see Langness 1965).

10. Photography

If one picture were really worth a thousand words, most ethnographic reports could be shortened to perhaps fifteen pages of plates. Photography has played a rather minor role in ethnography. Its value as a supplement to written records is unquestioned, but it must be remembered that the camera is selective as well as objective, so that the taking and interpretation of photographs is difficult. *Ethnographic films* are difficult and expensive to make. Like life histories and psychological tests, motion pictures can be meaningful only when the fundamental cultural patterns of a social group are fully understood and good rapport has been established. An ethnographic film made for teaching or esthetic purposes will be very different from one intended solely as a record of observations. Good films of any of these types are still extremely rare. The most successful have been collaborations between an experienced ethnographer and an imaginative professional filmmaker.

A recent innovation in the use of photography involves the analysis of pictures taken by members of the society being studied. For instance, John Adair has taught several Navajos to make and edit motion pictures on themes of interest to them, and Hal Kagan has experimented with having Colombian peasants each take a series of still photographs that they feel express certain cultural values. These "texts" can then be analyzed. Adair and Kagan are the first to use this technique in nonliterate societies.

11. Artifact collection

Many ethnographers bring back from the field artifacts that illustrate the arts and crafts of the societies they have studied. Such collections may be analyzed by experts in primitive technology, and ultimately find their way into museums. An ideal ethnographic collection will include samples of all the major tool types used by a society. For the larger artifacts, native craftworkers can often be persuaded to make accurate scale models. Artifacts, however, are nearly useless without careful notes that tell where they were made and describe materials, manner of production and distribution, and ways they are used.

Artifact collections constitute the principal data for archaeological inferences. The archaeologist's field notes must accurately describe the location of and relations among *traces and products of past human behavior* that he recovers. Modern archaeology often aims at the reconstruction of the history and total way of life of prehistoric human communities. For these purposes it requires careful study of every shred and sherd of evidence that can be recovered from a site. The field archaeologist must be a specialist in the excavation, preservation, and restoration of crumbling architectural features, fragile textiles, brittle bones, and all sorts of other cultural remains—from pottery fragments to plant seeds. He must identify and plot the position of each find, labeling and cataloging even apparently insignificant objects. And he must interpret these finds in terms of the reconstructed environment and the archaeological context from which they came.

12. Document collection

Particularly in working with literate societies, anthropologists gather documents—diaries, baptismal records, epitaphs, graffiti, newspapers, letters, and so forth. These documents require interpretation to extract the structural and historical information they contain. Sometimes the relevant documents for ethnohistorical study must be sought at some distance from the society under study. For example, Latin Americanists may consult the royal archives of Spain or Portugal, and Indianists may need access to the records of British colonial agencies and trading companies.

The preceding list should give some idea of the kinds of records, texts, questionnaire responses, and test protocols that may be produced by a period of field work. The quality of each type of record is a result of the skill of the ethnographer and the conditions under which she has to work. The goal of all these techniques is to reduce observations of human behavior to forms that can be analyzed to disclose regularities at various levels of cultural patterning. Texts (in the broad sense of the word) provide the evidence for general statements that the ethnographer makes about the culture of the group she has studied.

INFERENCES FROM TEXTS

Anthropologists can make certain kinds of inferences from field data of their own and of others. Anthropologists analyzing their own data make use of unrecorded memories and of intuitions derived from the period of field research; however, all inferences should derive from, and be documented by, written texts, photographs, and artifact collections—that is, from evidence that could in principle be analyzed by any competent anthropologist, with roughly comparable results. The extent to which analyses of the same materials differ is a measure of the degree of subjectivity that remains, and perhaps must remain, a part of anthropological inference.

The kinds of inferences made from records of observations depend in part on the nature of the materials: linguistic, ethnographic, archaeological. Starting with inferences of *structure*—that is, the categories and plans found in particular languages—we shall then consider the methods used to make

A		B	
q'an	'ripe'	q'anq'an	'rotten'
suk	'good'	suksuk	'delicious'
ras	'green'	rasras	'very green'
q'eq	'black'	q'eqq'eq	'jet black'
nim	'big'	nimnim	'very big'
kaq	'red'	kaqkaq	'very red'
saq	'white'	saqsaq	'very white'

FIGURE 11.1 Part of a Pocomchi Linguistic Text (from W. Merrifield *et al., Laboratory Manual for Morphology and Syntax* [Santa Ana, Calif.: Summer Institute of Linguistics, 1962], Problem 54).

historical, functional, and causal interpretations of materials from different periods or different cultural systems.

Linguistic Inference

Part of a linguistic text in Pocomchi (an Indian language of Guatemala) is given in Figure 11.1. From such a text (which has already been phonemically written), what inferences are possible? It appears that words such as those in column *B* can be formed by *reduplication* (repetition) of words such as those in column *A* and that this plan for word formation produces an *intensification* of meaning. Suppose now that the linguist finds in his text the word *suq*, 'sweet.' Is he justified in forming from *suq* another word, **suqsuq*, with the probably meaning 'very sweet'? In this case, the linguist or the Pocomchi child would be mistaken, for the meaning 'very sweet' is rendered in Pocomchi as *mas suq*: **suqsuq* simply does not occur in normal speech.

Language is described in terms of *categories* of sounds and meaningful sound combinations plus the *plans* associated with these categories. The plans make it possible to build words, sentences, and larger linguistic units (speeches, tales, and so forth) from a limited number of units. The linguist identifies significant categories and determines the plans that govern their combination by studying the *form and distribution of similar items.* He goes carefully through his text comparing items that partly resemble one another in form and/or meaning, and he charts their relationships to other such items. All apparent regularities are then stated as provisional linguistic rules (hypotheses) and carefully checked against other texts or elicited utterances.

The *minimal goal* of a linguistic description is to account for all of the material in the texts by showing that it is the manifestation of learned rules (plans) operating on learned categories of experience. The larger the corpus (number of texts) on which a description is based, the more valid a given set of rules is likely to be; yet so long as a linguistic description accounts for all the material in the texts, it meets the minimal goal stated above. Standard linguistic descriptions are composed of sections dealing with the sound system and the grammatical system, plus a dictionary that lists words (or morphemes) together with their meanings.

A more ambitious goal of linguistic description is to account for the *ability* of speakers of a language to produce and interpret an infinite number of sentences (see the discussion of productivity, p. 59). A *generative grammar* is intended not only to describe a finite corpus reliably but also to state the rules that would generate *all* and *only* those sentences that a native speaker would judge to be grammatical. A finite number of categories and plans can be used to generate an infinite number of sentences. Ideally, the linguist with a large enough corpus and an adequate theory of language should be able to describe *everything that a native speaker has to know in order to speak and understand his language.* This ideal has yet to be realized.

Even adult speakers occasionally produce ungrammatical sentences. Errors of performance, both accidental and deliberate, are quite common in spoken language, for linguistic rules are only shared conventions for speaking which, like other kinds of social rules, *may be violated.* A structural description gives the rules that channel behavior into expected patterns, but it cannot and does not claim to account for actual behavior. It seeks to specify the *competence* that members of a society must share if they are to understand one another's speech and actions and that enables them to judge the grammaticality of an utterance or the appropriateness of a social act.

Ethnographic Inference

Ethnography is the description of the structure and organization of single societies. Ethnographic descriptions may employ historical materials when they are available, but the traditional ethnography is *synchronic,* that is, limited to one period of time.

The texts on which ethnographic descriptions are based consist of records of social interaction together with native judgments of the meanings and appropriateness of such actions. From these concrete cases and evaluative statements, the ethnographer infers the shared expectations (social rules) that govern interaction.

Given a set of texts that constitutes an adequate sample of social interaction, how does an ethnographer formulate his description of the social system? As in linguistic analysis, he must go through his corpus, taking note of the *form and distribution of similar items*. In social analysis, however, the relevant units are kinds of persons (roles), kinds of groups (including institutions), conceptions of social space and time (situations), and the principles of organization that determine how the structure is put into action.

In the compass of this chapter it is possible to give only a brief example of ethnographic inference. Consider how an alien observer would formulate an ethnographic description of a great American institution, the college football game. If he had no access to the official rules, he would first attempt to observe and ask questions about several performances of the game. He will learn that football games take place during a particular part of the athletic year (football season) and usually on a specific day of the week. The next Saturday will find him sitting in the stands, busily taking field notes. He will ask questions of his fellow spectators, take pictures, interview coaches and team members, and collect a few documents and artifacts (game programs, an official ball, a penalty flag, and perhaps a model goal post). The coaches probably will not allow him to participate in the game, but he may attend a few practice sessions, if he can convince them that he is not a spy. Having built up a sizable corpus of texts, he will retire to try to make sense of them.

Any ethnography of the football game would have to include an *inventory of the categories* of persons, times, places, and objects, and the features that distinguish each from the others. It should also include the *plans associated with each category* and the ways they relate to one another. That is, the ethnography should state both the general behaviors expected of the category of players (as contrasted with other kinds of persons present, such as referees and spectators), and the specific actions expected of, say, a quarterback on a third-down play. These plans would be more than just the official rules: they should constitute a "grammar" of the game, indicating what combinations of units are possible (for example, four- and five-man lines) and how different units must be modified in various situations (for example, reaction of each team to an intercepted pass).

Furthermore, the ethnographer should describe *recruitment* to each of the categories of persons: How are coaches, referees, and players chosen? Who is paid and by whom? What kinds of persons attend the games as spectators or as band members? and so on. Our alien ethnographer might find that his attempts to study the recruitment of players met with some resistance, but this would lead him into a number of significant areas (the scouting system, training methods, athletic scholarships, and league regulations on eligibility) which would then require accumulation of data and careful analysis.

A person who had all this knowledge would know how to avoid breaking rules, but he would not necessarily be able to do anything right (for example, block, tackle, or catch a pass). Once again, we are talking about knowledge or competence rather than performance. Successful performance requires *skills* that can be gained only through practice and participation, and an *understanding* of organizational principles—in this case, the strategy of offensive and defensive play and team leadership. Although the principles of strategy and leadership can probably be verbally formulated, they would not be very useful to someone without firsthand experience in playing the game. This is true of rules of art and of maxims in general: they are of use only to those who have already acquired considerable skill and nonverbal comprehension (Polanyi 1964). These are limitations of any ethnography (or grammar), but not obstacles to its purpose: to state the structure within which meaningful human behavior takes place.

Whether it deals with a college football game or the kinship behavior of the Tallensi, ethnographic inference operates on a series of concrete cases to produce statements of regularities. From records of who did and said what, where, when, and to whom, the ethnographer *infers* the *recurrent patterns of behavior* and states them as plans (expectations) associated with categories of persons, objects, and situations. One's first interpretations are hypotheses that must be verified by further observations or texts. For example, the provisional interpretation that only members of the category "ends" may receive forward passes must be modified when he discovers cases in which "backs" may legally do so.

Many social rules are discovered by the ethnographer only when he is able to *observe the consequences of a violation.*

Informants may disagree as to whether a specific violation has taken place, but there will generally be a consensus as to what kind of behavior constitutes a violation (for example, being on the wrong side of the line of scrimmage when the ball is snapped) and how it should be penalized. Such judgments of appropriateness are among the most important clues to the existence of shared expectations.

There remains the problem of the relationship of the group or institution to its environment. A college football game is a highly artificial situation: it contributes only indirectly, if at all, to the biological survival of the spectators or the players. Occasionally, a football hero may be enabled to find a mate as a result of his athletic prowess, but this selective advantage is probably overshadowed by the dangers of his profession. For a winning team, victory in a game may be adaptive in that it leads to a championship, a good job offer (for players and coaches), and prominence for the college (which may make recruitment of players easier). The college may benefit from having a winning team, by recruiting sports-loving students and faculty, and by maintaining alumni interest with its accompanying financial support.

These adaptations are primarily on the level of the social environment. (See Figure 6.3.) A full understanding of cultural adaptation on all three levels is essential to a complete ethnographic description. This understanding must go beyond the statement of roles, groups, and situations to a consideration of the needs that they serve. Like tools, social structures have definite effects on the environment in which they operate, though their technological functions are not always easy to specify. When a group of women with hoes goes into a field to cultivate the ground, the function of the work group is in part the same as that of the tools: the women use their skills and energy to break up the soil into its component parts so that crops can grow and people can eat. But what about a political party, a church, a college faculty, or a football team? How can we describe their adaptive functions?

We have come to some rather intricate problems of social theory, and all that we can do here is to indicate the nature of the problems. To begin with, in Chapter 5 we defined three types of group functions—task, control, and expressive—each of which is present in every group, though in varying proportions. We also distinguished between explicit functions (of which the participants were overtly aware) and implicit functions (of which the participants are presumably unaware, but which were detected by the anthropologist). When anthropologists speak of a *structural-functional approach* (or theory), they mean one in which the structure of a group is related to the specific task, control, and expressive functions that it performs. Thus, members of a clan society may give various explicit reasons for the rule of clan exogamy, but the implicit function of producing social solidarity by the exchange of mates is seldom recognized by the participants themselves. Clans may also have important functions in relation to the physical/biological environment, as in societies where they control access to land or other resources, and they may function on the level of the internal environment by providing personal security and a sense of identity. All of these possibilities must be considered by the anthropologist.

In assessing the functions of a custom or institution, anthropologists must be particularly on guard against ethnocentrism. They must not judge a custom to be dysfunctional (harmful to the society) simply because they disapprove of its content, or nonfunctional just because they cannot immediately understand its purpose. For example, even if anthropologists disapprove of race prejudice, they must try to understand the part it plays in maintaining a status quo. Robert Merton (1957) has shown that some big-city political bosses provided necessary personal services to their constituents at a time when impersonal bureaucracies were ineffective in meeting genuine needs. Marvin Harris (1967) has suggested that the sacred cow of Hindu India—often cited as a destructive and worthless animal—actually performs essential adaptive functions by providing dung for fuel and fertilizer as well as oxen for plowing and transport. This does not mean that anthropologists have to endorse prejudice, bossism, or superstition, but they must avoid judging a practice before they understand its part in the total culture. All cultures have some *survivals* (functionless customs that have persisted from earlier periods), but in every culture the vast majority of customs, groups, and institutions *do* contribute to social continuity and the satisfaction of needs.

The discovery of social functions is only partly based on inferences from texts. When an ethnographer states that a given social ritual contributes to group solidarity or that an institution (such as a university) supports the traditional social class structure, she may be invoking theoretical notions that find no direct support in her texts. If, however, she can demonstrate that when the ritual is omitted, groups tend to break up, or that admission to a university depends on the applicants' social class and perpetuates their high status by giving graduates access to prestigious roles, then her statements have a firmer basis. The kinds of structures and functions that a particular anthropologist will detect in her materials depend largely on her theoretical training and interests. There are competing theories of description and explanation in modern cultural anthropology, and their use is still largely a matter of personal preference.

Archaeological Inference

Archaeological inference is similar to ethnographic inference, with two differences: the archaeologist is (1) limited to observation of the material remains and other traces of once-living cultures, and (2) more likely to be concerned with *diachronic* problems—questions of historical development and relationships. Archaeologists make extensive use of artifact collections. An archaeological text consists of a catalog of artifacts and a record of their positions at the time of excavation. Since archaeologists cannot observe these objects in use, they must *infer their history and functions from a detailed study of their form and distribution.* They can, however, make use of comparable ethnographic materials in forming their hypotheses.

Archaeologists use descriptive units similar to those discussed above. They define significant *categories of objects*: artifact types, buildings, fossil remains of plants and animals, and so forth. They compare them with known tool types or organisms and study their distribution relative to one another and to features of the natural environment.

On the basis of such information they try to characterize the culture of the people who once inhabited a site. They ask such questions as: How many people lived here and how long did they stay? What was the nature of their subsistence economy? Were they hunters, fishers, gatherers, agriculturalists, or some combination of these types? What was their social structure like? Is there evidence of large-scale social cooperation? Of social stratification? Of religious or artistic activity? And so on.

These are the same kinds of questions ethnographers ask about the communities they study, but archaeologists must find their answers indirectly, by examining cultural remains and in-

Careful measurement and records are essential to the correct interpretation of archeological sites, as at this "dig" in Ethiopia.

ferring their meaning. They must exercise extreme caution and avoid making unwarranted assumptions. Where extensive skeletal remains have been preserved (which is not usually the case), it must be remembered that they constitute only a *sample* of the total population; it must not be assumed that all the individuals represented in a cemetery lived at the same time. When population size is estimated from the remains of shelters, archaeologists must not assume that all of the detected structures were standing during the same period; nor should they estimate the number of persons per dwelling on the basis of modern standards of comfort. The nature of the shelters (materials, construction, form, and so forth) can give some indication of the permanence of habitation at the site, but even where substantial dwellings are found, it is dangerous to assume continuous occupation. For example, the Eskimo often build large wood and stone dwellings that they occupy only during certain seasons, living in perishable tents or igloos at other times.

Subsistence activities can be inferred from a variety of object types: projectile points, traps, fishhooks, hoes, seed grinders, containers; and the shells, bones, seeds, or pollen of various organisms can all be used as clues to the nature and relative importance of various economic activities. Paleobotanists and zoologists can often identify plant and animal species from fragmentary evidence, and in most cases can also determine whether organic remains are those of wild or domesticated varieties.

The skills of these and other specialists are very important to modern archaeology, for present-day archaeologists are more concerned with understanding the adaptation of prehistoric societies to their environments than were their predecessors, who tended to be collectors or historians. Thus, every scrap of evidence is inspected and items are collected which might formerly have been dismissed or overlooked: pollen samples, bits of charcoal for radioactive dating, broken tools and pieces of pottery—anything that might reveal the nature of human activities.

To infer the social structure of prehistoric societies, the archaeologist may draw on ethnographic parallels, but only with great care. The presence, for example, of a large-scale irrigation system or of monumental architecture does not necessarily indicate that the people lived in dense population centers. There is considerable evidence that the magnificent ceremonial centers of the Mayan civilization in Mesoamerica were fully occupied only on ritual occasions, and that the peasant population lived dispersed in small villages.

The degree of social stratification in an extinct society can sometimes be estimated from the quantity and quality of grave goods (material objects buried with a person). If most of the burials at a site contain a scattering of poor trinkets, but a few burials contain a variety of finely made weapons, containers, and ornaments, the archaeologist is probably justified in inferring the existence of a wealthy class.

Change in a culture over time may be inferred in a variety of ways. Within a single site, the most important evidence for length of occupation and for culture change comes from the *stratification of remains.* When a particular location has been inhabited for several generations, cultural evidence tends to accumulate. Usually, older materials are covered by more recent remains. This means that the archaeologist can, with caution, *translate spatial distributions into temporal sequences.* The principle of stratification states that, other things being equal, the lower down in a deposit, the older the objects uncovered. Thus in sites such as Olduvai Gorge, the caves of southern France, or the ancient mounds of the Near East, centuries of prehistoric occupation have left stratified remains that give a clear picture of human biological and cultural development in these regions.

Archaeologists can fit together several stratified sites with overlapping cultural sequences to produce a long-range picture of cultural development within a large region. Not all archaeologists, however, are content with just reconstructing particular historical sequences. The "new archaeology" (like the new linguistics) is much more ambitious. It is concerned with the causes of cultural variation rather than classification alone, and with general principles rather than conjecture about "influences" or "migrations." It insists that archaeologists must adhere to the scientific method of forming hypotheses and testing them against the data. As Lewis Binford has put it, "We attempt to explain similarities and differences in archaeological remains in terms of the functioning of material items in a cultural system and the . . . operation or evolution of the cultural systems responsible for the varied artifact forms, associations, and distributions observable in the ground" (1972:120).

This means that the topics that archaeologists can explore are limited only by their imagination in formulating hypotheses and by their ability to devise methods for testing them on available data. It also means that archaeology must "test the validity of explanatory principles currently in use and attempt to refine or replace them by verified hypotheses relating the significance of archaeological data to past conditions'' (Binford 1972:121). The goal is the formulation of *general laws of cultural process,* often emphasizing the role of long-range ecological processes in producing cultural change. This goal requires close cooperation among archaeologists, ethnologists, linguists, and specialists from many biological and physical sciences. It is a vast undertaking, but it does represent one way in which we may someday achieve a unified science of humanity.

COMPARATIVE METHODS

The most general goal of cultural anthropology can be stated as the attempt to *understand the similarities and differences among all human cultures and the processes that have produced them.* To achieve this purpose, we must compare all kinds of data on living and extinct societies, languages, technologies, and ideologies. For if we are to understand any culture—including our own—we must see it in relation to and in contrast with other cultures. Otherwise, we may attribute to ''human nature'' beliefs and behaviors that are only the conventions of a particular society.

Comparisons are carried out for at least three different, though related, purposes:

1. Historical—to reconstruct the sequences of development within and relationships among cultural systems. Historical studies may also deal with particular items within systems—for example, the history and spread of a particular word or technique rather than an entire language or technological system.

2. Functional/Causal—to understand the general principles of cultural development and integration. Although certainly not independent of historical understanding, this type of investigation involves comparisons among various historical traditions and the use of special cross-cultural methods.

3. Universals—to discover features that appear in every language and social system. They may be universals of content or of process. The anthropologist also attempts to trace such features to their sources in human biology or psychology, in culture history, and/or in the necessary constitution of cultural systems.

The ethnologist attempts to infer culture history from the *geographic distributions of social, technological, and ideological forms.* His goal is to trace the source and spread of various peoples and to understand the processes that lead to accept-

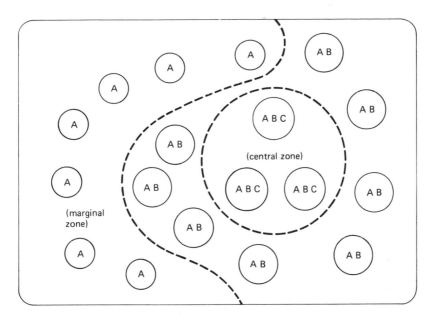

FIGURE 11.2 The Age-Area Principle. Mapping the geographic distribution of selected cultural elements (A, B, and C) makes it possible
tentatively to infer their relative age. For example, if each of the circles
above represents a different community and if A = radio, B = black-
and-white television, and C = color television, it might be inferred that
radio is the oldest invention (because of its wide distribution), followed
by black-and-white television (which has a more restricted distribution
and has not yet reached the marginal communities), while color television is the most recent, being found only in the central zone.

ance, rejection, and modification of cultural innovations. In
achieving these aims, the ethnologist makes use of certain assumptions similar to the archaeological principle of stratification. For example, in trying to infer the relative age of different
forms from their contemporary geographic distribution, he often
assumes that, other things being equal, the greater the spatial
spread of a form, the older it must be. This assumption is known
as the "age-area principle." (See Figure 11.2.)

As with the principle of stratification, other things are of
course *not* always equal, and the age-area principle must be
used with great caution. But in the absence of other evidence,
it is useful in forming hypotheses about temporal sequences
from spatial distributions. In much of Africa, for example, archaeological remains are few, because of the perishability of
materials used and the poor conditions for preservation; there-

fore, inferences from geographic distributions are heavily relied upon in reconstructing culture history. But in the last thirty years, increased archaeological activity in this region has led to a reevaluation of many historical reconstructions that were based solely on ethnographic comparisons and native legends. In many cases the previous reconstructions were confirmed, but in some cases they were shown to be inaccurate.

Many of the historical statements in the chapters on technological systems are the results of painstaking comparative research by ethnologists, supplemented by archaeological data when available. For example, the discussions of types of snowshoes, boats, and fire-making techniques are all based on detailed comparative ethnographic studies. The ethnologist plots the geographic distribution of the forms she is interested in, and analyzes the artifacts or practices into the smaller cultural elements of which they are composed. For example, an arrow is considered in terms of the type of point, shaft, feathers, and even the way the arrow is released. Using criteria of similarity and elaboration, culture historians make inferences about the origins and spread of various elements, describing the ways that they have been reinterpreted by borrowing societies and/or combined with other elements. In most culture historical studies, individuals are unknown or unimportant; the focus is on sequences of cultural developments in regional and sometimes worldwide contexts.

Traditional culture history has been criticized by many contemporary ethnologists for its arbitrary methods, untested assumptions, and insufficient attention to the social and environmental functions of the elements it studies. Some of these criticisms are doubtless justified, but the best culture historians have always been aware of these problems and have done their best to control them. What has really happened is that the interests of ethnologists have changed so that they are now asking different questions. In addition to tracing the development of specific regional traditions, ethnologists are interested in the processes of *adaptive change* and *culture growth.* They ask such questions as: What happens when groups with relatively similar cultures move into diverse environments? Can any general tendencies be found in the development of human culture as a whole?

The essays in *Evolution and Culture,* edited by Marshall Sahlins and Elman Service (1960), made an important distinction between general and specific cultural evolution. Studies of general evolution analyze the overall progressive trends in human culture as a whole; it is measured, as Leslie White first sug-

gested, by increasing human control over sources of energy
(see p. 195). Such studies are concerned with the emergence of
new levels of integration or principles of social organization
wherever they take place and without regard to environmental
adaptations. The study of specific evolution, on the other hand,
is concerned with the particular adaptations made by particular
regional cultures to their material and social environments. As
Sahlins and Service noted:

> The cultural anthropologist surveying the ethnographic and archae-
> ological achievements of his discipline is confronted by variety if
> nothing else. There are myriads of culture types, that is, of the cul-
> ture characteristic of an ethnic group or a region, and even greater
> variety of cultures proper, of the cultural organization of given co-
> hesive societies. How has this come about? In a word, through adap-
> tive modification: culture has diversified as it has filled in the variety
> of opportunities for human existence afforded by the earth. Such is
> the specific aspect of cultural evolution [1960:23].

Thus we are led to a view of cultural evolution that has many
similarities to the modern theory of biological evolution: new
forms (organic or cultural) arise and survive through adaptation
to changing environmental situations; but above and beyond
this specific process, there emerge new levels or "grades" of
organization that may be ordered in an ascending series. Just
as the biological "grade" of *monkeys* arose independently in
the Old and New Worlds from different groups of prosimian
ancestors, so did the cultural "grade" of *civilization* arise, more
than once in both hemispheres, from very different cultural traditions. (See Service 1975.)

Cross-Cultural Studies

Through long and intensive acquaintance with an alien culture,
the ethnographer is often able to discover the implicit function
of customs and institutions that seem bizarre and arbitrary on
more superficial acquaintance. But for the discovery of some
kinds of functional relations, comparative study is necessary.
For example, the function of a type of kinship terminology or
the consequences of some mode of enculturation can be understood only by systematic comparison of societies in which the
custom or trait is found with other societies in which it is *not*
present, and noting what appear to be the consequences for
other parts of the culture.
   Social anthropologists construct categories of customs that

can be applied cross-culturally: they study cross-cousin marriage, matrilineal descent, or dependency training in a variety of societies. While recognizing that the actual behaviors in each group are quite different, they still hope to discover some *regularities of form or process* that will show a functional relationship between the custom under study and some other part of the cultural system.

This kind of study has a long history. During the nineteenth century, Sir Edward Tylor coined the term "adhesion" to indicate those customs that were found together in more societies than would be expected if they coexisted just by chance. For example, Tylor was interested in the custom of mother-in-law avoidance, a social rule that forbids a man to speak to, or in some cases even to look at, his wife's mother. He studied a large number of ethnographic descriptions of societies in which this custom was observed and found that in the majority of them, the rule of postmarital residence was matrilocal—the man was expected to reside with his wife's kin. This adhesion—or as we would say today, *correlation*—does not explain either of the rules, but it does indicate the probability of a functional relation between them, and it indicates that any attempt to understand mother-in-law avoidance must take account of residence patterns (1889:245–269).

Using a similar cross-cultural correlational approach, George P. Murdock reached some general conclusions about the relative effect of three structural factors on kinship terminology. Although special *marriage rules,* such as sister exchange, have a notable effect on kinship terminology, the effect of *descent rules* on terminology is somewhat stronger. Murdock also found that *residence rules,* although they do affect terminology to some extent, are not so powerful as either of the two other factors. In decreasing order of their effect on kinship terminology, then, we have:

1. rules of descent (patrilineal, matrilineal, and so forth) and the kinship groups they produce;
2. marriage rules (polygamy, polyandry, monogamy, and so forth) and the kinds of families they produce;
3. residence rules (patrilocal, neolocal, bilocal, and so forth) and the local groupings they produce (1949:182–183).

The functional relationships among these three structural factors have also been studied. Murdock concludes that residence rules tend to be "progressive" rules: in the course of social change, it is the residence rules that are most likely to change *first*. This change eventually produces changes in the more "conservative" rules governing descent and marriage, which in turn have strong effects on kinship terminology. These findings support the conception of social structure as a *system* within which any change in one part has effects on all the other parts. But since residence rules are most responsive to environmental change, they also caution us to look *outside* of the social system for some of the factors that set change in motion.

Murdock's work was in part made possible by a research aid known as the Human Relations Area Files (HRAF), which he founded at Yale University during the 1930s. These files contain ethnographic information on several hundred societies, ranging from primitive tribes to national states. They are organized by culture area and are broken down into categories for indexing. These materials have been duplicated and are now available to researchers at most major universities and colleges. They make possible the rapid inspection of materials from a great variety of societies on any given cultural topic. For instance, if an ethnologist is interested in diet, wedding ceremonies, or clothing in some region of the world, he has only to go to the files, and in a few hours he can pull out and inspect a range of materials that would otherwise require many days or weeks to locate. HRAF also commissions and publishes integrative studies on cultural topics and regions. Summaries of various studies based largely on materials in the files are published in the journal *Ethnology.*

Another area of comparative research in which the cross-cultural approach has been used is the study of enculturation (or, more generally, culture and personality). In some of these studies, the investigators use *rating scales* on which the intensity of a custom is evaluated, rather than just its presence or absence. But the principle is the same: if one custom or personality trait can be shown to go with another more than random association would predict, the hypothesis that they are functionally related is felt to be validated. For example, John Whiting and Irvin Child have tried to show that cultural explanations of illness are functionally related to child-training practices (socialization). Without going into the details of their theory (which hinges on the Freudian concept of fixation), we may describe their general conclusions in regard to "oral explanations" of illness.

By "oral explanations," Whiting and Child mean the custom of attributing illness either to the ingestion of some material (food or poison) by the patient or to verbal spells and incantations performed by other people. They found that *there is a significant relationship between oral explanations of illness and the presence in a society of child-training practices likely to produce considerable anxiety about oral behavior* (sucking, eating, or speaking). The child-training practices believed to produce a high degree of "oral socialization anxiety" include such customs as early or severe weaning as well as excessive punishment in connection with oral behavior. They found that early weaning was highly correlated with the presence in a society of oral explanations for illness—beliefs that illness was caused by something eaten or spoken (1953:162).

The cross-cultural approach is used widely in ethnology, but it has raised as many questions as it has answered. Among the problems still to be solved in this area are the following:

1. Validity and comparability of the primary data (ethnographic sources)
2. Reliability of the rating procedures
3. Suitability and randomness of the sample
4. Allowance for geographic factors (control for the possibility of historical diffusion rather than functional relationship of customs)
5. Significance of the results

Each of these points could be discussed at great length, and numerous books and articles attempt to deal with them. We shall comment here only on the last point. In the case of Whiting and Child's data described above, what does it *mean* that early weaning and oral explanations of illness are found together in a high proportion of societies? To begin with, it does *not* necessarily mean that there exists a *causal relationship* between the two customs. A correlation must never be taken as proof of causation. Although it may be argued from these data, given several assumptions of Freudian psychology, that custom *A* (age of weaning) is the cause of custom *B* (oral explanations of illness), *at least three other possibilities* must be taken into account in this (or any other) case:

1. The supposed causal relationship between *A* and *B* could be reversed. In this example, perhaps people who believe that illness is caused by ingestion of harmful material tend to wean their children early as a form of protection.
2. Both *A* and *B* may be produced by some third factor, *C*, which is as yet unrecognized. (There is a high correlation

between the flowering of fruit trees and the northerly migration of birds, but most people recognize that there is a seasonal factor that controls both.)

3. The finding may be spurious because of an unintentionally biased sample. Statistical analysis says only how *improbable* a certain outcome is—it can never certify the validity of a finding. Indeed, statistical theory asserts that highly improbable combinations of factors *do* occur now and then simply by chance.

Thus the cross-cultural approach, even with the help of research aids such as the HRAF and techniques of statistical inference, cannot guarantee valid findings. And even the most plausible *post hoc* explanations of correlations must be carefully questioned. It is only when a hypothesis based in theory has *preceded* the testing of a relationship that the correlation can be taken as support for the hypothesis.

For these and other reasons, ethnological inference remains, to a large extent, an *art*. In most arts, valid results are produced only when talented workers apply their knowledge and skills to a vast domain of phenomena. For the ethnologist, this domain consists of the facts discovered by ethnography, linguistics, and archaeology. And these subfields, too, have their "artistic" qualities. As Evans-Pritchard has observed:

> The work of the anthropologist is not photographic. He has to decide what is significant in what he observes and by his subsequent relation of his experiences to bring what is significant into relief. For this he must have, in addition to a wide knowledge of anthropology, a feeling for form and pattern, and a touch of genius [1954:82].

CULTURAL UNIVERSALS

Anthropologists have been interested for a long time in the question of whether cultural universals exist. It should be obvious that any answers to this question must be based on a wide range of comparative data. But even though we will never be able to study all human societies in detail, the more we know, the better are our chances of arriving at valid generalizations. For example, it is now well established that all human societies have language systems that are entirely adequate to their communication needs; as recently as fifty years ago, however, some scholars maintained that "primitive languages" were crude, incomplete, or unable to express certain kinds of concepts. These ideas are no more valid than the travelers' tales that claimed that members of such-and-such a group had to supplement their speech with gestures and thus were unable to communicate in the dark—probably because they huddled around a fire at night. Yet without scientific study of primitive languages and cultures, such statements could not be effectively refuted.

Today we have a great deal of ethnographic material on which generalization can be based. Some statements of universals are actually classifications of cultural subsystems, which, while useful, do not tell us anything about the *content* of these systems. In this book, we have used an implicit classification that is made explicit in Figure 11.3.

Another classification of the "universal cultural pattern" is that suggested by Clark Wissler in his *Man and Culture*. Wissler classified the "facts of culture" under nine headings: speech, material traits, art, mythology and scientific knowledge, religious practices, family and social systems, property, government, and war. Wissler also suggested that certain cultural contents are found in all human societies. For example:

> All the historic cultures, however primitive, knew fire. They also knew its value in the preparation of food. In every case they knew, or formerly knew, how to chip stone. The principle of the knife was known and the fundamental idea of the drill. Likewise, the art of twisting string, or the making of cord; as to weaving, there was not one that did not understand the fundamental step. The fact that some of them went no further is not to the point. . . . We can go even farther, for there were common beliefs. The belief in a soul or spiritual counterpart of some kind . . . is universal. Again, the idea that evil fortune can be avoided by the strict observance of formulated prohibitions, or taboos, as they are often called, is equally so [1923:73–77].

Let us suppose that we have discovered a number of valid cultural universals. How are they to be understood? That is, why are certain particular acts, beliefs, and items found in all human societies while others are not? There are at least three kinds of explanations for the universality of a given category of culture. They may be summarized as follows:

1. The universal may be rooted in human biological needs and thus constitute a prerequisite for human social life. For example, food preparation and care of the young, part of every culture, are also present in the animal world wherever a species is capable of a varied diet and where the young are born relatively helpless. Without *some* way of performing these tasks,

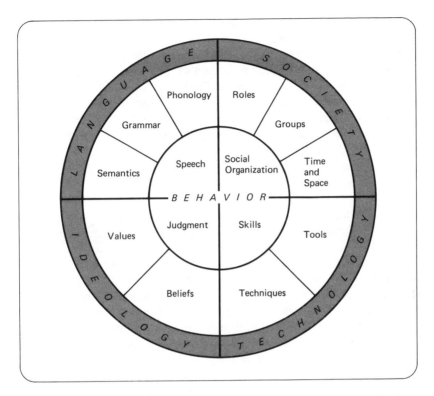

FIGURE 11.3 The Major Subsystems of Culture: Language, Society, Technology, and Ideology. The middle ring contains the major structural components of each subsystem; in the center are the behaviors that manifest the various subsystems.

the society (animal or human) could not survive; but the human capacity for culture elaborates a group's solution into a complex social tradition.

2. The universal may be an exceedingly ancient invention that has had time to diffuse (spread) around the world. For example, the use of fire or the basic techniques of chipping stone-cutting tools are "technical traits" (to use Wissler's phrase) that were first developed hundreds of thousands of years ago and have had ample time to spread or be carried over the face of the earth—whether from one or several centers of invention. We can, today, see the rapid spread of other traits from the places of their invention (for example, the smoking of tobacco, which spread from the New World to Europe in the sixteenth century and since then over most of the world; and the use of metal cutting tools, which is now universal). Diffusion may have been slower in past ages, but it was just as inevitable.

3. Universals may be the result of the convergence of cultural forms due to their adaptive advantage. That is, similar traits or techniques may have been independently invented many times and may have persisted or replaced other items because of their functional value for the group. This is a frequent explanation for the universality of the incest taboo, the notion being that groups without some such rule would suffer the social and biological disadvantages of inbreeding, while those with such a taboo would of necessity establish cooperative bonds with other social groups—relationships that would operate to their advantage in the struggle for survival.

These three types of explanation are not mutually exclusive. Given a human biological need (say, temperature regulation), the development of a culture trait that helps to meet this need (such as fire, dress, or shelter) is very likely to spread, whether it is invented once, twice, or many times. Similarly, explanations of the historical (2) and functional (3) types are as applicable to regional or nonuniversal traits as they are to true universals. In some cases, one type of explanation may seem more plausible than another. For example, the *norm of reciprocity* has been claimed to be universal (Chapter 6); but even if it is only very widespread, an explanation of its distribution based on its implicit function (production of social solidarity through exchange) is more plausible than one that claims the norm was "invented" at some early time and then diffused. Both functional relationships and historical diffusion play important roles in culture history. Some social anthropologists who look only for functional explanations may neglect much more obvious historical ones (Bock 1967).

A final type of universal that has interested some anthropologists may be called a *value universal*. Although cultural anthropology teaches us not to evaluate other societies by an ethnocentric standard, it does not preclude the possibility that at least some values are found in every culture. Indeed, the norm of legitimacy (which places a negative value on birth out of wedlock) and the norm of reciprocity (which positively values repayment of obligations) may be instances of value universals.

One other possible value universal is suggested by the work of Lévi-Strauss (p. 249). It may be that in every culture there are certain *oppositions* that must be maintained, and although cultures may phrase them in different ways, some kinds of boundaries are essential to individual and social continuity. For example, every culture makes a distinction between the living and the dead, and devotes a good deal of ritual energy to maintaining this boundary. The line between life and death may be drawn in very different places according to social conventions (for example, the dispute in modern medicine as to whether "brain death" or "circulatory death" is the proper criterion of the life/death distinction). But *some* such convention is essential to human social life. Similarly, every culture seems to make and defend oppositions between sacred and profane and between nature and culture. It may well be that the most profound differences among cultures have to do with the ways in which they draw these universal distinctions, while the most profound similarities flow from the common "human nature" that makes us draw them.

RESPONSIBILITIES OF THE ANTHROPOLOGIST

In this chapter we have been concerned with method. But as a wise man once said, an excessive concern with technique, whether in science, art, or love, frequently leads to impotence. Let us then discuss some of the purposes of anthropology, and the responsibilities that accompany these purposes.

To begin with, anthropologists have certain responsibilities to their profession. As social scientists, they are committed to use critical intelligence, to choose genuine social issues for investigation, and to carry through their research with energy and imagination. In the last analysis, the scientific method means to do your damnedest while being ready to admit mistakes. Anthropologists also have a responsibility to work for an *integrated* science of humanity. This task is becoming increasingly difficult owing to specialization and fragmentation within the discipline. For example, within just a few days I noted (in print) the following designations for "kinds of anthropology":

Structural anthropology	Psychedelic anthropology
Psychological anthropology	Humanistic anthropology
Applied anthropology	Educational anthropology
Economic anthropology	Political anthropology
Ecological anthropology	Urban anthropology
Behavioral anthropology	Development anthropology
Linguistic anthropology	Radical anthropology
Cognitive anthropology	Visual anthropology
Medical anthropology	Symbolic anthropology

and these are in addition to the conventional subfields of physical, cultural, and social anthropology! Such specialization is perhaps inevitable, if only because the number of professional anthropologists has doubled in the last ten years; but it also means that our understanding of human beings and culture will become fragmented if we do not actively strive for an integrated view.

Anthropologists also have certain *ethical* responsibilities to their profession. One good rule for the ethnographer is "Don't mess up so bad that nobody can ever work there again." There are a number of communities (and even countries) where American anthropologists are not welcome because of the alleged misbehavior of their colleagues. Certainly, anthropologists should avoid becoming involved in dishonest or undercover kinds of research, the results of which cannot be freely disclosed and published. But equally important are the responsibilities of anthropologists to the people they study. As Roy Wagner has stated, we are obliged to deal with other peoples "on a basis of equality and mutuality." People of other cultures may be *subjects* of study, but should not be treated as mere *objects* of research, or as means to the ethnographer's selfish ends.

Anthropology may well be the study of human beings, but what if the human beings don't want to be studied, or don't realize the possible consequences for their lives of having anthropologists poking around in their societies? Times have changed. Primitive and Third World peoples have a new sense of their cultural identity, and for many, the anthropologist has become a symbol of imperialism. People are no longer uncertain about the social role of anthropologists—as far as they are concerned, anthropologists are simply "tools of neocolonialism." At the very least, they are asking: Why should we let you study us? What will be the benefits to our community? And they have forced many anthropologists to rethink their notions of responsibility and obligation. We have always hoped that our work would not harm the people we studied; but we must now ask ourselves—given that our own careers are advanced by doing research—whether we should not ensure some positive benefits (intellectual and/or economic) to the subjects of our inquiry. For example, several ethnographers have arranged for any royalties from the publication of their field research to be paid into a medical or scholarship fund for people of the community.

The situation becomes much more complex when anthropologists, on the basis of their analyses, deliberately attempt to produce changes in the communities they have studied. Even when the changes are in line with what "the people" want, there is a great deal of uncertainty about long-range consequences, about the degree of intracommunity consensus, and about the reaction of institutions in the larger society. And when they are undertaking applied anthropology on behalf of some external agency (business corporation, government bureau, or foreign aid group), anthropologists must carefully consider the uses that might be made of their findings and policy recommendations. (See Weaver 1973:5–61.)

Finally, anthropologists also have responsibilities to the public that supports their research and teaching efforts, and to the students who sit in their classes. Quite aside from the application of anthropological knowledge and techniques to practical social problems, I believe that anthropologists have an obligation to make available to the public ("popularize," if you like) the valid findings of their science, and actively to combat the myths and fallacies that threaten our civilization. These include the myth of racial superiority, the ethnocentric assumptions of all peoples, and sensational distortions such as "man, the killer ape." We must also beware of *anthropocentrism:* the assumption that we are the most important species and that whatever is good for humanity is good for the planet. There are many historical examples of cultures that became extinct because they ignored the relation of human society to the larger environmental system. It will be ironic if our principal advance over the ancient civilizations turns out to be our ability to pollute and degrade the environment with greater speed and efficiency.

RECOMMENDED READING

Robin Fox, *Encounter with Anthropology*. New York: Harcourt Brace Jovanovich, 1973. Delightful essays on social structure in Ireland and North America, plus provocative statements on biology and culture. Cited here especially for the introductory essay on "Anthropology as a Vocation."

Myron Glazer, *The Research Adventure*. New York: Random House, 1972. Interesting discussion of the "promise and problems of fieldwork," using material from anthropology and sociology, including the author's own experiences doing field work with Chilean students in a time of revolution. Highly readable and provocative.

Rosalie H. Wax, *Doing Fieldwork*. Chicago: University of Chicago Press, 1971. Detailed and extremely honest accounts of the anthropologist's three major field experiences, two with contrasting American Indian groups and the third with Japanese-Americans interned during World War II.

Thomas Weaver, ed., *To See Ourselves.* Glenview, Ill.: Scott, Foresman, 1973. An anthology of readings dealing with "anthropology and modern social issues," and including excellent selections on the social responsibility of the anthropologist and the ethical dilemmas connected with intervention in other cultures.

Douglass R. Price-Williams, *Explorations in Cross-Cultural Psychology.* San Francisco: Chandler & Sharp, 1975. Excellent brief treatment of the problems involved in using psychological methods across cultural boundaries. Critical and sensible statements on personality studies and the "cultural relativism of intelligence."

EPILOGUE
CULTURE AND FREEDOM

A major concern of this book has been the great *paradox of culture*—the fact that culture frees people by binding them. As with language, the benefits of other cultural systems come only as people accept their constraints. The very process of enculturation, which makes possible communication and interaction among the members of a society, excludes them from participation in other traditions. The child who learns a particular set of linguistic, social, and ideological conventions will probably never feel entirely comfortable with a different set. All too often, such children grow into intolerant adults who are afraid to let loose, even for a moment, of the categories and plans they learned in childhood. They are thus disqualified from having a genuinely new experience of the world.

Throughout the book I have stressed the conventional basis of cultural phenomena. The criteria that we use in categorizing colors, sounds, kin, or diseases, the ways in which we structure time and space, and the standards we use in evaluating goodness or beauty are all creations of our predecessors. They *could have been different*. In some other society they may be either ignored or reversed.

Yet beneath the multiplicity of phonological and kinship systems, we know that there lie a few *basic oppositions*, rooted in

321

the givens of human biology, thought, and society: vowel/consonant, male/female, older/younger, individual/group, sacred/profane, and so forth. Anthropologists have shown the ways in which cultures have erected superstructures of great complexity on these foundations. Perhaps it is not too much to hope that other cultural subsystems will someday yield to a similar kind of analysis.

Culture is a wonderful creation. Words and social roles were necessary inventions. We need categories in order to deal with the complexity of the real world. The inability to form general concepts (to "see the forest for the trees") is a serious block to understanding, but when we substitute the role for the whole person, or when we mistake the word for the thing, there is a danger of losing contact with our direct experiences. Categories are essential to communication, but most categories either lump together experiences that share a few attributes while being uniquely different in other respects, or give separate labels to events that are actually different aspects of the same underlying process. For example, the tendency to label all non-Western peoples as "savages," or all nonconformist youths as "hippies," indicates both prejudice and a striking lack of imagination.

Ernest Schachtel has suggested that most of us cannot remember the first years of childhood because the culture categories (schemata) into which we have learned to force our memories are too narrow to accommodate the richness of those early, direct experiences. In his essay "On Memory and Childhood Amnesia," he says that "the world of modern Western Civilization has no use for . . . experiences of the quality and intensity typical of early childhood." Yet Schachtel believes that "memory cannot be entirely extinguished in man, his capacity for experience cannot be entirely suppressed by schematization. It is in those experiences which transcend the cultural schemata [and] those memories . . . which transcend the conventional memory schemata, that every new insight and every true work of art have their origin" (1959:107).

I agree that genuine creativity and spontaneity depend on being able to break through the labels, stereotypes, and conventions of an arbitrary tradition. Does this mean that cultural categories are merely artificial annoyances to be brushed aside whenever possible and by any means (including the use of drugs) that are available? No, I think not. And for two reasons.

First of all, breaking through the conventions does not guarantee truth, happiness, or creativity. Without discipline, the results may be just childish, sloppy, or bizarre. Great artists and scientists do go beyond the conventional wisdom of their day. But their insights are based in part on their understanding of the achievements as well as the deficiencies of their predecessors. They develop their new contributions by contrasting or integrating their ideas with what they have received from the past. Paradoxically, this process often restructures traditions and thus revitalizes them, so that they can continue to be of use to the people of each successive "modern" period. Furthermore, the innovator's creations must somehow be communicated to contemporaries: otherwise they would remain hazy elements of a private world and be doomed to die with the innovator.

This problem of communicating new insights brings me to the second point. In the absence of shared expectations and understandings, people become inarticulate: communication and meaningful interaction quickly break down. This is why revolutionary and utopian movements, be they political, religious, or artistic, must develop an in-group jargon and culture or perish. The sense of loving cooperation and empathy that often occurs during or after a great crisis (what Victor Turner has called "communitas") cannot last indefinitely. If its benefits are to continue, they must be consolidated into institutional forms that seem—to some participants—the exact opposite of the open, egalitarian experience that they valued (Turner 1969). This leads some to despise Establishment culture and even to despair of ever communicating through ordinary language. But this, in turn, can lead to a vicious circle of withdrawal, suspicion, failure of communication, hostility, further withdrawal, and so on. The dialectic between person and institution is an unavoidable part of the human condition. (See Sisk 1970.)

For thousands of generations humans have used cultural means to solve their adaptive problems. The reliance on tools and rules in addition to genes has enabled *Homo sapiens* to become the dominant species on our planet. Since one cannot learn "culture" in the abstract, every human being must rely on the traditions of the group in which he or she is enculturated. This reliance entails many positive benefits for the individual, especially for the powerful and privileged; but even the most exploited castes owe their survival to the society that exploits them. They participate in its traditions even as they rebel against them. In Michael Polanyi's eloquent phrase, "Our believing is conditioned at its source by our belonging" (1964:322).

Does this mean that we are stuck with whatever culture we happen to be born into? Again, I think not. There is a certain nobility in loyalty to a tradition, provided that one tries to develop the best in it. On the other hand, the better we know and understand ourselves, our own traditions, and those of others, the more free we become—even though we may at first shrink from the anxiety and responsibility that accompany such consciousness of freedom. Since cultures are integrated systems, we cannot borrow bits and snatches from here and there and expect them automatically to add up to a meaningful way of life. But the wider our knowledge of other cultures and the deeper our understanding of cultural processes, the more likely we are to find something beautiful, meaningful, and useful. Human freedom includes the freedom to believe.

I suggest that we should start with our own traditions, developing and adding to them in a spirit of *play,* trying not to take ourselves too seriously, recognizing that the rules are conventional, but striving to create something good and beautiful out of the materials at our disposal. People who speak several languages generally agree that the second and third are the hardest; thereafter, learning a new language becomes easier each time. Speaking many languages does not guarantee scientific insights into linguistic processes; but I believe that it does give the individual greater freedom by making available different modes of thought, understanding, and expression. This development of flexibility and potential for creativity also comes from knowing a variety of cultures. For this reason, I believe anthropology should be part of every liberal arts curriculum. To quote Dorothy Lee: "When I study other cultures . . . I am enabled to see my culture as one of many possible systems of relating the self to the universe, and to question tenets and axioms of which I had never been aware" (1959:2).

Ethnocentrism, suspicion of the unfamiliar, and hostility toward outsiders are understandable (and even occasionally useful) in a small, isolated society, struggling for survival. In a vast civilization built with the ideas and labor of people from every corner of the earth, such attitudes are no longer adaptive. Modern technology can bring the sights, sounds, and thoughts of distant traditions within easy reach in books or on film and records. Truly "cultured" people are free to enjoy these experiences because they *do not feel threatened* by them. They know their own tradition and recognize both its values and its limitations. Contacts with alien peoples and places are pursued as much for the esthetic satisfactions they bring as for any practical purpose. As Robert Redfield once observed:

In coming to understand an alien way of life, as in coming to understand an alien art, the course of personal experience is essentially the same: one looks first at an incomprehensible other; one comes to see that other as one's self in another guise. This widening of our comprehension of the human has been going on, I suppose, since the day thousands of years ago, when some primitive hunter relaxed his suspicion of or hostility to the people over the hill long enough to think to himself, "Well, I guess those fellows have something there after all." It goes on today, in spite of all the hatreds and conflicts between peoples. Slowly, for one or another of us, the vision and comprehension of humanity, both in its extraordinary variety of expressions and its fundamental sameness, is widened [1959:39].

The "widening of our comprehension of the human" should, I believe, be a continuing goal for anthropology. If this book has increased the readers' awareness of cultural diversity, it has contributed to that goal.

GLOSSARY

Italicized terms are defined elsewhere in the glossary.

acculturation Culture change as a result of continuous, firsthand contact between societies.

adaptation, cultural Learned *plans* for coping with environmental demands, whether from the physical/biological environment or the external social system.

affinity a *criterion* that separates *ego's* blood relatives (consanguines) from in-laws (affines).

age-area principle In *ethnology,* the assumption that—other things being equal—cultural elements that are widespread are older than those with a more restricted distribution.

age-grading Any division of a social group or *institution* into categories based primarily on age.

age-set A social group with *recruitment* based on the similar age of its members; an age-set may move as a unit through a series of age-grades.

agriculture Any system of cultivation making use of the plow, usually in connection with an animal or mechanical source of energy.

American Anthropologist The journal of the American Anthropological Association, published since 1888; devoted to general articles and book reviews. A sister journal, the *American Ethnologist,* contains more specialized articles on ethnology and social anthropology.

Review of Anthropology, Annual Starting in 1972, a useful collection of articles reviewing recent developments in various subfields of anthropology. Between 1959 and 1971, the *Biennial Review of Anthropol-*

ogy (Stanford University Press, ed. B. Siegel and others) was issued in odd-numbered years. This is probably the best single source for evaluation of and bibliography on current ideas and methods.

anthropocentrism The attitude that *Homo sapiens* is the most or the only important species on this planet. See *ethnocentrism*.

anthropology The study of human beings and their works. It includes physical anthropology, which deals with humans as a biological species—their anatomy, physiology, and development—and cultural anthropology, which is concerned with the behavior of people as members of organized societies.

anticipation A principle of *social organization* that calls for the preparation of personnel, resources, and setting before the initiation of recurrent social *situations*.

apes Gorillas, chimpanzees, orangutans, and gibbons, plus extinct members of the biological family *Pongidae,* but not including monkeys.

approach, cross-cultural In ethnology, *techniques* for *inferring* culture history by comparisons of several related cultures. In social anthropology, techniques for making functional/causal inferences by comparisons of historically unrelated societies.

approach, ecological In ethnology, examination of the relationship of cultural systems (or subsystems) to the larger environmental systems in which they operate and to which they must adapt.

approach, structural-functional Techniques for inferring the social functions of *relationships* and *insti-*tutions within a society by careful examination of their structure.

archaeology, prehistoric The subfield of cultural anthropology that deals with inferences about extinct societies.

artifact Any portion of the material environment that has been deliberately modified for human use.

association A social group with voluntary recruitment based on some common interest of its members.

Australopithecinae A subfamily within the family *Hominidae*; contains extinct "man-apes" that lived in the Old World between 1 and 5 million years ago.

authority As part of a leadership role, legitimate command over the actions of others (followers).

avunculocal A *rule of residence* that assigns a couple to the household or community of the groom's mother's brother.

Benedict, Ruth F. (1887–1948) A student of *Boas*. Her innovative studies emphasized the unique configurations of each culture and the relation of culture to personality. Major works include *Patterns of Culture, The Chrysanthemum and the Sword,* and *An Anthropologist at Work* (ed. M. Mead).

bifurcation A *criterion* that separates ego's relatives on "mother's side" from those on "father's side," that is, according to the sex of the linking relative.

bilateral A rule of *kinship group* formation which permits membership on the basis of genealogical ties through males and/or females.

Boas, Franz (1858–1942) German-born and trained in the natural sciences, he became the father of American academic anthropology. At Columbia University he trained a generation of major scholars. His works include *Race, Language, and Culture* (collected papers) and *The Mind of Primitive Man*.

career, social A sequence of social roles through which some set of individuals is expected to pass.

castes *Endogamous* social groups based on descent and ranked in a rigid *hierarchy,* each caste usually having specific ritual and/or technical functions.

categories, cultural Learned classes of persons, objects, or events, conventionally associated with learned *plans* for action or interaction.

clans *Descent groups* composed of several *lineages;* although clan membership does not require that actual genealogical links be known, there is usually an ideology of descent from a common founder. When the founder is given an animal name, we speak of a totemic clan.

class, social A division of a *societal group* into ranked subgroups with recruitment based on a variety of criteria and with movement of individuals among groups at least theoretically possible.

collaterality A *criterion* that separates ego's lineal relatives (direct ancestors and descendants) from collaterals (all others).

conformity Compliance with the expectations embodied in a given *social structure;* includes choice among legitimate alternatives.

cosmology The part of an *ideology* that is concerned with the nature and origin of the universe and with humans' position in it.

criterion, kinship A *binary opposition* used to divide a set of relatives into two subsets. See *affinity, collaterality, bifurcation, decedence*.

cross-cousins Children of ego's mother's brother (matrilateral) or father's sister (patrilateral).

culture Learned *categories* of experience conventionally associated with learned *plans* for action. Refers both to specific cultures of societal groups and to human culture as a whole.

culture, paradox of The inescapable fact that acceptance of any cultural system frees the individual at the same time that it constrains behavior.

Current Anthropology An international journal containing special review articles with commentary, announcements, and extensive correspondence. Published since 1960 by the University of Chicago and sponsored by the Wenner-Gren Foundation.

decedence A *criterion* that separates those kin who are linked to *ego* by living relatives from those whose links are deceased.

descent groups Kinship groups to which ego is assigned by an automatic recruitment rule. See *patrilineal, matrilineal, double descent*.

diachronic study An examination of cultural systems at two or more points in time, emphasizing history and change. See *synchronic study*.

double descent A kinship system in which *ego* belongs to both the father's *patrilineal* group and the mother's *matrilineal* group.

dual organization A division of a societal group into two halves (Fr., moieties), usually with reciprocal social functions and with recruitment based on descent.

Durkheim, Emile (1858–1917) French sociologist whose pioneering work influenced the development of British social anthropology. His books include *The Division of Labor in Society* and *The Elementary Forms of the Religious Life*.

ego The individual, sex unspecified, who is taken as a point of reference in a *genealogy* or kinship chart.

eidos Integrating principles of belief that give consistency to an *ideology*.

enculturation The process of learning one's culture; often synonymous with socialization, though the latter term sometimes refers to deliberate techniques of child-training.

endogamy A *marriage rule* specifying that ego should select a mate from within a given category of persons. See also *exogamy*.

esthetics, anthropological The study of judgments of beauty in different societies.

ethnocentrism The attitude that one's own culture is the highest and constitutes a standard for judging all other cultures. See *relativism, cultural*.

ethnography The subfield of cultural anthropology that formulates descriptions of social, technological, and ideological systems.

ethnohistory The subfield of anthropology that uses materials from ethnography and archaeology in conjunction with documentary evidence for the reconstruction of culture history.

ethnology The subfield of cultural anthropology that compares materials provided by *ethnography*, usually to draw historical inferences. See also *social anthropology*.

Ethnology Published since 1962 by the University of Pittsburgh, this journal emphasizes studies in Africa and the Pacific as well as cross-cultural studies employing the *Human Relations Area Files*.

ethnosemantics The study of systems of meaning as embodied in other languages with special attention to *folk taxonomies* and *binary oppositions*.

ethos Integrating patterns of value that give coherence to an *ideology*.

evaluation The general process of judging persons, objects, or events relative to some culture standard (for example, of beauty, grammaticality, or morality); may involve classification and/or ranking.

evolution, biological The well-supported theory that by known genetic mechanisms, higher and more recent forms of life have developed, as a result of adaptive change, out of lower and more ancient forms.

evolution, cultural The plausible theory that complex forms of culture and society have developed, as a consequence of adaptive change, out of simpler forms, although the mechanisms are not clearly understood.

evolution, moral The unlikely notion that human moral behavior (or at least human standards of judgment) have improved in some absolute sense over the million or so years of human existence.

exogamy A *marriage rule* specifying that *ego* should select a mate from outside of a given category. See also *endogamy*.

function, adaptive The way(s) in which a given *tool* helps to satisfy human needs.

function, social The way(s) in which any cultural element contributes to the survival of the society and/or continuity of the culture in which it is found.

genealogy A record of the (alleged) relations of descent, co-descent, and marriage among a set of persons.

grammar The rules that influence the verbal behavior of speakers of some language; also, a linguist's attempt to formulate these rules, excluding the *phonology*. See also *morphology, syntax*.

group, corporate A clearly bounded social group whose members share in some "estate," material or nonmaterial.

group, kinship Any social group to which members are recruited by virtue of kinship connections. See *descent groups*.

group, residential A category of persons who customarily live in the same area of *social space* and who share some *plans* for interaction. Typical residential groups found in most societies are the household (domestic group) and the local community (whether mobile or sedentary).

group, societal The group composed of all the members of a given society.

Herskovits, Melville J. (1895-1963) Best known for his studies of black culture in the Old and New World, he founded the first major U.S. program in African studies at Northwestern University. A student and biographer of *Boas,* he was among the first to appreciate the value of economic theory to anthropology. Works include *Economic Anthropology, Cultural Dynamics, Dahomean Narrative* (with F. Herskovits), and *The Myth of the Negro Past.*

hierarchy Any arrangement of parts from high to low, whether in terms of power, wealth, or prestige, or any other criterion.

Hominidae The human biological family, including *Homo sapiens, Homo erectus,* and the *Australopithecinae*; all members of this family except the modern variety of *Homo sapiens* are now extinct.

Homo erectus The species most closely related to and ancestral to *Homo sapiens*; includes Java man, Peking man, and other extinct varieties that flourished about a half-million years ago.

Homo sapiens The biological label for the human species, including both *Neanderthal* and modern varieties, which have flourished for the last 100,000 years.

horticulture Any system of food cultivation that does not employ the plow, though it may use "intensive" techniques such as fencing, irrigation, or fertilization.

human "The maker of tools, rules, and moral judgments." *Homo sapiens,* though sometimes used more generally to refer to all of the *Hominidae*. See also *anthropocentrism*.

Human Organization The journal of the Society for Applied Anthropology, published since 1941; contains articles and commentary on the application of anthropological theory and methods to social problems.

Human Relations Area Files An extensive, cross-indexed catalog of ethnographic information on more than 600 societies, used as a research tool in cross-cultural studies.

ideology Cultural subsystem consisting of beliefs and values shared by the members of a social or societal group.

inference In anthropology, reasoning from regularities in the form and distribution of human behavior (and products of behavior) to the cultural elements that *influence* that behavior to produce the perceived regularities.

influence The relationship between *cultural categories* and *plans* and the behavior of persons who share these learned elements.

innovation Any behavior that violates the rules or general expectations associated with a *social situation,* from a slightly novel choice to a completely original action. See also *invention*.

institutions, social Relatively self-contained subgroups within which several *social careers* are organized into a system.

institutions, total Institutions in which at least some persons spend all of their time, such as boarding schools or mental hospitals.

integration, group A quality of solidarity or cohesiveness within or between social groups, generally produced by the exchange of equivalent values among members. See also *reciprocity, norm of*.

invention Any social, linguistic, or technological *innovation* that violates cultural rules by the omission, rearrangement, substitution, or combination of expected elements.

Journal of Anthropological Research Published since 1945 by the University of New Mexico, it contains articles on all fields of anthropology with emphasis on theory-oriented research. Before 1973 it was known as the *Southwestern Journal of Anthropology*.

kindred A *bilateral kinship group,* often vaguely bounded, and with optional *recruitment*. Each individual may be the focus of his or her own personal kindred, or the stem kindred may revolve around a particularly important individual.

Kluckhohn, Clyde K. M. (1905–1960) A background in the classics gave Kluckhohn a unique perspective on many anthropological problems. He is best known for his intensive studies of the Navajo, and he was an innovator in studies of values, personality, and religion. Works include *Navaho Witchcraft, Mirror for Man,* and *Culture and Behavior* (ed. R. Kluckhohn).

Kroeber, Alfred L. (1876–1960) A student of *Boas,* Kroeber (who had been trained in the humanities) had a lifelong fascination with style in culture and with processes of cultural growth and change. His contributions to all fields of cultural anthropology are enormous. Major works include *Anthropology* (1948), *Style and Civilization,* and *The Nature of Culture* (collected papers).

language A subsystem of *culture* consisting of *categories* of sound associated with *plans* for speaking. See also *speech*.

legal system Cultural *categories* and *plans* relating to the settlement of disputes within and among *societal groups*.

lineages *Exogamous descent groups,* often localized, with automatic *recruitment* based on known or fictional genealogical relationships.

linguistics, anthropological A subfield of cultural anthropology that is concerned with the *language* systems and *speech* behavior of all human groups.

Lowie, Robert H. (1883–1957) Another student of *Boas,* he brought careful scholarship and sensitivity to his field studies of the Crow Indians and his comparative studies in the Plains and elsewhere. The Lowie Museum of Anthropology is in Berkeley, California, where he and *Kroeber* taught for many years. Major works include *Primitive Society* (a response to *L. H. Morgan*), *The Crow Indians,* an autobiography, and collected papers (ed. C. Du Bois).

Malinowski, Bronislaw (1884–1942) Polish-born and trained in the natural sciences, he became a founder of *social anthropology* and of a variety of functionalism that emphasized the relationship between *institutions* and human needs. Known for his intensive field work in and publications on the Trobriand Islands. Major works include *Argonauts of the Western Pacific, The Coral Gardens and Their Magic,* and *Magic, Science and Religion.*

Man Formerly the *Journal of the Royal Anthropological Institute,* this publication includes articles on cultural and social anthropology, and brief but excellent book reviews.

marriage rule A *recruitment rule* stating the preferred or permitted *categories* from which a given *ego* may select a mate. See also *endogamy, exogamy.*

matrilineal A rule of *descent* that assigns *ego* to the *kinship group* of his or her mother.

matrilocal A rule of *residence* that assigns a couple to the household or community of the bride's parents.

method, comparative In *linguistics,* techniques for reconstructing the parental form or *protolanguage* of two or more related languages. In *ethnology,* see *approach, cross-cultural.*

moiety See *dual organization.*

morality, absolute Judgment of the rightness of actions according to an unvarying (cultural) standard.

morality, situational Judgment of the rightness of actions according to standards that take account of particular circumstances.

Morgan, Lewis Henry (1818–1881) Pioneering American anthropologist, lawyer, and believer in *cultural evolution,* he founded the comparative study of kinship systems and was a student of the Iroquois. Works include *Ancient Society* and the *Journals* (ed. L. White).

morpheme An ordered set of *phonemes* associated, in a given language, with a minimum unit of meaning; includes roots and affixes.

morphology In linguistics, the study of how *morphemes* are combined into larger meaningful units (words) and the modifications that they undergo in the process.

Nacirema A societal group in North America having unusually backward customs (and spelling!).

Neanderthal A variety of *Homo sapiens* that flourished between 50,000 and 100,000 years ago, at the end of the Ice Age.

neolocal A rule of *residence* that assigns a couple to a separate household of their own.

nuclear family A *kinship group*

composed of a married couple together with their unmarried offspring; may or may not correspond to a *residential group* (household).

opposition, binary A two-way contrast between categories of persons, objects, or events; for example, vowel/consonant, sacred/profane, raw/cooked, affine/consanguine.

organization, social Processes involving individual *anticipation, conformity, adaptation,* and *innovation,* in response to the requirements of a given *social structure*. See *reciprocity, norm of*.

parallel cousins Children of ego's mother's sister (matrilateral) or father's brother (patrilateral). See also *cross-cousins*.

participant observation In *ethnography,* the technique of learning and collecting data while taking part in the daily life of the society.

pastoralism A system of food production based on herding and (usually) husbandry of domesticated animals.

patrilineal A *rule of descent* that automatically assigns *ego* to the *kinship group* of his or her father.

patrilocal A *rule of residence* that assigns a couple to the household or community of the groom's parents.

phonemes Meaningless but significant *categories* of vocal sound which signal differences of meaning in a given *language*. Selections and combinations of these units of sound make up *morphemes*.

phonology The study of the sound system of language, that is, *phonemes—* their distinctive features, variant forms, and distributions.

phratry An association among several clans, often sharing a common *marriage rule* or other *social function*.

placebo effect An apparent cure of illness brought about by the confident administration of a chemically inert medication, as, for example, sugar pills or a saltwater injection.

plans, cultural A set of learned, hierarchically organized expectations that *influence* sequences of behavior in some social group; conventionally associated with one or more *cultural categories*.

polygamy Any *marriage rule* permitting *ego* to have more than one spouse at the same time. More particularly, "polyandry," which allows a female ego to have plural husbands, and "polygyny," which allows a male ego to have plural wives.

Pongidae A family within the order *Primates,* consisting of the living and extinct *apes*. See also *Hominidae*.

Primates An order of mammals that includes *humans* (living and fossil forms), the *apes,* the monkeys, and several other species, living and extinct.

productivity In *linguistics,* refers to the fact that speakers of a language can produce (generate) an infinite number of grammatical utterances; in *ethnography,* refers to a similar capacity on the part of group members—their ability to behave in novel but socially appropriate ways.

Radcliffe-Brown, Alfred R. (1881–1955) With *Malinowski,* a founder of *social anthropology,* "R-B" was a master of comparative studies of *social structure* (in Australia and Africa). His functionalism is still basic to British social anthropology. Major works include *The Andaman Islanders, Structure and Function in Primitive Society*.

reciprocity, norm of A possibly *universal* principle of *social organization* which demands that individuals should help, and not hurt, those others who have benefited them; a general plan for interaction which can take over in the absence of (or in addition to) more specific expectations.

recruitment, rule of A device for assigning classes of individuals to social *roles* and *careers* according to factors of birth (ascription) and/or other criteria (achievement). See also *criterion, kinship; rules*.

Redfield, Robert (1897–1958) Trained in the law and familiar with sociological theory, Redfield pioneered in the study of peasant societies and the civilizations of which they form a part. His works include *The Little Community, Folk Culture of Yucatan,* and two volumes of collected papers (ed. M. P. Redfield).

reduplication In *linguistics,* a *plan* for producing words with modified or different meanings by repeating syllables; for example, "mama," "gogo," "aku-aku."

reinterpretation The assignment of new "meanings" to borrowed cultural elements.

relationship, social Any pair of social *roles* for which there exist cultural *plans* for interaction; for example, father/son, doctor/patient, but not *patient/son.

relativism, cultural The attitude that beliefs and practices must be understood in terms of the culture of which they form a part. See also *ethnocentrism*.

relativism, ethical The attitude that moral/ethical judgments cannot or should not be made cross-culturally, but must be relative to the standards of a particular social group.

revitalization movements Social movements that deliberately attempt to construct a more satisfying culture, often by supernatural means; examples are the cargo cults of Melanesia and the Ghost Dance in North America.

rite of passage A ritual event in which individuals move from one social position (*role*) to another, usually through the three stages of separation, transition, and incorporation.

role, kinship A social role to which *ego* is assigned (recruited) as a consequence of actual or putative genealogical connection.

role, personal A category of persons consisting of a single individual together with his or her style of interacting; the label for such a role is the individual's personal name or alias.

role, social Any *category* of persons that, in a given society, is associated with a conventional *plan* for interaction with one or more other categories of persons.

role, societal The category consisting of all members of a society together with their general rights and obligations as such.

rules, descent Rules that assign *ego* to a kinship group on the basis of the group affiliation of one parent. See also *matrilineal, patrilineal, double descent*; compare with *bilateral*.

rules, marriage Rules that specify eligible or ineligible spouses on the basis of ego's social category or group membership.

rules, residence Rules that assign *ego* to some residential group (household, local community, and so forth) at one or more points in his or her social career; for example, at time of marriage, or when first child is born.

Sapir, Edward (1884–1939) American linguist and ethnologist who inspired many fine students to follow his example of intensive field work in Indian languages and cultures. With *Benedict* he founded "culture and personality" studies. Major works: *Language* (1921) and collected papers (ed. D. Mandelbaum).

semantic differential A technique for measuring the connotative meanings of terms in any language.

shaman A part- or full-time ritual specialist who performs religious and curing ceremonies in behalf of his clients and social group.

social anthropology The subfield of cultural anthropology that compares materials provided by *ethnology* and *ethnography* to draw functional, causal, and universal inferences. See also *approach, cross-cultural*.

sociolinguistics The subfield of *linguistics* that studies the relationships between *language* and social systems, including the ethnography of communication.

specialization, role Refers to the development in food-producing societies of individuals who devote most or all of their time to ritual, political, or specialized technical activities.

speech Vocal behavior *influenced* by some *language* system(s), and from which the language may be inferred.

stratification, principle of In archaeology, the assumption that—other things being equal—the deeper an *artifact* is found, the greater its age. See also *age-area principle*.

stratification, social The existence within a society of ranked subgroups. See also *castes; class, social; hierarchy*.

structure, social *Categories* of persons and associated *plans* for interaction characteristic of any social or societal group. See also *career, social; institutions, social; relationship, social*.

swidden system A form of *horticulture* that involves cutting and firing of vegetation (slash-and-burn) prior to planting.

synchronic study An examination of a cultural system at one point in time, emphasizing the description of structure. See also *diachronic study*.

syntax In *linguistics,* the rules that specify how words can and must be combined into larger meaningful units (phrases, sentences, and so forth), including rules of order, agreement, and transformation.

taxonomy, folk A "native" classification of some set of objects, persons, or events; for example, color terms, plant names, kinship terms. See also *ethnosemantics*.

technique A belief about the relationship between means and ends characteristic of some *social role* or group; includes expected ways of employing the human body and/or tools to modify the environment.

technology The cultural subsystem consisting of categories of *tools* together with plans for their manufacture and use, as well as other *techniques* for producing changes in the material environment.

territory Area of *social space* associated with particular individuals or social groups.

text Any record of observations of behavior (or the products of behavior), including field notes, photographs, test responses, documents, and so forth.

tool An artifact used to augment human ability to act upon the physical world.

Tylor, Sir Edward B. (1832–1917) Critical scholarship and encyclopedic knowledge set him off from most of his British contemporaries. Tylor used the comparative method (with statistical verification) to infer culture history and functional relationships, and to postulate universal concepts. Major works: *Primitive Culture, Anthropology*.

universals, cultural Elements or processes that are found in all cultural systems.

universals, linguistic Elements or processes that are found in all human *languages*.

values, social Conceptions of the desirable that are characteristic of a given social group, often forming a system with integrating patterns. See also *ethos*.

BIBLIOGRAPHY

Alland, Alexander, Jr.
   1975 Adaptation. Annual Review of Anthropology 4:59–74.

Arensberg, Conrad
   1955 American Communities. American Anthropologist 57:1143–1162.

Ariès, Philippe
   1974 Western Attitudes Toward Death from the Middle Ages to the Present. Baltimore: Johns Hopkins University Press.

Aronson, E., and J. Mills
   1959 The Effect of Severity of Initiation on Liking for a Group. Journal of Abnormal and Social Psychology 59:177–181.

Banfield, Edward C.
   1958 The Moral Basis of a Backward Society. New York: Free Press.

Barnett, Homer G.
   1953 Innovation: The Basis of Cultural Change. New York: McGraw-Hill.

Barth, Fredrik, ed.
   1969 Ethnic Groups and Boundaries. Boston: Little, Brown.

Bateson, Gregory
   1958 Naven. 2nd ed. Stanford: Stanford University Press.

Beattie, John
   1960 Bunyoro: An African Kingdom. New York: Holt, Rinehart and Winston.

Benedict, Ruth
1934 Patterns of Culture. New York: Houghton Mifflin.
1946 The Chrysanthemum and the Sword. New York: Houghton Mifflin.

Bennett, John W., ed.
1975 The New Ethnicity. Perspectives from Ethnology. St. Paul: West Publishing Company.

Berlin, Brent, and Paul Kay
1969 Basic Color Terms. Berkeley: University of California Press.

Berne, Eric
1964 Games People Play. New York: Grove Press.

Bettelheim, Bruno
1971 The Informed Heart. New York: Avon Books.

Bidney, David
1953 The Concept of Value in Modern Anthropology. *In* Anthropology Today. Alfred L. Kroeber, ed. Pp. 682–699. Chicago: University of Chicago Press.

Binford, Lewis R.
1972 An Archaeological Perspective. New York: Seminar Press.

Birket-Smith, Kaj
1965 The Paths of Culture. Madison: University of Wisconsin Press.

Boas, Franz
1955 Primitive Art. New York: Dover.

Bock, Philip K.
1966 The Micmac Indians of Restigouche. National Museum of Canada, Bulletin 213, Ottawa.
1967 Love Magic, Menstrual Taboos, and the Facts of Geography. American Anthropologist 69:213–217.
1968 Peasants in the Modern World. Albuquerque: University of New Mexico Press.
1974 Modern Cultural Anthropology. 2nd ed. New York: Knopf.
1977 Interdependence in Anthropology. *In* Interdependence: An Interdisciplinary Study. Archie J. Bahm, ed. Pp. 16–27. Albuquerque: World Books.
1978 Micmac. *In* Handbook of North American Indians. Vol. 15. Bruce Trigger, ed. Washington, D.C.: Smithsonian Institution.

Bohannon, Paul
1963 Social Anthropology. New York: Holt, Rinehart and Winston.

Bottomore, T. B.
1966 Classes in Modern Society. New York: Vintage.

Brown, Ina C.
1963 Understanding Other Cultures. Englewood Cliffs, N.J.: Prentice-Hall.

Brown, Paula
1968 Social Change and Social Movements. *In* Peoples and Cultures of the Pacific. Andrew P. Vayda, ed. Pp. 465–485. Garden City, N.Y.: Natural History Press.

Cancian, Frank
1963 Informant Error and Native Prestige Ranking in Zinacantan. American Anthropologist 65:1068–1075.

Caudill, William, and Helen Weinstein
1969 Maternal and Infant Behavior in Japan and America. Psychiatry 32:12–43.

Chomsky, Noam
1957 Syntactic Structures. The Hague: Mouton.

Cohn, Bernard
1955 The Changing Status of a Depressed Caste. *In* Village India. McKim Marriott, ed. Chicago: University of Chicago Press.

Conklin, Harold C.
1955 Hanunoó Color Categories. Southwestern Journal of Anthropology 11:339–344.

Cory, H.
1955 The Buswezi. American Anthropologist 57:923–952.

D'Andrade, Roy G.
1976 A Propositional Analysis of U.S. American Beliefs about Illness. *In* Meaning in Anthropology. Keith H. Basso and Henry A. Selby, eds. Albuquerque: University of New Mexico Press.

Davenport, William
1959 Nonunilinear Descent and Descent Groups. American Anthropologist 61:557–572.

Deng, Francis
1972 The Dinka of the Sudan. New York: Holt, Rinehart and Winston.

Driver, Harold E., and William C. Massey
1957 Comparative Studies of North American Indians. Transactions of the American Philosophical Society 47(2):165–456.

DuBois, Cora
1955 The Dominant Value Profile of American Culture. American Anthropologist 57:1232–1239.

Dundes, Alan
1962 Earth-Diver: Creation of the Mythopoeic Male. American Anthropologist 64:1032–1051.

Durkheim, Émile
1947 The Division of Labor in Society. New York: Free Press. (First published, 1893.)

Elbert, Samuel H.
1951 Hawaiian Literary Style and Culture. American Anthropologist 53:345–359.

Elwin, Verrier
1947 The Muria and their Ghotul. Bombay: Oxford University Press.

Endleman, Robert
1967 Personality and Social Life. New York: Random House.

Evans-Pritchard, E. E.
1940 The Nuer. London: Oxford University Press.
1954 Social Anthropology. New York: Free Press.

Fallers, Lloyd
1955 The Predicament of the Modern African Chief: An Instance from Uganda. American Anthropologist 57:290–305.

Feder, Ernest
1971 The Rape of the Peasantry: Latin America's Landholding System. Garden City: Anchor Books.

Firth, Raymond
1951 Elements of Social Organization. London: Watts.

Fitch, J., and D. Branch
1960 Primitive Architecture and Climate. Scientific American 203(6):134–144.

Ford, Clellan S., and Frank A. Beach
1951 Patterns of Sexual Behavior. New York: Harper.

Forde, C. Daryll
1963 Habitat, Economy and Society. New York: Dutton.

Fortes, Meyer and E. E. Evans-Pritchard, eds.
1940 African Political Systems. London: Oxford University Press.

Foster, George R.
1961 The Dyadic Contract: A Model for the Social Structure of a Mexican Peasant Village. American Anthropologist 63:1173–1192.
1967 Tzintzuntzan. Boston: Little, Brown.

Frake, Charles O.
1961 The Diagnosis of Disease among the Subanun of Mindinao. American Anthropologist 63:113–132.
1964 How to Ask for a Drink in Subanun. American Anthropologist 66(6, Part 2):127–132.

Frank, Jerome D.
1963 Persuasion and Healing. New York: Schocken.

Franklin, Karl J.
1963 Kewa Ethnolinguistic Concepts of Body Parts. Southwestern Journal of Anthropology 19:54–63.

Frazer, Sir James
1953 The Golden Bough. Abridged edition. New York: Macmillan.

Freedman, Daniel
1974 Human Infancy: An Evolutionary Perspective. Hillsdale, N.J.: Lawrence Erlbaum Associates.

Fried, Morton H.
1967 The Evolution of Political Society. New York: Random House.

Gardner, Peter M.
1966 Symmetric Respect and Memorate Knowledge: The Structure and Ecology of Individualistic Culture. Southwestern Journal of Anthropology 22:389–415.

Gearing, Fred
1958 The Structural Poses of 18th Century Cherokee Villages. American Anthropologist 60:1148–1157.

Gerth, Hans, and C. Wright Mills, eds.
1958 From Max Weber: Essays in Sociology. New York: Oxford University Press.

Gladwin, Thomas
1962 Latency and the Equine Subconscious. American Anthropologist 64:1292–1296.
1970 East is a Big Bird: Navigation and Logic on Puluwat Atoll. Cambridge: Harvard University Press.

Goffman, Erving
1959 The Presentation of Self in Everyday Life. Garden City, N.Y.: Anchor Books.
1961 Asylums. Garden City, N.Y.: Anchor Books.
1963 Stigma. Englewood Cliffs, N.J.: Prentice-Hall.

Goody, Jack R., ed.
1958 The Developmental Cycle in Domestic Groups. New York: Cambridge University Press.
1973 The Character of Kinship. New York: Cambridge University Press.

Gouldner, Alvin
1960 The Norm of Reciprocity: A Preliminary Statement. American Sociological Review 25:161–178.

Guillemin, Jeanne
1975 Urban Renegades: The Cultural Strategy of American Indians. New York: Columbia University Press.

Hall, Edward T.
1959 The Silent Language. Garden City, N.Y.: Doubleday.

Hallowell, A. Irving
1960 Ojibwa Ontology, Behavior, and World View. *In* Culture in History. S. Diamond, ed. New York: Columbia University Press.

Harris, Marvin
1967 The Myth of the Sacred Cow. Natural History Magazine 76:6–12A.

Hart, C. W. M., and Arnold Pilling
1964 The Tiwi of North Australia. New York: Holt, Rinehart and Winston.

Heilbroner, Robert L.
1961 The Worldly Philosophers. Revised ed. New York: Simon and Schuster.

Herskovits, Melville J.
1952 Economic Anthropology. New York: Knopf.
1964 Cultural Dynamics. New York: Knopf.

Herskovits, Melville J., and Frances Herskovits
1958 Dahomean Narrative: A Cross-Cultural Analysis. Evanston, Ill.: Northwestern University Press.

Hoebel, E. Adamson
1960 The Cheyennes. New York: Holt, Rinehart and Winston.

Hogbin, Ian
1964 A Guadalcanal Society: The Kaoka Speakers. New York: Holt, Rinehart and Winston.

Holmberg, Allan
1969 Nomads of the Long Bow. Garden City, N.Y: Anchor Books.

Hsu, Francis L. K.
1961 American Core Values and National Character. *In* Psychological Anthropology. F. L. K. Hsu, ed. Pp. 209–230. Homewood, Ill.: Dorsey Press.

Hughes, Everett C.
1958 Men and their Work. New York: Free Press.

Huntingford, G. W. B.
1960 Nandi Age-Sets. *In* Cultures and Societies of Africa. Simon and Phoebe Ottenberg, eds. Pp. 214–226. New York: Random House.

Hyman, Charles
1966 The Dysfunctionality of Unrequited Giving. Human Organization 25:42–45.

Hymes, Dell
1974 Foundations in Sociolinguistics: An Ethnographic Approach. Philadelphia: University of Pennsylvania Press.

Kluckhohn, Clyde
1968 The Philosophy of the Navajo Indians. *In* Readings in Anthropology. Vol. 2. 2nd ed. Morton Fried, ed. Pp. 674–699. New York: Crowell.

Kluckhohn, Clyde, and Dorothea Leighton
1946 The Navaho. Cambridge: Harvard University Press.

Kluckhohn, Florence, and Fred Strodtbeck
1961 Variations in Value-Orientations. Evanston, Ill.: Row, Peterson.

Kroeber, Alfred L.
1909 Classificatory Systems of Relationships. Journal of the Royal Anthropological Institute 39:77–84.
1948 Anthropology. New York: Harcourt, Brace.

Kuhn, Thomas
  1964 The Structure of Scientific Revolutions. Chicago: University of Chicago Press.

LaBarre, Weston
  1970 The Ghost Dance: The Origins of Religion. New York: Delta Books.

Landauer, T. K., and J. W. M. Whiting
  1964 Infantile Stimulation and Adult Stature of Human Males. American Anthropologist 66:1007–1028.

Langness, Lewis L.
  1965 The Life History in Anthropological Science. New York: Holt, Rinehart and Winston.

Leach, Edmund R.
  1966 Anthropological Aspects of Language: Animal Categories and Verbal Abuse. *In* New Directions in the study of Language. Eric Lenneberg, ed. Pp. 23–64. Cambridge: M.I.T. Press.

Lee, Dorothy
  1959 Freedom and Culture. Englewood Cliffs, N.J.: Prentice-Hall.

Lee, Richard B., and I. DeVore, eds.
  1968 Man the Hunter. Chicago: Aldine.

Leeds, Anthony J.
  1960 The Ideology of the Yaruro Indians in Relation to Socio-Economic Organization. Antropológica 9:1–10.

Lévi-Strauss, Claude
  1953 Social Structure. *In* Anthropology Today. A. L. Kroeber, ed. Pp. 524–553. Chicago: University of Chicago Press.
  1963a The Bear and the Barber. Journal of the Royal Anthropological Institute 93:1–11.
  1963b Totemism. Boston: Beacon Press.
  1966 The Savage Mind. Chicago: University of Chicago Press.

Lienhardt, Godfrey
  1966 Social Anthropology. London: Oxford University Press.

Linton, Ralph
  1936 The Study of Man. New York: Appleton-Century.
  1955 The Tree of Culture. New York: Knopf.

Lomax, Alan, and others
  1968 Folk Song Style and Culture. American Association for the Advancement of Science, Publication No. 88. Washington, D.C.

Lowie, Robert H.
  1948 Social Organization. New York: Holt, Rinehart and Winston.
  1956 The Crow Indians. New York: Holt, Rinehart and Winston.

Malinowski, Bronislaw
  1955 Magic, Science and Religion. Robert Redfield, ed. Garden City, N.Y.: Anchor Books.
  1961 Argonauts of the Western Pacific. New York: Dutton.

Mayer, Philip and Iona
1970 Socialization by Peers: The Red Xhosa Youth Organization. *In* Socialization: The Approach from Social Anthropology. P. Mayer, ed. London: Tavistock.

McAllester, David P.
1964 Enemy Way Music. Papers of the Peabody Museum, Vol. 41, No. 3. Cambridge, Mass.

Mead, Margaret
1935 Sex and Temperament in Three Primitive Societies. New York: William Morrow.
1949a Coming of Age in Samoa. New York: Mentor Books.
1949b Male and Female. New York: William Morrow.

Meighan, Clement
1966 Archaeology: An Introduction. San Francisco: Chandler.

Mercier, P.
1954 The Fon of Dahomey. *In* African Worlds. Daryll Forde, ed. London: Oxford University Press.

Merton, Robert K.
1957 Manifest and Latent Function. *In* Social Theory and Social Structure. Pp. 19–84. New York: Free Press.

Miller, George, Eugene Galanter, and Karl Pribram
1960 Plans and the Structure of Behavior. New York: Holt, Rinehart and Winston.

Miller, Walter B.
1958 Lower Class Culture as a Generating Milieu of Gang Delinquency. Journal of Social Issues 14:5–19.

Miner, Horace
1956 Body Ritual among the Nacirema. American Anthropologist 58:503–507.

Morgan, Lewis H.
1871 Systems of Consanguinity and Affinity of the Human Family. Washington: Smithsonian Institution.

Montagu, Ashley
1972 Touching: The Human Significance of the Skin. New York: Harper & Row.

Mumford, Lewis
1961 The City in History. New York: Harcourt Brace and World.

Munroe, Robert L., and Ruth H. Munroe.
1975 Cross-Cultural Human Development. Monterey, Calif.: Brooks/Cole.

Murdock, George P.
1949 Social Structure. New York: Macmillan.
1960 How Culture Changes. *In* Man, Culture, and Society. Harry Shapiro, ed. New York: Oxford University Press.

Murphy, Gardner
1947 Personality: A Biosocial Approach to Origins and Structure. New York: Harper & Brothers.

Nader, Laura, and Thomas W. Maretzki, eds.
1973 Cultural Illness and Health. American Anthropological Association, Anthropological Studies, Number 9.

Nash, Manning
1958 Machine Age Maya. American Anthropological Association, Memoir 87.
1966 Primitive and Peasant Economic Systems. San Francisco: Chandler.

Newman, Philip L.
1964 "Wild Man" Behavior in a New Guinea Highlands Community. American Anthropologist 66:1–18.
1965 Knowing the Gururumba. New York: Holt, Rinehart and Winston.

Oliver, Douglas L.
1955 A Solomon Island Society. Boston: Beacon Press.

Opler, Morris E.
1945 Themes as Dynamic Forces in Culture. American Journal of Sociology 51:198–206.
1968 The Themal Approach in Cultural Anthropology and Its Application to North Indian Data. Southwestern Journal of Anthropology 24:215–227.

Parsons, Talcott
1948 Essays in Sociological Theory, Pure and Applied. New York: Free Press.

Pehrson, Robert
1954 Bilateral Kin Groups as a Structural Type. Journal of East Asiatic Studies 3:199–202.

Pelto, Pertti J., and Gretel H. Pelto
1975 Intra-cultural Diversity: Some Theoretical Issues. American Ethnologist 2:1–18.

Piddocke, Stuart
1965 The Potlatch System of the Southern Kwakiutl: A New Perspective. Southwestern Journal of Anthropology 21:244–264.

Polanyi, Michael
1964 Personal Knowledge. New York: Harper Torchbooks.

Price-Williams, Douglass R.
1975 Explorations in Cross-Cultural Psychology. San Francisco: Chandler & Sharp.

Radcliffe-Brown, A. R.
1952 Structure and Function in Primitive Society. New York: Free Press.

Redfield, Robert
  1941 The Folk Culture of Yucatan. Chicago: University of Chicago Press.
  1953 The Primitive World and Its Transformations. Ithaca: Cornell University Press.
  1956 Peasant Society and Culture. Chicago: University of Chicago Press.
  1959 Aspects of Primitive Art. New York: Museum of Primitive Art.

Redfield, Robert, and A. Villa Rojas
  1962 Chan Kom: A Maya Village. Chicago: University of Chicago Press. (First published, 1934.)

Riesman, David, and others
  1950 The Lonely Crowd: A Study of the Changing American Character. New Haven: Yale University Press.

Rivière, P. G.
  1974 The Couvade: A Problem Reborn. Man 9:423–435.

Russell, W. M. S.
  1968 The Slash-and-Burn Technique. Natural History Magazine, March.

Sahlins, Marshall D.
  1961 The Segmentary Lineage: An Organization of Predatory Expansion. American Anthropologist 63:322–345.

Sahlins, Marshall D., and Elman R. Service, eds.
  1960 Evolution and Culture. Ann Arbor: University of Michigan Press.

Schachtel, Ernest G.
  1959 Metamorphosis. New York: Basic Books.

Schneider, David M.
  1968 American Kinship. Englewood Cliffs, N.J.: Prentice-Hall.
  1976 The Meaning of Incest. Journal of the Polynesian Society 25:149–169.

Schneider, Harold K.
  1966 Turu Esthetic Concepts. American Anthropologist 68:156–160.

Service, Elman R., ed.
  1975a Profiles in Ethnology. 3rd ed. New York: Harper & Row.
  1975b Origins of the State and Civilization. New York: Norton.

Simmel, Georg
  1955 Conflict and The Web of Group Affiliations. New York: Free Press.

Sisk, John P.
  1970 Person and Institution. Notre Dame, Ind.: Fides Publishers.

Slater, Philip
  1970 The Pursuit of Loneliness. Boston: Beacon Press.

Spiro, Melford
  1958 Children of the Kibbutz. Cambridge: Harvard University Press.

Stern, Theodore
1963 Ideal and Expected Behavior as Seen in Klamath Mythology. Journal of American Folklore 76:23–28.

Stover, Leon E.
1974 The Cultural Ecology of Chinese Civilization. New York: Mentor Books.

Turner, Victor
1969 The Ritual Process. Chicago: Aldine.

Tylor, Edward B.
1889 On a Method of Investigating the Development of Institutions; Applied to Laws of Marriage and Descent. Journal of the Royal Anthropological Institute 18:245–269.
1958 The Origins of Culture. New York: Harper Torchbooks. (Part I of Primitive Culture, first published 1871.)

van den Berghe, Pierre L., and David P. Barash
1977 Inclusive Fitness and Human Family Structure. American Anthropologist 79:809–823.

van Gennep, Arnold
1960 The Rites of Passage. Chicago: Phoenix Books. (First published 1908.)

Veblen, Thorstein
1953 The Theory of the Leisure Class. New York: Mentor Books.

Vizinczey, Stephen
1965 In Praise of Older Women. New York: Bantam Books.

Wagley, Charles
1968 Tapirapé Shamanism. *In* Readings in Anthropology, Vol. 2. 2nd ed. Morton Fried, ed. Pp. 617–635. New York: Crowell.

Wallace, Anthony F. C.
1956 Revitalization Movements. American Anthropologist 58:264–281.
1970 Culture and Personality. 2nd ed. New York: Random House.

Weaver, Thomas, ed.
1973 To See Ourselves. Glenview, Ill.: Scott, Foresman.

Wheeler-Voegelin, E.
1949 Earth-Diver. *In* Standard Dictionary of Folklore, Mythology and Legend. Vol. 1. M. Leach, ed. P. 334. New York: Funk and Wagnalls.

White, Leslie A.
1949 The Science of Culture. New York: Grove Press.
1960 The World of the Keresan Pueblo Indians. *In* Culture in History. Stanley Diamond, ed. New York: Columbia University Press.

Whiting, John W. M., and Irvin L. Child
1953 Child Training and Personality. New Haven: Yale University Press.

Whiting, John W. M., Richard Kluckhohn, and Albert Anthony
1958 The Function of Male Initiation Ceremonies at Puberty. *In* Readings in Social Psychology. 3rd ed. E. Maccoby, T. Newcomb, and E. Hartley, eds. New York: Holt, Rinehart and Winston.

Whiting, John W. M. and others
1966 Field Guide for a Study of Socialization. Six Cultures Series, Vol. 1. New York: Wiley.

Whorf, Benjamin Lee.
1956 Language, Thought, and Reality. John Carroll, ed. Cambridge: M.I.T. Press.

Wilson, E. O.
1975 Sociobiology: The New Synthesis. Cambridge: Belknap Press.

Wilson, Monica
1963 Good Company: A Study of Nyakyusa Age-Villages. Boston: Beacon Press.

Wissler, Clark
1923 Man and Culture. New York: Crowell.

Wittfogel, Karl
1957 Oriental Despotism. New Haven: Yale University Press.

INDEX

Aborigines, Australian, 38, 122, 198, 209
Acceptance of innovations, 221–222
Acculturation, 157–158
Achievement, recruitment by, 72–73, 93
Adair, J., 292
Adaptation, 133, 156–160, 306
Adaptive function, 169
Adhesions, 308
Affinal kin, 77
Affinity, criterion of, 80
Age-area principle, 305
Age-grades, 40, 126
Age roles, 89
Age-sets, 125–128
Age villages, 127
Aggregation, 109–110, 119
Agriculture, 195, 203
Alland, Alexander, Jr., 339
Allophone, 53
Alloying, 215
Alternatives, 26–28, 147, 150–152

Ambilocal residence, 107, 147
American Anthropologist, 327
Amoral familism, 246
Ancestor cults, 229
Andaman Islanders, 195
Anglo-Saxons, 114
Animal master, 198
Annealing, 215
Anthropocentrism, 317
Anthropology, 3, 221, 277, 279f.
   cultural, 15, 300, 304
   fields of, 15–16, 315
   goal of, 325
   medical, 208
   physical, 15
   social, 16
Anticipation, 143–147
Apache Indians, 32
Arapesh Mountain, 27
Archaeology, 15, 292
   inference in, 300f.
   new, 303
Arensberg, Conrad, 110, 339
Ariès, P., 339

A NOTE ON THE TYPE

The text of this book has been set in a computer version of a type face called Helvetica—perhaps the most widely accepted and generally acclaimed sans-serif face of all time. Designed by M. Miedinger in the 1950s in Switzerland and named for its country of origin, Helvetica was first introduced in America in 1963.